RELATED TITLES FOR GRADUATE SCHOOL ADMISSIONS

Get Into Graduate School: A Strategic Approach

Get Your M.B.A. Part-Time: For the Part-Time Student with a Full-Time Life

GMAT

GMAT with CD-ROM

GMAT Verbal Workbook

GMAT 800

GRE & GMAT Exams Math Workbook

GRE Biology

GRE Psychology

GRE Exam

GRE Exam with CD-ROM

GRE Exam Verbal Workbook

GRE Exam Vocabulary Flashcards Flip-O-Matic

Test Prep and Admissions

GRE® & GMAT® Exams
Writing Workbook

By the Staff of Kaplan Test Prep and Admissions

Simon & Schuster

NEW YORK · LONDON · SYDNEY · TORONTO

Kaplan Publishing
Published by Simon & Schuster
1230 Avenue of the Americas
New York, NY 10020

Contributing Editor: Ray Ojserkis
Executive Editor: Jennifer Farthing
Project Editor: Sandy Gade and Megan Gilbert
Production Manager: Michael Shevlin
Interior Page Layout: Jan Gladish
Cover Design: Cheung Tai

Manufactured in the United States of America
Published simultaneously in Canada
January 2005
10 9 8 7 6 5 4 3 2 1

ISBN 0-7432-6201-8

Table of Contents

kaptest.com/publishing

The material in this book is up-to-date at the time of publication. However, the Educational Testing Service may have instituted changes in the test or test registration process after this book was published. Be sure to check **gre.org** or **mba.com** for updates. If there are any important late-breaking developments—or any changes or corrections to the Kaplan test preparation materials in this book—we will post that information online at **kaptest.com/publishing**. Check to see if there is any information posted there for readers of this book.

kaplansurveys.com/books

What did you think of this book? We'd love to hear your comments and suggestions. We invite you to fill out our online survey form at **kaplansurveys.com/books**. Your feedback is extremely helpful as we continue to develop high-quality resources to meet your needs.

HOW TO USE THIS BOOK

Kaplan has prepared students to take standardized tests for more than 50 years; longer than the GRE and GMAT have even been around. Our team of researchers and editors know more about preparation for these exams than anyone else, and you'll find their accumulated knowledge and experience in this book.

The GRE and GMAT are standardized tests, and so, while every test is not identical, every test covers the same content in essentially the same way. This is good news for you; it means that by studying the material in this book, you can prepare for the Analytical Writing tasks you can expect to encounter on test day.

The main focus of this book is reviewing the writing and logic skills you need to get a good score on the Analytical Writing section of the GRE or GMAT. Strategic reviews and practice will help you brush up on all the skills you'll need for test day.

If possible, work through this book a little at a time over the course of several weeks. Writing is a process and it's hard to do it all at once.

The *GRE & GMAT Exams Writing Workbook* is divided into several chapters, each serving its own very important purpose. With careful review and practice, the content and strategies contained in this book will help you to score your best on the GRE or GMAT.

Getting Started

The first thing you need to do is find out exactly what to expect on the GRE or GMAT. In the first chapter of this book, we'll provide you with background information on the Analytical Writing sections of each test. The next chapter provides all the information you need to know about how your essays are scored and what your scores mean.

Once you know about what to expect on the test, chapters three and four cover essential information for writing a top-scoring essay. We cover grammar, mechanics, and style as well as strategies for writing effective paragraphs and essays. We'll also review logic terminology (for the Argument essays) as well as the Kaplan Five-Step Method to help you do your best. The final chapters of this workbook cover sample GRE and GMAT prompts. Using these prompts, you can practice the skills you have learned to write strong essays. In addition to sample prompts, we've also included sample top-scoring essays so you can review the qualities that earn an essay a high score. You'll find a word list at the end of the book containing over 500 vocabulary words and definitions to help you craft wining essays.

KAPLAN
Test Prep and Admissions

A SPECIAL NOTE FOR INTERNATIONAL STUDENTS

About 250,000 international students pursue advanced academic degrees at the master's or Ph.D. level at U.S. universities each year. This trend of pursuing higher education in the United States, particularly at the graduate level, is expected to continue. Business, management, engineering, and the physical and life sciences are popular areas of study for international students.

If you are an international student planning on applying to a graduate program in the United States, you will want to consider the following.

- If English is not your first language, you will probably need to take the Test of English as a Foreign Language (TOEFL®) or show some other evidence that you're proficient in English prior to gaining admission to a graduate program. Graduate programs will vary on what is an acceptable TOEFL score. For degrees in business, journalism, management, or the humanities, a minimum TOEFL score of 600 (250 on the computer-based TOEFL) or better is expected. For the hard sciences and computer technology, a TOEFL score of 550 (213 on the computer-based TOEFL) is a common minimum requirement.

- You may also need to take the Graduate Record Exam (GRE®) or the Graduate Management Admission Test (GMAT®) as part of the admission process.

- Since admission to many graduate programs and business schools is quite competitive, you may want to select three or four programs you would like to attend and complete applications for each program.

- Selecting the correct graduate school is very different from selecting an undergraduate school. You should research the qualifications and interests of faculty members teaching and doing research in your chosen field. Also, select a program that meets your current or future employment needs, rather than simply a program with a big name.

- Begin the application process at least a year in advance. Be aware that many programs offer only August or September start dates. Find out application deadlines and plan accordingly.

- Finally, you will need to obtain an 1-20 Certificate of Eligibility in order to obtain an F-1 Student Visa to study in the United States.

Kaplan English Programs*

If you need more help with the complex process of graduate school admissions, or assistance preparing for the TOEFL, GRE, or GMAT, you may be interested in Kaplan's programs for international students. Kaplan English Programs were designed to help students and professionals from outside the United States meet their educational and career goals. At locations throughout the United States, international students take advantage of Kaplan's programs to help them improve their academic and conversational English skills, raise their scores on the TOEFL, GRE, GMAT, and other standardized exams, and gain admission to top programs.

General Intensive English

Kaplan's General Intensive English classes are designed to help you improve your skills in all areas of English and to increase your fluency in spoken and written English. Classes are available for beginning to advanced students, and the average class size is 12 students.

TOEFL and Academic English

This course provides you with the skills you need to improve your TOEFL score and succeed in an American university or graduate program. It includes advanced reading, writing, listening, grammar, and conversational English. You will also receive training for the TOEFL using Kaplan's exclusive computer-based practice materials.

GRE for International Students

The Graduate Record Exam (GRE) is required for admission to many graduate programs in the United States. Nearly one-half million people take the GRE each year. A high score can help you stand out from other test takers. This course, designed especially for non-native English speakers, includes the skills you need to succeed on each section of the GRE, as well as access to Kaplan's exclusive computer-based practice materials and extra verbal practice.

GMAT for International Students

The Graduate Management Admissions Test (GMAT) is required for admission to many graduate programs in business in the United States. Hundreds of thousands of American students have taken this course to prepare for the GMAT. This course, designed especially for non-native English speakers, includes the skills you need to succeed on each section of the GMAT, as well as access to Kaplan's exclusive computer-based practice materials and extra verbal practice.

Other Kaplan Programs

Since 1938, more than 3 million students have come to Kaplan to advance their studies, prepare for entry to American universities, and further their careers. In addition to the above programs, Kaplan offers courses to prepare for the SAT®, LSAT®, MCAT®, DAT®, USMLE®, NCLEX®, and other standardized exams at locations throughout the United States. To get more information or to apply to any of Kaplan's programs, contact us at:

Kaplan English Programs
700 South Flower, Suite 2900
Los Angeles, CA 90017 USA

Phone (if calling from within the United States): (800) 818-9128
Phone (if calling from outside the United States): (213) 452-5800
Fax: (213) 892-1364

Website: www.kaplanenglish.com
Email: world@kaplan.com

*Kaplan is authorized under federal law to enroll nonimmigrant alien students.
Kaplan is accredited by ACCET (Accrediting Council for Continuing Education and Training).

Chapter One: **About the Analytical Writing Section**

The Graduate Record Examinations (GRE) General Test and the Graduate Management Admission Test (GMAT) are produced and administered by the Educational Testing Service (ETS) as tools to assist in the screening of applicants for graduate schools (GRE) and business schools (GMAT). ETS introduced the Analytical Writing sections of the GRE and the GMAT in response to the perception that many otherwise well-qualified applicants lack adequate writing skills to cope with the demands of their degree programs. The score is intended to provide admissions personnel with a measure of an applicant's ability to *read analytically*, *reason logically*, and *write persuasively*.

It is important to understand that, although the GRE and GMAT are used by a diverse group of institutions where students face a broad array of reading and writing tasks, the Analytical Writing section actually assesses a rather specific set of skills. Analytical reading entails the ability to critique an argument, isolating and evaluating the evidence as well as the unstated assumptions on which that argument is founded. Logical reasoning involves marshalling evidence to support your own argument, as well as evidence to refute alternative arguments under consideration. Persuasive writing means formulating complex ideas in a coherent, well-organized, and well-written essay of four to six paragraphs. Other kinds of reading, reasoning, and writing may be useful—even indispensable—in your field, but they are not tested by the Analytical Writing section.

GENERAL DESCRIPTION OF THE ANALYTICAL WRITING SECTION

For both the GRE and the GMAT versions of the Analytical Writing section, you are required to write two essays. In one, you will be asked to present your perspective on an issue of a very general nature; in the other, you will be asked to critique an argument. Each prompt can be answered without the need for specialized knowledge of any particular subject, and great care is taken to ensure that the difficulty level of the prompts is consistent.

All of the prompts currently being used for both GRE and GMAT Analytical Writing sections are published on the ETS website. The GRE offers approximately 245 prompts for each essay type, while the GMAT offers approximately 130 Argument prompts and 170 Issue prompts.

Writing On the Computer

Analytical Writing essays must be composed on a computer at an authorized testing center. The software provides for simple text manipulation, such as cut-and-paste. There is no spell checker or any other of the tools you may be used to. A tutorial prior to the start of the test will give you an opportunity to familiarize yourself with the software, but if you are not accustomed to composing at the computer, or if your typing is particularly slow or inaccurate, you should make time to practice. (The computer labs at your local Kaplan center are equipped with equipment and software that simulate actual test conditions.)

KAPLAN
Test Prep and Admissions

GRE ESSAYS

The two writing tasks for the GRE Analytical Writing section are called "Present Your Perspective on an Issue" and "Analyze an Argument." You will have 45 minutes to complete the Issue task and only 30 minutes to complete the Argument task.

Present Your Perspective on an Issue Task

The Issue task is presented as a brief statement of opinion expressed in one to three sentences—most often one. The accompanying instructions require you to give your views on the issue in question. As the name of the task suggests, your assignment is to "present your perspective on the issue." You may agree, disagree, or take a position somewhere in between. You are also told to support your view with "relevant reasons and/or examples."

Essentially, you will not be graded on your position or on the nature of the evidence you marshal in support of that position—as long as that evidence clearly supports your conclusion.

While the Issue task gives you quite a bit of freedom in shaping your response, do not presume upon the humor or good nature of the graders. Even if you may find the presented opinion completely inane, restrain yourself. At all costs, avoid frivolity. Dreams, gossip, and conjecture may be part of your "experience," but they are not appropriate evidence for a serious discussion of an issue.

Remember, you will have a choice of two different prompts. Because the prompts are already posted online, you should not spend much of your time on test day deciding which prompt you will answer. Also, be sure to follow test instructions on identifying for readers to which essay you're responding.

Analyze an Argument Task

The Argument task is presented as a passage of three to seven sentences (usually four or five) that is generally preceded by a single-sentence "contextualizer" which defines the source of the text. (Some of the GRE prompts do not provide context.) Here are some typical contextualizers:

- The following appeared as a memo from…
- The following appeared in a press release issued by…
- The following appeared as part of an article published in…

The "argument" in the Argument prompt is a theory, proposal, or prediction, with supporting evidence. Some of the prompts are proposals to improve the performance of a commercial enterprise; others relate to community development, educational policy, and health or safety. You are not expected to have any specific expertise in any of these fields. The instructions only ask you to "discuss how well reasoned you find this argument."

A primary consideration in scoring is "focus": you will be penalized if you stray from the task of critiquing the given argument. Do not be tempted by a provocative prompt to give your own opinions on the topic, or to offer alternative proposals, or to raise other (more important) questions. Absolutely everything in your essay must bear directly on the strength or weakness of the argument presented in the prompt.

GMAT ESSAYS

The two writing tasks for the GMAT Analytical Writing section are called "Analysis of an Issue" and "Analysis of an Argument." You will have 30 minutes to complete each of the essays.

Analysis of an Issue Task

The Issue task is presented as a brief statement of opinion expressed in one to three sentences—most often one. The accompanying instructions require you to give your views on the issue in question. The GMAT instructions specify that you may draw your "reasons and/or examples" from your personal "experience, observations, or reading." You will not be graded on your position or on the nature of the evidence you use in support of that position—as long as that evidence clearly supports your conclusion.

While the Issue task gives you quite a bit of freedom in shaping your response, do not presume upon the humor or good nature of the graders. Even if you may find the presented opinion completely inane, restrain yourself. At all costs, avoid frivolity. Dreams, gossip, and conjecture may be part of your "experience," but they are not appropriate evidence for a serious discussion of an issue.

Analysis of an Argument Task

The Argument task is presented as a passage of three to seven sentences (usually four or five), generally preceded by a single-sentence "contextualizer" which defines the source of the text. Here are some typical contextualizers:

- The following appeared as a memo from…
- The following appeared in a press release issued by…
- The following appeared as part of an article published in…

The "argument" in the Argument prompt is a theory, proposal, or prediction, with supporting evidence. Most of the prompts are proposals to improve the performance of a commercial enterprise; others relate to community development, educational policy, and health or safety. You are not expected to have any specific expertise in any of these fields.

Timing

According to ETS researchers, the amount of time allotted for impromptu essay writing does not significantly affect validity: an individual may produce a better essay if allowed more time, but the order of ranking of individuals in tested groups remains essentially the same regardless of the time factor. However, as you are practicing writing essays under the pressure of limited time, you should definitely apply the time limit accorded by the exam you will be taking.

What Is an E-rater®?

GMAT essays are now graded by one human grader and one automatic grader. Human graders are trained to apply "holistic grading" guidelines according to which the entire essay is assessed without reference to a strict checklist of criteria. The E-rater is a computerized system that calculates a score based on more than fifty quantifiable characteristics of each essay. ETS researchers claim that the E-rater arrives at scores that are as reliable as those assigned by human graders; studies find that 90% of the essay scores given by humans and the E-rater are identical or adjacent, a figure that compares favorably with results involving two human graders. In those cases where the human grader and the E-rater disagree by two or more points, a second human grader is called in to make a final decision.

The instructions first ask you to "Discuss how well reasoned you find this argument." They elaborate on this requirement with the following points:

1. You must analyze the line of reasoning, evaluating the pertinence and effectiveness of evidence that is presented in support of the argument's conclusion or recommendation.

2. You must point out the unstated assumptions that underlie the argument. If those assumptions are questionable, you should explain why.

3. You must cite alternative explanations, facts, counterexamples, or other evidence that would weaken the argument's conclusion.

4. You must discuss what kinds of additional evidence or changes in the line of reasoning would make the argument stronger as well as those that would make it weaker.

The instructions do not actually state that "you must" do all of these things: most are presented as suggestions. However, if you want to achieve a top score you should consider these points non-negotiable.

Not only must you attend to all four of the advisory points, but you must also rigorously avoid any other considerations. A primary consideration in scoring is "focus": you will be penalized if you stray from the task of critiquing the given argument. Do not be tempted by a provocative prompt to give your own opinions on the topic, or to offer alternative proposals, or to raise other (more important) questions. Absolutely everything in your essay must bear directly on the strength or weakness of the argument presented in the prompt.

What about Scoring?

Scoring varies slightly between the GRE and GMAT. To learn about how your essays are scored, be sure to read chapter two.

THE NEXT STEP

At this point you may be feeling reassured and confident. After all, the analytical writing tasks are relatively simple and straightforward. Strategically, this confidence is ill-advised. Simply writing a grammatically correct essay on a topic does not guarantee you a top score.

By reviewing the chapters in this book you will learn how to deal with the Analytical Writing tasks. You will be well prepared enough that you will feel comfortable with the time limits and secure in the knowledge that you know precisely what is expected of you.

Chapter Two: **Essay Scoring**

Approximately 10–15 days after your test date, you will receive your score on the Analytical Writing section. On both the GRE and the GMAT, you will receive a cumulative score from 0 to 6 for your two essays. Each essay is scored by at least two different graders. If the two scores for any essay are identical, the essay receives that score. If the scores differ by a single point, they are averaged. If the graders disagree by more than one point, a third grader is brought in to adjudicate the score. Your score on the Analytical Writing section will be the average of your two essay scores, rounded off (if necessary) to the nearest half-point.

Here's how a typical Analytical Writing score might be derived:

	Grader 1's Score	Grader 2's Score	Average Score
"Issue" Essay Score	4	5	4.5
"Argument" Essay Score	4	5	4.5

Issue Essay Score	Argument Essay Score	Final Score
4.5	5.0	5.0

It should be notes that while scores range from 0–6, about 90 percent of all scores on both the GRE and the GMAT fall between 2 and 5. The "mean" or average score for both tests is also about the same, around 4.2.

ETS sends this composite score to the institutions you designate; the individual essay scores and the actual essays are not made available to admissions personnel.

The use made of your test scores by colleges and universities is determined by those institutions. ETS provides guidelines for interpretation of scores and suggestions as to how the scores should be used, but the actual policies are set by the schools themselves.

Essay Scoring at a Glance

Both the GRE and GMAT essays are scored on a six-point scale that can be summarized as follows:

6: Outstanding

5: Strong

4: Adequate

5: Limited

2: Seriously flawed

1: Fundamentally deficient

0: Off topic, or not consisting of words in English

NS: No Score

The Analytical Writing sections of the GRE and GMAT share many similarities, but also have some interesting differences with regards to the scoring. Let's first begin by reviewing the similarities, starting with the scoring "rubric," which is almost identical for the two tests.

THE SCORING RUBRIC

GRE and GMAT essays are scored "holistically." A holistic score emphasizes the interrelation of different thinking and writing qualities within an essay—such as content, organization, and use of language—and tries to denote the unified effect. Four main areas are considered in coming up with a score. The essays should:

1. **Follow directions**. Essentially, this means—is the essay relevant to the issue or argument? For the issue essay, does the author (a) identify and take a position on the issue and (b) support the position with examples or evidence? For the argument essay, does the author (a) understand the argument's conclusion, evidence, and assumptions and (b) discuss why the argument is or is not convincing? This seemingly simple point is actually critical to success. No essay, no matter how well written, can receive a high score if it does meet the basic requirement of following directions and addressing the topic at hand.

2. **Reason soundly**. Does the essay draw a clear and insightful conclusion? Is the evidence persuasive, and does it logically and naturally lead to the conclusion? Does the essay clearly demonstrate how the evidence supports the conclusions?

3. **Be organized**. Does the essay state and maintain a clear and consistent position? Are evidence and conclusion placed close together and clearly linked? Does the author use transitions and keywords to maintain a smooth and logical flow and highlight important points? Is the overall effect one of clarity and focus or of randomness and lack of cohesion?

4. **Use language well**. Does the author use appropriate and expressive vocabulary, avoiding repetition, needless jargon, and overly poetic language? Is the sentence structure strong and varied, neither too short and choppy nor too dense and complex? Does the author avoid excessive errors in grammar, usage, spelling, or idiom that could obscure the meaning of the essay?

ESSAY DESCRIPTIONS

The following table provides a brief description of a typical essay of each type at each score level.

Score	Issue Essay	Argument Essay
6.0	Demonstrates a keen grasp of all facets of the issue; takes a perceptive position on the issue; uses logical and persuasive evidence to support this position; is tightly focused and well-organized; uses language that is descriptive, varied and precise; contains only minor errors in usage and grammar	Demonstrates deep understanding of the argument's structure; insightfully identifies and critiques key assumptions; provides compelling support for the critiques; offers ways to improve argument; is tightly focused and well-organized; uses language that is descriptive, varied and precise; contains only minor errors
5.0	Demonstrates clear and in-depth understanding of the issue; presents a thoughtful position on the issue; uses relevant examples to support the position; is focused and organized; language and sentence structure are clear and have some variety; contains only minor errors in usage and grammar	Demonstrates clear grasp of the argument's structure; understands key assumptions; critique is based on examining validity of assumptions; is focused and organized; language and sentence structure are clear and have some variety; contains only minor errors in usage and grammar
4.0	Demonstrates a basic ability to grasp and take a position on the issue; position on the issue is clear; most if not all evidence is relevant; focus and organization are strong enough to avoid detracting from the argument; conveys meaning with clarity; contains no major errors in grammar, usage, or mechanics	Demonstrates competence in analysis and writing; identifies evidence and conclusions; critique is based on assessment of assumptions; focus and organization are strong enough to avoid detracting from the argument; conveys meaning with clarity; contains no major errors in grammar, usage, or mechanics.
3.0	Demonstrates some understanding of the issue but has clear weaknesses, including at least one of the following: position on the issue (if any is stated) is superficial or imprecise; evidence is often not cogent; organization and focus are inconsistent; language does not convey meaning with clarity; contains some major errors in standard written English or frequent minor errors	Demonstrates some capacity for analysis but has conspicuous shortcomings, including at least one of the following: fails to identify evidence and conclusion clearly; fails to address some key assumptions; critique is illogical or tangential; organization and focus are inconsistent; language does not convey meaning with clarity; contains some major errors in standard written English or frequent minor errors

Score	Issue Essay	Argument Essay
2.0	Demonstrates a very limited capacity for analytical writing; discussion of and position on the issue (if any) lacks depth, clarity and insight; evidence (if any) is generally not compelling or relevant; provides little organization or structure; problems with language, grammar, and sentence structure are severe and/or persistent	Demonstrates only a limited ability to analyze an argument; does not show grasp of argument's structure; analysis based more on personal opinion than on a logical critique of assumptions; provides little organization or structure; problems with language, grammar, and sentence structure are severe and/or persistent
1.0	Demonstrates a near-total lack of analytical writing competence; shows little or no understanding of the issue —or does not even address the issue; is unfocused, unstructured, disorganized; has major errors in grammar, language, and sentence structure which greatly obscure the writer's meaning	Demonstrates lack of ability to conduct analysis and write clearly; shows little or no understanding of the argument's evidence, conclusion, or assumptions— or does not even address the argument; is unfocused, and disorganized; has major errors in grammar, language, and sentence structure which greatly obscure the writer's meaning

A score of zero is reserved for "unscorable" essays—essays that completely ignore the essay topic. For this reason you shouldn't spend your entire allotted time on an essay section typing over and over again: "I hate ETS. This essay assignment is awful." If you do so, you will be rewarded with a score of zero. On the GRE, if no essay response is given for either of the two essay tasks, an NS (No Score) is reported for the entire section. If an essay response is provided for only one of the two writing tasks, the task for which no essay response is provided will receive a score of zero. On the GMAT, if no essay response is given for either of the essay tasks, both essays will receive a score of zero, for a final score of zero.

THE SCORING PROCESS

As noted, both the GRE and the GMAT come up with a single score between 0 and 6 for the Analytical Writing section. On the GRE, each essay will be read by two human graders. On the GMAT, each essay will be graded twice, once by a human grader and once by the E-rater—a computer program designed by ETS to reduce test administration costs. More on the E-rater in a bit—for now just know that ETS justifies its use of the E-rater based on the high agreement between the scores given by the E-rater and those given by human graders.

In holistic scoring, graders are trained to assign scores on the basis of the overall quality of an essay in response to the assigned task. As aforementioned, if the two assigned scores differ by more than one point on the scale, the discrepancy is adjudicated by a third GRE or GMAT reader. Otherwise, the two scores are averaged. The final scores on the two essays are then averaged and rounded up to the nearest half-point.

ABOUT THE E-RATER®

Those of you who are just planning to take the GRE move along; this section is just for GMAT test takers. It's time to get acquainted with the E-rater. Obviously, ETS loves the E-rater, and its for-profit subsidiary, ETS Technologies, has had considerable success selling the program on a subscription basis to colleges as an automated essay-scoring program. It also offers the E-rater to people like you who are preparing for the GMAT, through its product Essay Insight℠. For $20, you can write two essays on real topics and have them scored by the E-rater. If you wish to try this product after you've finished with this book, it can be purchased at www.mba.com/mba/Store/.

But before you plop down your hard-earned cash for the opportunity to have two essays graded by the E-rater, let's face some facts. A computer program cannot follow the thread of an argument. It cannot even follow the grammar of an essay very well, as anyone who's ever used a grammar check program can tell you. In fact, these are just some of the reasons why ETS has not yet attempted to use the E-rater as an essay grader on the GRE.

So how do the E-rater's scores manage to correlate so well with those of human graders? And what does this mean to you and the way you should approach writing your essays?

First of all, you may find it insulting to have your essays graded by a computer program, but you shouldn't sweat it too much. The E-rater works like a search engine, much like Google™ and other Internet search engines. The E-rater employs a huge database that stores hundreds of scored sample responses for each ETS-approved essay topic. The computer program scans your essay and then determines how well it stacks up against the scored essays on the same topic in its database. If your essay is similar to the 6.0 essays in its database, then your essay will receive 6.0 points. If it's similar to 5.0 essays, then it will receive receives 5.0 points, and so on. In other words, if you write an essay that is very similar to a high-scoring essay in the E-rater's database, then you will get a high score.

Fooling the E-rater is easy if you are able to identify what it favors and what it does not. In fact, ETS has conducted its own study to find out how easy it is to trick the E-rater and found that it's quite easy—and the good news for you is that it's much easier to fool the E-rater into awarding you a higher score than the essay merits than the other way around. We are not suggesting that you write your essays with the specific goal of fooling the E-rater. But it is helpful to understand the process by which the E-rater mimics a human grader. Let's review the four areas used to come up with a score, to see how the E-rater analyzes these areas.

1. **Follow directions.** For the E-rater, this amounts to trying to assess whether the essay responds to the assigned topic. It does this by analyzing the essay's use of prompt-specific vocabulary. In order to be rewarded for following the directions well, you should try to use not only the words in the essay prompt, but also synonyms and related terms that would likely appear on a high-scoring essay. For instance, let's say an Issue essay asks for you to take a stand on the following: "Business leaders have a responsibility to give back to the communities in which

they operate." You should try to think of synonyms and related phrases to use in the essay, e.g., *business leader*: entrepreneur, chief executive officer or CEO, corporation, captain of industry, capitalist; *responsibility*: obligation, duty, accountability; *community*: locality, neighborhood; *related phrases*:
citizen, shareholder, philanthropy, etc.

2. **Reason soundly.** Of course the E-rater is completely incapable of following the reasoning of an essay. What it can do is search the essay for the use of transitional words that tend to be used in well-reasoned essays. In particular, the E-rater rewards the use of:

   - *Evidence and conclusion words*: because, since, for example, therefore, thus, so, etc.
   - *Contrast words*: however, but, although, conversely, nonetheless, still, yet, whereas, etc.
   - *Continuation words*: likewise, similarly, in addition, also, moreover, furthermore, etc.

3. **Be organized.** The E-rater rewards the use of an easy-to-follow structure, most clearly indicated by the use of paragraphs—with an introduction, body paragraphs, and a conclusion—that make appropriate use of the continuation words noted above.

4. **Use language well.** The E-rater rewards the correct use of grammar and the proper spelling of words, as well as syntactical variety (this just means varying the word choice, as we already recommended regarding the essay prompt words), and sentence structure variety. To vary your sentence structure you should try to mix up long sentences with short ones. Finally, it's important to give yourself enough time to proofread your essay for grammar and spelling errors.

Fortunately, the following chapters will help you to do all of the above as a matter of habit. So no matter how you feel about the E-rater as a grading tool, you can learn how to get a great score from it.

MAXIMIZING YOUR SCORE ON THE ANALYTICAL WRITING SECTION

Of course, that's what this book is all about. Right now we just want to offer a few pointers to set you off in the right direction, now that you understand how your essays are scored. Learning to do the following is essential to getting a high score on the essays.

Understand Your Task

In particular, we want to make sure you recognize the difference between an Issue essay and an Argument essay. In their rush to start writing their essays, some test takers have been known to mistake one assignment for the other, with disastrous consequences for their final score. This tends to happen more commonly on the GMAT, where either type of essay may appear first. For the Issue essay, your job is to take a stand on the stated topic and support it with relevant examples or reasons. Here's an example of an Issue essay prompt.

> The vote should be extended to minors between the ages of 14 and 18. This would encourage America's youth to take a greater interest in politics and government and allow them to have some say in policies that have a direct impact on their lives.
>
> Discuss the extent to which you agree or disagree with the opinion expressed above. Support your views with reasons and/or examples from your own experience, observations, or reading.

Note that you must take a stand on the issue. While it's good to acknowledge both sides of the issue, particularly in the introductory paragraph, you must declare your position. To achieve a high score you must attempt to persuade the reader that, despite the counterarguments, your position is the correct one.

Thus, your body paragraphs should explain your reasons for choosing the position you've taken, as well as counter the arguments that someone with the opposite position would likely make. Make absolutely sure that your side will "win out" in your introduction and conclusion.

For the Argument essay, your job is to analyze the given argument, regardless of whether or not you agree with its conclusion. This involves breaking down the argument, identifying the author's conclusion, evidence, and any underlying (but unstated) assumptions. You must then present a case for why the author's argument is or (more often) is *not* convincing. Often, this will hinge on the soundness of the underlying assumptions. In addition, you should indicate how the argument might be made more convincing. Here's an example of an Argument essay prompt.

The following appeared in a memo from the president of a wine distributor with customers throughout the United States.

> "For many years our company has distributed a wide variety of both domestic and imported wines. Last year, however, four out of five of our best-selling wines were produced in California. Furthermore, a recent survey by *Wine Connoisseur* magazine indicates an increasing preference for domestic wines among its subscribers. Since our company can reduce expenses by limiting the number of wines we distribute, the best way to improve our profits is to discontinue selling many of our imported wines and concentrate primarily on domestic wines."
>
> Discuss how well reasoned you find this argument. **In the discussion be sure to analyze the line of reasoning and the use of evidence in the argument. For example, you may need to consider what questionable assumptions underlie the thinking and what alternative explanations or counterexamples might weaken the argument's conclusion. You may also address possible changes in the argument that would make it more logically sound, and what, if anything, would help you better evaluate its conclusion.**

Note: We have placed a large portion of the above directions in bold. This is because these directions appear only in GMAT essay prompts. It would be helpful if these directions were also included in the GRE essay prompt, because the task is exactly the same even if it's less clearly spelled out. Note that you are asked to analyze the line of reasoning—not to agree or disagree with the final conclusion. This involves examining the evidence and underlying assumptions. You should also realize that no matter what argument you are given, it will contain some questionable underlying assumptions or shaky evidence. You may ultimately show that the argument could be made persuasive, if certain assumptions are shown to be valid or certain pieces of evidence are shown to truly support the conclusion, but the given argument on the GRE or GMAT Analytical Writing section will never be completely sound as written. So, your job is to root out the holes in the argument. For instance, whenever a survey is used in an argument, such the preceding *Wine Connoisseur* magazine survey, you should always ask yourself whether the survey is truly representative and useful to the argument or whether it could contain some sort of bias that undermines its credibility.

GMAT test takers may be at an advantage when it comes to taking apart an argument, since studying for the Critical Reasoning portion of the Verbal section of the GMAT should help to prepare students for the task of breaking apart an argument. If you want to learn more about the concepts and terminology related to analyzing an argument, refer to chapter four.

Use Your Time Wisely

Even test takers who are seasoned essay writers are likely to feel stress when trying to produce completed essays under the extreme time pressure of the GRE or GMAT Analytical Writing section. Whether you are given 45 minutes or 30 minutes for your writing assignment, it takes discipline and a good strategy to produce an essay that:

- effectively and insightfully addresses the writing task
- is well organized and fully developed, using appropriate example to support ideas
- displays an effective use of language, demonstrating variety in sentence structure and range of vocabulary

Fortunately, this book can teach you effective strategies that will allow you to produce an effective essay in the allotted time. With practice you will develop the discipline you will need to earn a top score. Remember: to maximize your score, you need to focus on writing what the scorers will reward—AND NOTHING ELSE. That's what we are here to teach you.

Address Your Weaknesses

Depending upon your own particular strengths and weaknesses you may need to spend more time in certain chapters of this book than others. For instance, if you are not a native English speaker, you may need to spend more time on the "Writing Strong Sentences" chapter of this book. If your main problem is not *how* to write using the rules of standard written English but *what* to write, you may need to concentrate on the "Writing Strong Paragraphs and Essays" chapter of this book.

This book is designed to break down the elements of writing a superior essay and make them second nature to you. With study and practice, the process of writing superior essays for the GRE or GMAT should become reflexive and automatic. When that happens you can produce stronger, clearer, and more complete essays, and that is the true key to maximizing your score on test day.

Chapter Three: **Writing Strong Sentences: Grammar, Mechanics, and Style**

Strong sentences are the building blocks of effective and top-scoring essays. This chapter takes a detailed look at the nuts and bolts of sentences: the most important things you need to know (or review) to help you earn a top score on the Analytical Writing section. Our **Eight Maxims of Effective Sentences** cover the essentials of grammar and usage, mechanics, and style, including everything from subject-verb agreement to semicolons, from parallel structure to point of view. Throughout this chapter, you'll find specific tips and strategies to help you earn top scores from both the E-rater and the human grader.

Let's start with some observations based on our research.

- In terms of the mechanics of writing, the graders do not set the bar extremely high. A comma splice here and some wordiness there won't ruin your essay. Your paper absolutely does not have to be perfect to get a 6. However, the fewer excuses you give readers for docking your score, the better. We'll give you guidelines to help you avoid potentially costly mistakes.

- Many so-called grammar rules are regularly broken by good writers. But the E-rater can't distinguish between rules that you break for effect and rules that you break because you don't know better; it simply assumes the latter. We'll review the rules so you can play it safe.

- It is possible to write in a rather personal, even idiosyncratic, style, and still get a top score. Bear in mind, however, that the E-rater will certainly not be moved by wit, eloquence, or any signs of personality. As for the human grader, after reading hundreds and hundreds of responses to the same question, he or she may be impressed by a well-turned phrase. Or, he or she may be cranky and impatient with anything that looks like posturing. We'll show you how to write with a style that will boost your score.

EIGHT MAXIMS OF EFFECTIVE SENTENCES

There are dozens and dozens of writing rules and guidelines, and it can be easy to feel overwhelmed by them, especially when you're under pressure to prepare for an exam. To help you remember what's most important and feel more in control on test day, we've organized those rules and guidelines around eight maxims of effective sentences. Use these eight principles as your guide for the Analytical Writing tasks.

MAXIM 1: BE CORRECT

Both the E-rater and the human reader will expect your writing to follow the conventions of Standard Written English. This section covers the most important rules of grammar, usage, and mechanics as well as the most frequently confused words.

Grammar and Usage

Verb Forms and Tenses

Though a few grammar errors alone won't necessarily bring down your score, certain types of errors are more likely to strike your human readers as more egregious than others. Verb mistakes are among the most damaging, so here's a detailed review of common kinds of errors.

Helping. Helping or auxiliary verbs do just that: they help you express exactly when an event will or did take place (e.g., future, past perfect, and conditional tenses). They also convey very specific meanings. Though we often use them interchangeably, *may* and *can* actually have two different meanings. *May* expresses permission while *can* express-es ability; thus the question "may I?" is actually very different from the question "can I?"

Here's a list of specific helping verb meanings:

can/could	ability	A radio ad <u>could</u> really expand our customer base.
may/might	permission	You <u>may</u> see the director now.
	possibility	We <u>may</u> benefit considerably from a radio ad.
should	expectation	We <u>should</u> have the results of the survey by Friday.
	recommendation	You <u>should</u> conduct a customer satisfaction survey.
must (have/had)	necessity	We <u>must have</u> the survey results by Friday.
will/shall/would	intention	We <u>shall</u> deliver the survey results by Friday.

Troublesome Verbs. Time to review those three sets of verbs that tend to give writers so much trouble: *lie/lay*, *rise/raise*, and *sit/set*.

The key to choosing the right word is to remember which verb in each pair is **transitive** and which is **intransitive**. A transitive verb needs an object to receive its action (you can think of it as <u>trans</u>ferring its action to the object). An intransitive verb does not take an object; it performs the action on itself.

<u>Intransitive</u> (no object)		<u>Transitive</u> (takes an object)	
lie	to rest or recline	**lay**	to put or place (something)
rise	to go up	**raise**	to lift or move (something) up
sit	to rest	**set**	to put place (something)

A pneumonic trick to remember which verbs are intransitive: the first vowel in each word is *i*.

> After hours of negotiating, Barker had to <u>lie</u> down and take a nap.
> After hours of negotiating, Barker <u>lay</u> his <u>head</u> upon the table and fell asleep.

> Nolan likes to <u>rise</u> at 4:30 so he can work for several hours before breakfast.
> The Federal Reserve <u>raised</u> the <u>interest rate</u> for the third time this quarter.

> Justine is going to <u>sit</u> in the back of the room and observe the training class.
> I've <u>set</u> <u>everything</u> you'll need for the conference call on your desk.

Subjunctive and Conditional. The subjunctive voice is actually a simple form but one that has been slipping out of everyday usage over the last several decades. However, it is still required for grammatically correct sentences. The subjunctive is primarily used to express something that is wished for or contrary to fact. To form the subjunctive, use the base form of the verb for all persons and numbers. The only exception is also the most frequently used subjunctive verb, *to be*. The subjunctive of *to be* is *were*:

> If I <u>were</u> in your position, I would ask for a second opinion.
> The mayor wishes [or wished] that the commercial tax base <u>were</u> larger.

Phrases such as *it is* (or any other tense of the verb *to be*) *necessary that...* also take the subjunctive form. Other adjectives and adjectival phrases that may be used in this expression include *vital, essential, indispensable, preferable, advisable, just as well, better,* and *best.*

> CORRECT: It is essential that the President <u>recognize</u> the limits of his mandate.
>
> CORRECT: Is it really necessary that we all <u>study</u> the law in order to protect ourselves from nuisance lawsuits?
>
> CORRECT: The CEO suggested that the secretary <u>revise</u> the report before releasing it.

Watch Out for Would!

A conditional sentence does not normally have *would* in the *if* clause. The exception is when *would* means *be willing to*, as in *If you would dry the dishes, I'll wash them*. In most cases, *would* or *would have* in the *if* clause is wrong:

INCORRECT: If the town would have raised taxes, it wouldn't have gone bankrupt.

CORRECT: If the town had raised taxes, it wouldn't have gone bankrupt.

INCORRECT: If we would have been more prepared, we would have landed the account.

CORRECT: If we had been more prepared, we would have landed the account.

Practice 1

Find and correct the mistake(s) in the following sentences. Answers are found on page 73.

1. Most of us wish that our parents will be better prepared to face retirement.

2. While we may wish that our physical conditioning would be better, few of us are prepared to invest the time and effort in the kind of exercise and diet that might help us achieve it.

3. Does it make sense to wish that we were armed with lethal claws and teeth like other animals?

4. Although it is simple to mouth words of support for the work of others, it is preferable that they are given negative feedback where it applies.

5. Many scientists recommend that the government make an effort to preserve every species.

6. Judging from recent pricing patterns, it is imperative that the American government begins to regulate retail milk prices.

Gerunds and Infinitives. Although gerunds look like verbs because they end in *–ing*, they are actually nouns:

Kinsley's organization promotes awareness of global <u>warming</u>.

Infinitives are formed by combining *to* + the verb base: *to warm*.

The main mistake people make with gerunds and infinitives is using the wrong from after a conjugated verb. Fortunately, if you are a native speaker of English, you can usually hear right away when this kind of error is made:

INCORRECT: Kinsley hopes <u>promoting</u> awareness of global warming.

CORRECT: Kinsley hopes <u>to promote</u> awareness of global warming.

For some verbs, either a gerund or infinitive will do, though sometimes one sounds a little better than the other:

CORRECT: Kinsley's goal is <u>to promote</u> awareness of global warming. [best choice]

CORRECT: Kinsley's goal is <u>promoting</u> awareness of global warming. [also correct]

The verbs *like, hate,* and other words that express preference fall into this either/or category. But many verbs can only take one form. Here are some general guidelines for when to use infinitives and gerunds.

Gerunds should always follow prepositions and the following verbs:

admit	enjoy	quit
appreciate	escape	recall
avoid	finish	recommend
cannot help	imagine	resist
consider	keep	risk
delay	miss	suggest
deny	postpone	tolerate
discuss	practice	
dislike	put off	

Infinitives generally follow these verbs, even when separated by a noun or pronoun:

advise (I <u>advise</u> you <u>to go</u> to graduate school)

agree (We <u>agree</u> <u>to stop</u> fighting.)

allow (Please <u>allow</u> us <u>to present</u> you with this award for your service to the community.)

ask (They have <u>asked</u> us <u>to write</u> a proposal for developing the Tulman Park area.)

beg	force	refuse
bother	hope	remind
cause	manage	require
claim	need	tell
command	offer	urge
convince	order	venture
decide	persuade	want
encourage	plan	warn
expect	pretend	wish
fail	promise	

CORRECT: The CEO <u>advised</u> the stockholders not <u>to sell</u> before reading the latest report.

CORRECT: The CEO <u>recommended</u> <u>waiting for</u> the quarterly report before making a decision.

Subject-Verb Agreement

Is it "he go" or "he goes"? Native speakers of English can generally count on their inner ear to pick the right form without any conscious thought. But in long, complex sentences or sentences with indefinite pronouns, even native speakers can sometimes make mistakes.

First, the principle: Subject-verb agreement means that the subject must agree (be equal to) the verb in number. A singular subject (*she*) must have a singular verb (*understands*); a plural subject (*they*) must have a plural verb (*understand*). Here's a review of the most common kinds of subject-verb agreement errors.

Indefinite Pronouns. *Every, each, everyone, everybody, anyone,* and *anybody* are all grammatically singular, even though they tend to have plural meanings.

INCORRECT: Each of us <u>have</u> completed a review of our department.

CORRECT: Each of us <u>has</u> completed a review of our department.

INCORRECT: Anyone who <u>attempt</u> to change my mind will only be disappointed.

CORRECT: Anyone who <u>attempts</u> to change my mind will only be disappointed.

With these expressions there are often problems of pronoun-antecedent agreement as well as issues of political correctness when you need a singular pronoun to refer to both men and women. You might want to avoid them altogether and use *all* instead:

INCORRECT: <u>Every</u> one of the delegates has cast <u>their</u> vote.

CORRECT: <u>Every</u> one of the delegates has cast <u>his or her</u> vote.

CORRECT: <u>All</u> of the delegates have cast <u>their</u> votes.

Practice 2

The following sentences contain various problem areas in subject-verb agreement. Of the two choices provided, choose the verb form that matches the subject of the sentence. Answers are found on pages 73–74.

1. Many people in New York **travel/travels** by subway.

2. Workers in New York often **commute/commutes** a long way to work.

3. Tourists in New York **expect/expects** to see the subway.

4. The "redbird"subway cars with a red body **has/have** been a common sight in New York until recently.

5. The streets of large cities such as New York **is/are** under-cut by complex networks of subway tunnels.

6. Today, the economy of New York and other large cities **is/are** booming.

7. New Yorkers with a good income **is/are** less likely to commute by subway.

8. A worker with a long commute **does/do** not want to spend hours on the subway.

9. A private car, although convenient, **pollutes/pollute** the air.

10. Parking in one of New York's many overcrowded garages **is/are** also a problem.

11. Every day, Joe and Carla **rides/ride** the subway to work.

12. Every day, Joe or Carla **rides/ride** the subway to work.

13. Every day, Joe's sisters or Carla's sisters **rides/ride** the subway to work.

14. Every day, Joe's sisters or Carla **rides/ride** the subway to work.

15. Every day, Carla or Joe's sisters from Long Island **rides/ride** the subway to work.

16. Everyone **enjoys/enjoy** a summer vacation.

17. Nobody **has/have** fun when the Cyclones lose a game.

18. Either of the answers **is/are** valid in response to that question.

19. Each of the students **bring/brings** a book to class every day.

20. Many **is/are** obsessed with reality television these days.

Prepositional Distracters. Errors frequently creep in when the grammatical subject of the sentence is singular but includes a prepositional phrase with a plural object. Remember that the object in a prepositional phrase is never the true subject of the sentence. To help you identify this kind of error, read the sentence *without* the prepositional phrase. Correct the error by changing the verb to match the true subject, by moving the prepositional phrase, or by recasting the sentence so that the object of the preposition becomes the true subject. (The prepositional phrases are bracketed in the first two examples below.)

INCORRECT: The <u>aim</u> [of all promotional strategies] <u>are</u> to influence the shape of the demand curve.

CORRECT: The <u>aim</u> [of all promotional strategies] <u>is</u> to influence the shape of the demand curve.

CORRECT: All promotional <u>strategies</u> <u>have</u> the goal of influencing the shape of the demand curve.

CORRECT: All promotional <u>strategies</u> <u>aim</u> to influence the shape of the demand curve.

When a singular subject is modified by a prepositional phrase that seems to expand the subject, the verb nonetheless agrees only with the true subject.

CORRECT: The President, along with the Vice President and the members of the Cabinet, <u>is</u> the highest security risk in times of crisis.

CORRECT: The <u>President</u> and the <u>Vice President</u>, together with the members of the Cabinet, <u>are protected</u> by numerous security officers.

Other common expressions that function in a similar way are *besides, as well as, in addition to,* and *not to mention.*

Practice 3

Find and correct the mistake(s) in the following sentences. Answers are found on page 75.

1. The installation of video cameras in public areas certainly add a measure of security but may eventually erode our right to privacy.

2. Competition for grades, jobs, and mates ultimately benefit society.

3. The main flaw in most of these arguments are the reliance upon unsupported inferences.

A Note about British English

Although ETS graders are not supposed to penalize test takers for applying British grammatical norms, it is best to stick to American norms in instances where British and American grammar differ. In British English, for example, collective nouns are plural.

CORRECT (U.S.): Air Novitrans has a fleet of twelve aging aircraft.

CORRECT (UK): Air Novitrans have a fleet of twelve aging aircraft.

We would advise test-takers to play it safe by following American conventions:

RISKY: A group of professors representing a dozen of our top universities have testified that tenure is an outmoded and counterproductive academic custom.

SAFE: A group of professors representing a dozen of our top universities has testified that tenure is an outmoded and counterproductive academic custom.

Other Interrupters Subject-verb agreement errors are also common when the subject and the verb are separated by an intervening adverbial or adjectival phrase.

INCORRECT: At the national level, each <u>government</u>, regardless of the prevailing economic and political institutions, <u>formulate</u> policies that regulate the international marketing efforts of both domestic and foreign firms.

CORRECT: At the national level, each <u>government</u>, regardless of the prevailing economic and political institutions, <u>formulates</u> policies that regulate the international marketing efforts of both domestic and foreign firms.

INCORRECT: The political <u>cartoon</u> depicting the prime minister as a cowboy corralling immigrants <u>have caused</u> a great deal of controversy.

CORRECT: The political <u>cartoon</u> depicting the prime minister as a cowboy corralling immigrants <u>has caused</u> a great deal of controversy.

Group Nouns. Group or collective nouns refer to a class or group and are almost always treated as singular because they emphasize the group as a single unit or entity. When the context of the sentence makes it clear that the writer is referring to the individual members of the group, then the noun is treated as plural. Group nouns include *audience, class, committee, company, family, firm, government, group, jury, team,* as well as proper names referring to companies and other corporate entities. (Relevant pronouns and verbs are also underlined in the following examples to emphasize agreement.)

INCORRECT: The research <u>group</u> meet weekly to discuss <u>their</u> progress.

CORRECT: The research <u>group</u> meets weekly to discuss <u>its</u> progress.

CORRECT: The <u>members</u> of the research <u>group</u> meet weekly to discuss <u>their</u> progress.

INCORRECT: The <u>jury</u> <u>is</u> engaged in a heated debate.

CORRECT: The <u>jury</u> <u>are</u> engaged in a heated debate. [Calls attention to the individual members and their opinions.]

CORRECT: The <u>members</u> of the <u>jury</u> <u>are</u> engaged in a heated debate.

Be careful with *a number of* and *the number of. A number of* means *some*, and is plural. *The number* (whether or not it is followed by a prepositional phrase) is singular.

CORRECT: A <u>number</u> of politicians <u>have</u> urged passage of a Constitutional amendment making same-sex marriage illegal.

CORRECT: The <u>number</u> of politicians who refuse donations from political action groups <u>is</u> extremely small.

Practice 4

Find and correct the mistake(s) in the following sentences. Answers are found on page 75.

1. The entire team of scientists were allergic to the very chemicals they were studying.

2. The research team is scheduled to conclude its work this week.

3. A number of Internet companies is doubtless preparing to challenge Google for dominance of the search engine market.

Compound Subjects. First, the easy part: a subject that consists of two or more nouns connected by *and* takes the plural form of the verb.

CORRECT: The <u>Trash-Site Safety Council</u>, a public interest non-profit organization, and <u>Eco-Farms International</u>, an association of organic farmers, <u>are monitoring</u> development of upstate landfill projects.

Either/Neither. Now the trickier part. When the subject consists of two or more nouns connected by *or* or *nor*, the verb agrees with the CLOSEST noun.

CORRECT: Either the senators or <u>the President is</u> misinformed.

CORRECT: Either the President or the <u>senators are</u> misinformed.

Practice 5

Find and correct the mistake(s) in the following sentences. Answers are found on page 75.

1. The CEO, along with the Board of Directors, are responsible for any infraction of the corporation's environmental protection policy.

2. Either the Attorney General or his senior assistants has the option of prosecuting such violations.

3. Neither the professor nor the students have any strong interest in postponing the end of classes.

Pronouns

When you answer the telephone and someone asks for you, do you reply "This is she" or "This is her"? Pronouns are marvelously useful in that they save us from having to repeat the names of people and objects over and over. But there are several kinds of pronoun errors that can plague even seasoned writers.

Pronoun-Antecedent Agreement. Though it may sound right to say "Each delinquent client has now paid their bill in full," the pronoun *their* is incorrect. The subject is singular: *each client*. The verb is also singular: *has*. Thus the pronoun must also be singular to agree with *client*, its **antecedent** (the word a pronoun replaces or refers to):

CORRECT: Each delinquent <u>client</u> has now paid <u>its</u> bill in full.

Mistakes often occur when the antecedent is an indefinite pronoun. Singular indefinite pronouns include the following:

anybody	everybody	nobody
anyone	everyone	somebody
anything	everything	someone
each	neither	something
either	no one	

These are singular antecedents that require singular pronouns:

INCORRECT: I have asked <u>everyone</u> to write down <u>their</u> preferences for travel accommodations.

CORRECT: I have asked <u>everyone</u> to write down <u>his or her</u> preferences for travel accommodations.

Plural indefinite pronouns include *both, few, many,* and *several*. They are plural antecedents that require plural pronouns:

INCORRECT: I have carefully considered your offers, and <u>both</u> are appealing, but <u>it</u> is simply too costly.

CORRECT: I have carefully considered your offers, and <u>both</u> are appealing, but <u>they</u> are simply too costly.

Some indefinite pronouns—*all, any, most, none,* and *some*—can be either singular or plural depending upon the noun or pronoun to which the indefinite pronoun refers. Here are some examples (notice also how the verbs changes to agree with the subjects):

SINGULAR: Does <u>any</u> <u>owner</u> still have <u>his or her</u> original deed?

PLURAL: Do <u>any</u> of the <u>owners</u> still have <u>their</u> original deeds?

SINGULAR: <u>None</u> of the <u>waste product</u> can be recycled, so it must be stored in an airtight container and placed in underground storage.

PLURAL: <u>None</u> of the <u>waste products</u> can be recycled, so they must be stored in airtight containers and placed in underground storage.

Correct Pronoun Case. So what's the correct response when someone asks for you on the telephone? Answer: "This is <u>he</u>" or "This is <u>she</u>" or "It is <u>I</u>." Why? Because in this situation the pronoun is functioning as a subject and must be in the subjective case.

	Subjective case	Objective case
singular	I	me
	you	you
	he/she/it	him/her/it
plural	we	us
	you	you
	they	them
relative pronoun	who	whom

Whenever the pronoun functions as a subject, use the subjective case. Whenever the pronoun functions as an object, use the objective case. Remember that pronouns in prepositional phrases are *always* objects.

> INCORRECT: Wiler promised to keep the content of our conversation between <u>he</u> and <u>I</u>.
>
> CORRECT: Wiler promised to keep the content of our conversation between <u>him</u> and <u>me</u>.
>
> INCORRECT: To <u>who</u> should I address a letter of complaint?
>
> CORRECT: To <u>whom</u> should I address a letter of complaint?

Pronouns in comparative *than* clauses are always subjects because a verb always follows the pronoun, even if that verb is only implied:

> INCORRECT: We have been in business much longer than <u>him</u>.
>
> CORRECT: We have been in business much longer than <u>he</u>.

The second version is correct because the sentence includes an unstated but understood verb at the end: *We have been in business much longer than he has.* Here's another example:

> INCORRECT: The Jensens are more likely to get the contract than <u>us</u> because they have more up-to-date equipment.
>
> CORRECT: The Jensens are more likely to get the contract than <u>we</u> [are] because they have more up-to-date equipment.

Other Pronoun Issues. Finally, two last comments about pronouns.

1. Don't forget that **possessive pronouns do not use an apostrophe**. *Your* is a pronoun; *you're* is a contraction of *you are*.

> INCORRECT: When potential customers cancel <u>they're</u> orders, we need to carefully evaluate <u>they're</u> reasons for cancellation.
>
> CORRECT: When potential customers cancel <u>their</u> orders, we need to carefully evaluate <u>their</u> reasons for cancellation.

KAPLAN

Test Prep and Admissions

2. The relative pronouns **who/whom, that**, and **which** are often misused. Here are the guidelines:

Use *who/whom* when referring to people.

INCORRECT: Two entrepreneurs <u>which</u> have created multi-million dollar empires and <u>which</u> are under 30 will be the keynote speakers at the seminar.

CORRECT: Two entrepreneurs <u>who</u> have created multi-million dollar empires and <u>who</u> are under 30 will be the keynote speakers at the seminar.

Use *that* when referring to things.

INCORRECT: ABC Candles offers several candle-making classes <u>which</u> are very popular.

CORRECT: ABC Candles offers several candle-making classes <u>that</u> are very popular.

Use *which* to introduce clauses that provide information that is *not* essential to the sentence. Exception: if the clause refers to people, use *who*.

INCORRECT: ABC Candles, <u>that</u> is located on Elm Street, offers weekly candle-making classes.

CORRECT: ABC Candles, <u>which</u> is located on Elm Street, offers weekly candle-making classes. [The information *which is located on Elm Street* is not essential to the sentence.]

Modifiers

Modifiers are those words, phrases and clauses that serve to describe (modify) other words in a sentence. Here's the number one rule regarding modifiers: To keep your sentences clear and correct, always place your modifiers as close as possible to the word(s) they modify.

Misplaced Modifiers. If you violate the proximity rule, you're likely to end up with a misplaced modifier, which is exactly that—a modifier that is in the wrong place. These are usually quite easily corrected by moving the modifying clause or phrase right next to its subject.

INCORRECT: Satisfied and sleepy after a full bottle of milk, the mother laid her baby in the crib.

CORRECT: The mother laid her baby, satisfied and sleepy after a full bottle of milk, in the crib.

INCORRECT: Frightened by the threat of a bear market, the newspaper reported that investors were apprehensive about buying stocks.

CORRECT: The newspaper reported that investors, frightened by the threat of a bear market, were apprehensive about buying stocks.

Dangling Modifiers. Another common modifier error is the dangling modifier. Here the problem is that the subject of the modifying phrase or clause is different from the subject of the main clause or is simply unclear.

> DANGLER: Having studied countless sick cows, they were placed on a diet of organic feed and antibiotics.

[The subject of the introductory participle *having studied* would have to be scientists, veterinarians, or some other group; but the subject of the main clause, *they*, refers to the cows themselves.]

> UNDANGLED: Having studied countless sick cows, the veterinarians placed the cows on a diet of organic feed and antibiotics.

Practice 6

Find and correct the mistake(s) in the following sentences. Answers are found on page 75.

1. Looking at the data carefully, the premises simply will not support the conclusion.

2. Having selected an appropriate brand name, there are still many obstacles to successful marketing of the new product.

3. In this argument, an essential inference is that to pass the course the exam must be taken.

Adjectives and Adverbs. A few short words about adjectives (which modify nouns and pronouns) and adverbs (which modify verbs, adjectives, and other adverbs) to help prevent some common errors:

1. *Good* is an adjective; *well* is an adverb.

   CORRECT: Irina made several <u>good</u> suggestions for revising the application process.
   CORRECT: The new application process is working very <u>well</u>.

2. Use the adjective *less* to modify singular nouns representing a quantity or degree. Use *fewer* to modify plural nouns or things that can be counted.

   INCORRECT: There are <u>less</u> benefits to outsourcing than we first believed.
   CORRECT: There are <u>fewer</u> benefits to outsourcing than we first believed.

3. The comparative form should be used when comparing two things. The superlative should be used when comparing three or more things.

   Comparative: *-er* or *more/less*
       heavier, more innovative

   Superlative: *-est* or *most/least*
       heaviest, most innovative

4. Don't double up. Only one negative or one comparative is needed.

INCORRECT: So far we have been <u>more luckier</u> than last year with the weather during our sidewalk sales.

CORRECT: So far we have been <u>luckier</u> than last year with the weather during our sidewalk sales.

INCORRECT: We <u>don't</u> have <u>no</u> doubt that our plan will increase business.

CORRECT: We <u>don't</u> have <u>any</u> doubt that our plan will increase business.

Parallel Structure

An essential element of proper sentence construction is parallel structure, which is really another variation on the idea that items in a sentence should be balanced. Parallelism means that similar elements in a series, list, or two-part construction (e.g., *not only/but also*) should be expressed in parallel grammatical form: all nouns, all infinitives, all gerunds, all prepositional phrases, or all clauses.

INCORRECT: All business students should learn word processing, accounting, and how to program computers.

CORRECT: All business students should learn word <u>processing</u>, <u>accounting</u>, and computer <u>programming</u>.

The parallelism principle applies to any words that might begin each item in a series: prepositions (in, on, by, with, etc.), articles (*the, a, an*), helping verbs (*had, has, would,* etc.) and possessives (*his, her, our,* etc.). Either repeat the word before every element in a series or include it only before the first item. Anything else violates the rules of parallelism. In effect, your treatment of the second element of the series determines the form of all subsequent elements.

INCORRECT: He invested his money <u>in</u> stocks, <u>in</u> real estate, and a home for retired performers.

CORRECT: He invested his money <u>in</u> stocks, <u>in</u> real estate, and <u>in</u> a home for retired performers.

CORRECT: He invested his money in <u>stocks</u>, <u>real estate</u>, and <u>a home</u> for retired performers.

When proofreading, check that each item in the series agrees with the word or phrase that begins the series. In the above example, *invested his money* is the common phrase that each item shares. You would read "He *invested his money in real estate, (invested his money) in stocks,* and *(invested his money) in a home for retired performers.*"

A number of two-part sentence constructions also call for you to always express ideas in parallel form. These constructions include:

X is as _____ as Y.

X is more/less _____ than Y.

The more/less X, the more/less Y.

Both X and Y . . .

Either X or Y . . .

Neither X nor Y . . .

Not only X but also Y. . .

X and *Y* can stand for as little as one word or as much as a whole clause, but in any case the grammatical structure of *X* and *Y* must be identical.

INCORRECT: The downturn in sales was attributed not only to <u>the recession</u> but also <u>because</u> a new competitor entered the market.

CORRECT: The downturn in sales was attributed not only to <u>the recession</u> but also <u>to the fact that</u> a new competitor entered the market.

INCORRECT: Generally, <u>the profits from sales of</u> everyday necessities are not nearly as spectacular <u>as from</u> luxury items.

CORRECT: Generally, <u>the profits from sales of</u> everyday necessities are not nearly as spectacular as <u>those from the sale of</u> luxury items.

It is often rhetorically effective to use a particular construction several times in succession to emphasize a particular idea or series of thoughts. The technique is called parallel construction, and it is effective only when used sparingly because it works on a larger (multiple-sentence) scale. Here's how parallel construction should be used:

CORRECT PARALLELISM: As a leader, Lincoln inspired a nation to throw off the chains of slavery; as a philosopher, he proclaimed the greatness of the little man; as a human being, he served as a timeless example of humility.

The repetition of the sentence structure (*As a X, Lincoln Y...*) provides a strong sense of rhythm and organization to the sentence and alerts the reader to yet another aspect of Lincoln's character. However, careless writers sometimes use a parallel structure for expressions of *dissimilar* structure.

INCORRECT: They are sturdy, attractive, and cost only a dollar each. [The phrase *They are* makes sense preceding the adjectives *sturdy* and *attractive*, but cannot be understood before *cost only a dollar each.*]

CORRECT: They are sturdy and attractive, and they cost only a dollar each.

Practice 7

Find and correct the mistake(s) in the following sentences. Answers are found on page 75.

1. For example, I would say that my roommate could be characterized as a poor student because he waited until the last minute to study for exams, wrote his lab reports without completing the assigned experiments, and his motivation was low.

2. It is reasonable for a Kravis Software sales representative to expect that he will have an opportunity to introduce his products at the meeting, that there will be a projector for his slide presentation, and prospective buyers will ask questions about the product.

3. We would like to hire someone who is eager, responsible, and works very hard.

Sentence Fragments

In real life, full-blown grammatically complete sentences are a rarity. Most speech takes the form of what would qualify as a "sentence fragment" if it occurred in writing. But for the Analytical Writing section, you'll want only complete sentences. Don't even risk a title: the E-rater will think that's a fragment, too.

What exactly is a fragment? An incomplete sentence (like this one). To be complete, a sentence must have both a subject and a verb *and* express a complete thought. Often fragments are dependent clauses that need another sentence to make a complete thought:

> FRAGMENT: <u>While we are reorganizing the department</u>. Harrison will be the interim office manager. [The first sentence is a dependent clause that cannot stand alone; *while* makes it depend upon the second sentence.]

These fragments have an easy fix: simply combine the dependent and independent clauses into one sentence.

> COMPLETE THOUGHT: While we are reorganizing the <u>department, Harrison</u> will be the interim office manager.

Other times a fragment is a clause or phrase missing a subject or verb, or both. The solution: add the missing subject or verb, or attach the lose clause or phrase to the core sentence.

> FRAGMENT: Cheyenne has been researching ways to conserve energy. <u>Without sacrificing production</u>.
> COMPLETE THOUGHT: Cheyenne has been researching ways to conserve <u>energy</u> <u>without</u> sacrificing production.

Sometimes a relative pronoun (*that, who, which*) causes the fragment, which can be corrected by simply deleting the pronoun.

FRAGMENT: Cheyenne, <u>who</u> has been researching ways to conserve energy without sacrificing production.

COMPLETE THOUGHT: Cheyenne has been researching ways to conserve energy without sacrificing production.

Practice 8

Some of the sentences in the following short passage are sentence fragments. Identify the fragments and fix them by adding or removing the necessary words to make complete sentences. Answers are found on page 76.

> Everyone feels shy. At some point in life. It is perfectly normal to be concerned about how strangers might view you in an unfamiliar situation. For example, a social gathering or new job. However, shyness can sometimes become a major difficulty. If a person feels overpowering anxiety about common situations such as going to the store, attending classes at school or even walking down the street. That anxiety can interfere with the person's ability to carry on a normal life. A few shy people develop a serious fear of strangers. Forcing them to restrict or avoid contact with people most of us interact with daily. Such as the mail carrier, co-workers or teachers. These people who feel overwhelmed by the mere thought of contact with a stranger. Such people may have agoraphobia.

_____

_____

_____

_____

_____

_____

_____

_____

Run-on Sentences

Run-ons are sentences that literally run right into each other sometimes there is a comma between them however a comma alone is not strong enough to separate two complete thoughts.

Okay, let's try that again:

Run-ons are sentences that literally run right into each other. Sometimes there is a comma between them; however, a comma alone is not strong enough to separate two complete thoughts.

There are four ways to correct run-on sentences:

1. **Separate the sentences with a period.**

   INCORRECT: Cheyenne has been researching ways to conserve <u>energy, she</u> will submit her findings by Friday.

   CORRECT: Cheyenne has been researching ways to conserve <u>energy. She</u> will submit her findings by Friday.

2. **Separate them with a comma *and* a coordinating conjunction (*and, or, for, nor, but, so* and *yet*).**

   CORRECT: Cheyenne wants to conserve <u>energy, but</u> she is worried about sacrificing production.

3. **Separate them with a semicolon. Use this option when the two ideas are closely related.**

   CORRECT: Cheyenne has been researching ways to conserve <u>energy; she</u> is also seeking more eco-friendly suppliers.

4. **Make one sentence dependent upon the other by adding a subordinating conjunction such as *since, because, while, although, during,* and *before*.**

   CORRECT: <u>Although it might mean slightly increased costs,</u> Cheyenne wants to use more eco-friendly suppliers.

It is also correct to separate the two sentences with a dash, but *only* if you wish to set the second sentence off for emphasis.

   CORRECT: Cheyenne wants to conserve energy—but only if it doesn't sacrifice production.

Note: *However* is not a subordinating conjunction; it is a conjunctive adverb. Use it with a semicolon, not a comma, to join two independent clauses.

   CORRECT: Cheyenne wants to conserve energy; however, she is worried about sacrificing production.

Mechanics

Mechanics refers to the rules for punctuation, capitalization, and spelling. With the E-rater, correct mechanics is especially important, because these are among the easiest mistakes for the program to find.

Punctuation

Comma. If you are one of those writers who finds comma rules confusing, you're in a bit of luck. In a few cases where a comma used to be required, the comma is now optional:

- before the conjunction (usually *and*) in a series
- before the coordinating conjunction joining two relatively short independent clauses
- following *brief* introductory adverbial expression

In all these cases, so long as there is no danger of ambiguity, ETS favors omitting the comma. That doesn't mean you *have* to omit it or that you will be penalized if you do; these are still grammar "gray areas." However, it does mean a little more freedom from comma worries.

That said, let's review the places where you *do* need a comma:

❍ To set off **appositive** or **non-restrictive** material within the sentence—that is, information that is relevant but not essential to the core sentence. (Obviously, if the material occurs at the beginning or the end of the sentence, only one comma will be needed.)

CORRECT: Early retirement was offered to eleven employees, all of whom have been employed for over 25 years.

CORRECT: Dwayne, who has been an employee for over 25 years, has accepted the offer of early retirement.

❍ To set off **transitional expressions**, **interjections**, or nouns of **direct address**:

CORRECT: Critics of the proposal, however, will doubtless focus on the unknown risks.

CORRECT: Nevertheless, the proponents of the proposal will surely prevail.

CORRECT: After we review your proposal, Mrs. Jenkins, we'll let you know our decision.

❍ To separate direct discourse from the speaker or source (unless the quoted phrase is very short):

CORRECT: I wonder, How can politicians fairly represent such a diverse constituency?

CORRECT: My supervisor informed me, with a straight face, "Your performance is too good for this department. You're making the rest of us look bad."

Note that quotation marks are only necessary for direct quotation of an utterance. Otherwise, they are not necessary:

CORRECT: The question is, Do we need more students?

○ Before a **coordinating conjunction** joining two independent clauses.

CORRECT: It was Kendra's first time interviewing a potential employee, and she was more nervous than the applicant.

○ After a long **introductory phrase or clause**.

CORRECT: Against the advice of his accountant, Auggie did not pay estimated taxes.

○ **Between two modifiers** that both modify the same word.

CORRECT: Hani is a perfect example of a self-educated, highly successful entrepreneur. [Both *self-educated* and *highly successful* modify *entrepreneur*.]

○ **Between items in a series**. Again, the comma before the *and* and last item is optional.

CORRECT: To furnish her new office, Anna bought two filing cabinets, a spacious oak desk, a matching swivel chair, and several framed Ansel Adams photographs. [Remember that the comma before *and* is optional.]

○ Anywhere else it's needed **to prevent confusion**.

CORRECT: When you think about it, it isn't really all that complicated.

Now, here are some cases where the comma is superfluous:

○ when a direct quotation ends in a question mark or an exclamation point but the sentence continues on, the comma must be omitted:

INCORRECT: "Millions for defense, but not one cent for tribute!," the newspapers proclaimed.

CORRECT: "Millions for defense, but not one cent for tribute!" the newspapers proclaimed.

○ after very short introductory adverbial expressions if there is no danger of confusion:

INCORRECT: Every winter, the number of fatal traffic accidents increases due to adverse driving conditions.

CORRECT: Every winter the number of fatal traffic accidents increases due to adverse driving conditions.

○ around restrictive (essential) phrases

INCORRECT: Teachers and principals, in the public school system, have been lobbying for more funding for the arts.

CORRECT: Teachers and principals in the public school system have been lobbying for more funding for the arts.

○ before words quoted indirectly

INCORRECT: The Supreme Court has ruled that, no evidence gathered by illegal surveillance methods entered into the trial record.

CORRECT: The Supreme Court has ruled that no evidence gathered by illegal surveillance methods entered into the trial record.

○ *after* a coordinating conjunction

INCORRECT: Every nation must take measures to protect itself from terrorist attacks,
but, the rights of citizens to due privacy and equal protection under the
law must be protected.

CORRECT: Every nation must take measures to protect itself from terrorist attacks,
but the rights of citizens to due privacy and equal protection under the
law must be protected.

Practice 9

Find the mistake(s) in the following sentences. Answers are found on pages 76–77.

1. Elementary schools must impart the tools necessary, to
teach the basic skills.

2. The role, of providing lifelong assistance to disabled people,
belongs to the government which can muster the vast
resources needed to properly care for the ill.

3. Advocates of the proposed law however, will most likely
insist on the need to forestall improper sharing of intellectual property, and classified information.

4. All the support for this argument is either flawed superfluous or irrelevant.

5. In fact it is just as likely that some other cause can
explain why the products at the uptown factory are
cheaper to produce.

6. Although discounted the evidence of the second survey is
actually more informative to this argument.

Period. How and when to use a period may seem straightforward, but especially when
it comes to quotations and abbreviations, there are specific rules you need to follow.

○ An indirect question embedded within a declarative sentence ends with a period, not
a question mark.

INCORRECT: We must consider why white-collar crime has risen so rapidly?

CORRECT: We must consider why white-collar crime has risen so rapidly.

❍ Only one period should appear at the end of a sentence, even if the sentence ends in an abbreviation or a directly quoted sentence. Likewise, a period cannot be combined with a question mark or exclamation mark.

INCORRECT: Investigators recently reported, "The mysterious pollutants have been traced to the Trenton-based Kwalitee Products, Inc.".

INCORRECT: Investigators recently reported, "The mysterious pollutants have been traced to the Trenton-based Kwalitee Products, Inc.."

CORRECT: Investigators recently reported, "The mysterious pollutants have been traced to the Trenton-based Kwalitee Products, Inc."

INCORRECT: Connor's brief fax consisted of only one word: "Help!".

CORRECT: Connor's brief fax consisted of only one word: "Help!"

❍ In abbreviations, no space follows internal periods. Where initials are used instead of names, the general practice is to leave internal spaces, although newspapers do not do so. If initials replace a name, the periods and spaces may be omitted. Whichever style you choose, be consistent.

INCORRECT: Many students feel that having the letters "Ph. D." after their name will make them more competitive on the job market.

CORRECT: Many students feel that having the letters "Ph.D." after their name will make them more competitive on the job market.

INCORRECT: Since the dissolution of the U. S. S. R., political instability has replaced political repression.

CORRECT: Since the dissolution of the U.S.S.R., political instability has replaced political repression.

❍ Periods are omitted from acronyms, words formed from the initial letters of a multi-word name: NATO (North Atlantic Treaty Organization), GOP (Grand Old Party, i.e., Republican Party), CEO (chief executive officer), etc. Many abbreviated company names are treated as acronyms: IBM, AOL, GM.

❍ When a quoted phrase appears at the end of a sentence, the period is placed within the quotation marks, even when it did not appear in the original next that is being quoted. (This is the American practice; the British practice is to place the period outside the quotation marks unless it was actually part of the original text.)

AMERICAN: The prevailing ethos of our westward expansion is summed up in the phrase "Manifest Destiny."

BRITISH: The prevailing ethos of our westward expansion is summed up in the phrase "Manifest Destiny".

Need we insist? It's an American test; use the American convention.

Practice 10

Find the mistake(s) in the following sentences. Answers are found on page 77.

1. We may well ask ourselves what colleges can possibly do to prevent cheating?

2. Does it actually make sense to ask whether people's lives are more meaningful now than one hundred years ago?

3. For years, the largest contingents of international peace-keepers have come from the U. K. and the U. S. A..

Semicolon. For the most part, you should use a semicolon only where you could also use a period—it is a punctuation mark that belongs primarily between two *independent* clauses. The difference between the semicolon and period is that a semicolon still keeps the two clauses together in one sentence. Thus, use a semicolon instead of a period when the two clauses are closely related and you want to keep a connection between them:

PERIOD: Hillary earned her bachelors degree in just two and a half years. She then went on to become a teacher of gifted children. [These two sentences are sequential, but not closely related.]

SEMICOLON: Hillary earned her bachelors degree in just two and a half years; she earned her masters in less than one. [These two sentences are closely related; they both deal with Hillary's speed in earning her degrees.]

The other time to use a semicolon is when one or more items in a list contain an internal comma. In this case you can avoid confusion by using semicolons instead of commas to separate the elements in the list.

CORRECT: Similar incidents have occurred in Houston, Texas; Nashville, Tennessee; and Davis, California.

Practice 11

Find the mistake(s) in the following sentences. Answers are found on page 77.

1. When a society is in agreement on the need to meet social objectives, government generally takes on a powerful role, in such cases, taxation, rather than simply raising money, becomes, in addition, a means of implementing those goals.

2. The assets of such an enterprise might include, for example, $30 million in real estate, equipment and infrastructure, $20 million in cash, investments, and accounts receivable, and $10 million in inventory.

3. Many of the food products marketed by McBurger are notoriously high in cholesterol, fat, and calories; the company's sales are therefore likely to decline over the next few years if new product lines are not introduced.

Colon. Less frequently used than commas and semicolons, but no less important, is the colon. The colon has three specific functions. Use a colon:

1. To introduce a list of three or more items if the list comes after an independent clause:

INCORRECT: Some of the benefits of the new system include: speed, accuracy, and significant savings.

CORRECT: Some of the benefits of the new system <u>include speed</u>, accuracy, and significant savings

CORRECT: There are three benefits of the new <u>system: speed</u>, accuracy, and significant savings.

Do **not** use a colon after *such as, for example,* or *including*:

INCORRECT: The new system offers many benefits, such as: speed, accuracy, and significant savings.

2. To introduce a quotation if it comes *after* an independent clause:

INCORRECT: As Thomas Edison said: "Genius is 1% inspiration and 99% perspiration."

CORRECT: I agree 100% with Thomas Edison: "Genius is 1% inspiration and 99% perspiration."

3. To introduce an explanation or summary of an independent clause:

CORRECT: There is one essential ingredient of success, and only one: perseverance.

CORRECT: The pitch was a complete failure: the client rejected every item in the proposal.

Hyphen and Dash. Often confused because they look alike, the hyphen (-) and the dash (—) perform very different functions. Use a **hyphen** to connect two or more words that work together as one object or modifier:

CORRECT: The <u>editor-in-chief</u> occasionally does restaurant reviews.

CORRECT: Our new partnership is clearly a <u>win-win</u> situation.

Use a **dash** to set off a word, phrase or clause for emphasis:

CORRECT: Pickering—who is just 26 years old—is the youngest CEO of a major corporation.

Question Mark. Use question marks only to indicate a *direct* question is being asked.

INCORRECT: We often wonder where the time has gone?

CORRECT: We often wonder, where has the time gone?

Do not place a question mark at the end of an indirect question unless the indirect question is itself is embedded in a question.

INCORRECT: A good leader should always ask herself who will follow her lead?

CORRECT: A good leader should always ask herself who will follow her lead.

CORRECT: Should a good leader always ask herself who will follow her lead?

Practice 12

Find the mistake(s) in the following sentences. Answers are found on page 77.

1. The prompt poses a simple question: Should the 55 mph limit should be restored?

2. The question posed is whether the 55 mph limit should be restored.

3. Is there an answer to the question of the feasibility of restoring the 55 mph speed limit?

Quotation Marks. Quotation marks enclose text that is a direct quote. They can also be used to indicate a word that is being used as a word.

INCORRECT: This building is zoned for residential office use, the realtor said.

CORRECT: "This building is zoned for residential office use," the realtor said.

CORRECT: The realtor said this building is zoned for residential office use.

INCORRECT: He used the term proactive five times in his introduction.

CORRECT: He used the term "proactive" five times in his introduction.

Here are a few important notes about quotation marks:

○ In American usage (unlike British), commas and periods should be placed <u>inside</u> quotation marks, even when they are not properly part of the quoted material.

CORRECT: J. D. Salinger's "Catcher in the Rye," a novel taught in American high schools for generations, caused a fundamental shift in attitudes toward "dirty language."

CORRECT: "Ask not what your country can do for you," urged the President. "Ask what you can do for your country."

○ Colons and semicolons, on the other hand, should *follow* the closing quotation mark.

CORRECT: I was not one who believed "my country right or wrong"; in fact, having come to age during the Viet Nam War, I tended to assume that our foreign policy was devoid of moral principle.

○ Question marks and exclamation marks should be placed <u>inside</u> the quotation marks when they are part of the quoted material and <u>outside</u> when they are not. When a question ends with a quotation that is itself a question, there will be only one question mark: the one inside the quotation marks.

INCORRECT: Doesn't the judge usually ask the jurors, "Have you reached a verdict?"?

CORRECT: Doesn't the judge usually ask the jurors, "Have you reached a verdict?"

CORRECT: The judge asked the jurors, "Have you reached a verdict?"

Apostrophe. The apostrophe is used to form most possessives and contractions, in addition to a few plurals (see above). Here are a few reminders to help you avoid apostrophe errors.

○ The apostrophe is used to show *possession*, not *plurality*:

INCORRECT: Americans eat million's of hamburger's every day.

CORRECT: Americans eat millions of hamburgers every day.

○ When adding a possessive apostrophe to a plural noun ending in *s*, place the apostrophe after the plural *s* and *omit* the possessive *s*.

INCORRECT: As new products are developed, the manager must devote some thought to those product's names.

INCORRECT: As new products are developed, the manager must devote some thought to those products's names.

CORRECT: As new products are developed, the manager must devote some thought to those products' names.

○ If the plural does *not* end in *s*, the possessive is formed, as usual, by adding apostrophe and then *s*.

INCORRECT: Some peoples' idea of a sacrifice is not watching TV for one evening.

CORRECT: Some people's idea of a sacrifice is not watching TV for one evening.

❍ If a singular noun ends in *s*, show possession by adding *'s*.

INCORRECT: Travis relied on Lukas' expertise to negotiate a fair contract.

INCORRECT: Travis relied on Luka's expertise to negotiate a fair contract.

CORRECT: Travis relied on Lukas's expertise to negotiate a fair contract.

❍ Remember that possessive pronouns do *not* take an apostrophe:

INCORRECT: The decision is our's [your's, her's, their's].

CORRECT: The decision is ours [yours, hers, theirs].

Practice 13

Find the mistake(s) in the following sentences. Answers are found on page 78.

1. Three principle's are at issue in this case.

2. Ultimately, a leader must be guided by her peoples wishes.

3. With very few exceptions, womens' rights have been adjudicated by the courts over the past few decade's.

4. Many Prince's of Wales' have served long terms as the heir to the crown of Great Britain, and Prince Charles' case is no exception.

The normal way to change a singular noun to plural is by adding *s* or *es*. But when it comes to numbers or other characters, the plural is usually formed by adding *'s*:

CORRECT: How many i's are there in the word *Mississippi*?

CORRECT: A valid email address cannot have two @'s.

Decades have traditionally been accorded apostrophes (e.g., 1990's). These days, however, it is becoming more common to omit the apostrophe (1990s), especially in the abbreviated form, which already uses an apostrophe to indicate the omission of the first two digits of the year:

CORRECT: Having grown up in the 1990s, I believe that world peace is an achievable goal.

UNACCEPTABLE: The '60's and '70's were years of turbulence in many countries.

ACCEPTABLE: The '60s and '70s were years of turbulence in many countries.

ACCEPTABLE: The sixties and seventies were years of turbulence in many countries.

Practice 14

Find the mistake(s) in the following sentences. Answers are found on page 78.

1. In most developing country's, up to 80% of the population lives in rural community's.

2. Republicans and Democrats alike may feel uncomfortable about running on their parties' platforms.

3. Human's are not the only primate's that have been known to murder their own kind: infanticide is well-documented among chimpanzee's, baboon's, and several species of monkeys.

Slash. The forward slash (/) has many uses.

It can mean per, as in m^3/sec (cubic meters per second).

It can mean and, as in w/d (washer and dryer).

It can indicate abbreviation, as in w/ and w/o (with and without).

In a non-technical academic essay such as the Analytical Writing section, you should avoid these informal or technical uses of the slash.

One other use of the slash is worth avoiding. Apparently, due to the popularization of *s/he* (read *she or he*) and other attempts to remedy the lack of a gender-neutral singular pronoun in English, the slash has in recent years been tossed around as a short form of *or*. This practice is not likely to gain acceptance in professional or academic prose any more than the use of *&* to replace *and*. Either spell out *or*, or let a single option suffice.

UNACCEPTABLE: A successful leader will convince/coerce his/her followers to lay aside their hostilities and focus on the challenges facing the community.

ACCEPTABLE: A successful leader will convince her followers to lay aside their hostilities and focus on the challenges facing the community.

Practice 15

Find the mistake(s) in the following sentences. Answers are found on page 78.

1. In the age of electronic media, reading books/magazines is not as important as it once was.

2. Consumers must have the confidence that they have an option to get a refund/exchange any online purchase that does not meet with their satisfaction.

3. Statistics for births/year/person can give a useful measure of a nation's reproductive status.

Practice 16

The following paragraph contains numerous errors in punctuation. Correct the errors and check your answers against the revised version found on pages 78–79.

(1) Abraham Lincoln described the U. S. government as being as he said in the Gettysburg Address "of the people by the people and for the people." (2) This notion I believe puts the priorities' between the achievements of institutions, and the achievements of governments, in proper perspective. (3) It is not a question, of the achievements of individuals v. s. the achievements of the government, that individual/government contrast is a false dilemma. (4) Rather it is the achievements of individuals which make up the achievements of a government that determine the greatness of a nation. (5) This is what Lincoln meant when he referred to the nations "unfinished work:" that each of us has a task to perform and those tasks determine what kind of nation we will live in. (6) With this fundamental argument in mind how can we not join with Lincoln in wishing that such a nation, "shall not perish from the earth"?

Capitalization

Capitalization is not rocket science, but it is easy to lose points for simple errors. These are the most important points to review.

First, the general principle is this: Capitalize proper nouns—the <u>specific</u> names of people, places, and things. Do not capitalize general items.

Specific	General
Souderton High School	my high school
Aunt Bettie	your favorite aunt
A-Plus Computer Services	computer repair company

Now some more specific guidelines. In a GRE or GMAT essay, you **must capitalize**:

○ the first word in a sentence. Avoid ellipsis points (...): even if you use them correctly, the E-rater is likely to become confused and decide that you have an uncapitalized sentence.

○ people's names, as well as titles when used with the name (Judge Blackwell) or, in the case of high officials, when used to refer to a particular person.

CORRECT: In the face of enormous resistance to his foreign policy, President Johnson announced that he would not run for re-election in 1968.

CORRECT: The President called a press conference to announce his decision.

CORRECT: The president of the United States is not chosen directly by the people.

○ names of places (but not "the" or "of," unless they fall at the beginning of a sentence), as well as adjectives derived from place names.

> CORRECT: The Library of Congress contains several exhibitions in its online gallery.
>
> CORRECT: There are several exhibitions in the Library of Congress's online gallery.

○ names of institutions (except, again, "the" or "of" and other minor words, unless they fall at the beginning of a sentence).

> CORRECT: I received my letter of acceptance from the University of Pennsylvania today.
>
> CORRECT: The University of Pennsylvania campus is just five miles from my home.

○ special events and periods (names of holidays, historical events, eras), but not centuries.

> CORRECT: The exhibit includes drawings and letters from the historic Battle of the Bulge.

○ names of countries, languages, and religions, and adjectives derived from them.

> CORRECT: In the tiny country of Bhutan, nearly every citizen is a Buddhist.

○ the stars, planets, and other celestial bodies and structures (the Milky Way, the Crab Nebula); ETS even capitalizes Earth, as well as Moon and Sun when referring to the Earth's moon and sun.

○ the first and all important words of publication titles, movies, songs, works of art.

> CORRECT: The British comedy "The Office," like the American comic strip "Dilbert," satirizes life behind the cubicle.

Do NOT capitalize:

○ any word simply for emphasis

> INCORRECT: The two essential characteristics of any leader are Decisiveness and Communication Skills.
>
> CORRECT: The two essential characteristics of any leader are decisiveness and communication skills.

○ the names of academic subjects, except when referring to the name of a particular course or to a department.

> INCORRECT: I plan to major in Anthropology and minor in French Literature.
>
> CORRECT: I plan to major in anthropology and minor in French literature.
>
> INCORRECT: This semester I am taking anthropology 101 and introduction to french literature.
>
> CORRECT: This semester I am taking Anthropology 101 and Introduction to French Literature.

○ seasons.

○ the first word of a sentence cited in indirect discourse.

> INCORRECT: Leah said She was enrolling in the executive MBA program.
> CORRECT: Leah said she was enrolling in the executive MBA program.

Practice 17

Find the mistake(s) in the following sentences. Answers are found on page 79.

1. During the Middle Ages and the most of the Renaissance, Philosophy was hardly distinct from Theology.

2. By the end of Spring, american and canadian University students have been enjoying their Summer Vacation for well over a month.

3. Widely regarded as the most important U. S. Trade Agreement in the past two decades, the U.S.-Canada Free Trade Agreement phased out all tariffs and quotas between the two countries by the end of the Twentieth Century.

4. Last year, doctor sanford was elected president of the brooklyn council. The president of the council meets regularly with the dean of students.

5. american independence day and memorial day occur during the summer, but labor day is in the fall.

6. The novels of william faulkner are set in the american south, and the author himself lived most of his life south of the mason-dixon line.

Spelling

Frequently Misspelled Words. Most of us could use a good review of these commonly misspelled words—especially those of us who have grown dependent upon the autocorrect feature on our computers.

absence: One *a*, two *e*'s.
accommodate, accommodation: Two c's, two m's
accompany: Two c's.
all right: Two words. *Alright* is *NOT* all right.
a lot: Always two words, never one; do not confuse with *allot*.
argument: No *e* after the *u*.
calendar: *A, e,* then another *a*.
campaign: Remember the *aig* combination.
cannot: Usually spelled as a single word, except where the meaning is "able not to."

> CORRECT: One cannot ignore the importance of conformity.
> CORRECT: Anyone can not pay taxes, but the consequences may be serious.

comparative, comparatively: Yes, *comparison* has an *i* after the *r*. These words don't.

conscience: Spell it with *science*.

correspondent, correspondence: No dance.

definite: Spell it with *finite*, not *finate*.

develop, development: No *e* after the *p*.

embarrass: Two *r*'s, two *s*'s.

every day (adv.): Two words with *every* modifying *day*. Note that there is also an adjective, *everyday*, meaning *commonplace, usual*.

> ADVERB: We see this error *every day*.

> ADJECTIVE: Getting stuck behind an elephant in traffic is no longer an *everyday* occurrence in Katmandu.

exaggerate: One *x*, two *g*'s.

foreign: Think of the *reign* of a *foreign* king.

grammar: No *e*.

grateful: Spell it with *grate*

harass: One *r*, two *s*'s.

independent, independence: No dance.

indispensable: It's something you are not *able* to dispense with.

judgment: No *e* on the end of *judge*.

leisure: Like *pleasure* but with an *i* instead of *a*.

license: In alphabetical order: *c* then *s*, not *lisence*.

maintenance: *main*, then *ten*, then *ance* (reverse alphabetical order for your vowels preceding *n*).

maneuver: Memorize the unusual *eu* combo.

no one: Two words. Don't be mislead by *nobody, nothing, everyone, someone*, and *anyone*.

noticeable: Notice that this one keeps the *e* when adding the suffix.

occur, occurred, occurrence: Double the *r* when you add a suffix beginning with a vowel.

parallel, unparalleled: Two *l*'s, then one.

parenthesis (pl. **parentheses**): Likewise, many other words of Greek origin are spelled with *-is* in the singular and *-es* in the plural; among the more common are **analysis, diagnosis, prognosis, synthesis, thesis.**

perseverance: Only two *r*'s—*sever*, not *server*. Remember that the *a* in the suffix keeps it from being all *e*'s.

professor, professional: One *f*.

pronunciation: Never mind *pronounce* and *pronouncement*: *pronunciation* has no *o* in the second syllable.

questionnaire: Two *n*'s, one *r*.

regardless: Not *irregardless*, an unacceptable yoking of *irrespective* and **regardless.**

responsible, responsibility: While the French and Spanish cognates end in *–able*, it's *–ible* in English.

separate: Look for "a rat" in separate.

unanimous: *un* then *an*.

vacuum: One *c*, two *u*'s.

Practice 18

The following paragraph contains several of the spelling errors described in this section. Locate and correct the commonly misspelled words. There are 37 spelling errors in the paragraph in all. Answers are found on page 80.

Many people think it is alright to except charitable assistance irregardless of their ability to secure financial indepandance for themselves. Other people think it can not effect them, or that they do not loose money, if these proffesional charity cases force the government to acomodate they're free reign. I would not be exxagerating if I said that noone lives in a vaccum, and all descent people need to be responsable for there own welfare to. I wander if it would of ever ocured too these folks to ascent to by food, clothing and shelter firsthand for people who will not altar their indiscrete financial habits. I think its unlikely. When your looking passed the question of whose paying for these goods and services, than your excepting there right to steel from you're pocket everyday.

Doubling Consonants. One of the most confusing issues in spelling is whether to double the final consonant when adding a suffix. *Beginning* or *begining*? *Traveling* or *travelling*? Here's the rule: If the final syllable is accented and the final vowel is short, the consonant is doubled. (Except for *c*, because *c* before *e* or *i* is softened to an *s* sound; we simply add a *k* instead: e.g. *picnic, picnicked.*)

short vowel:	hop	hopped
	fat	fatten
	set	setting
long vowel:	hope	hoped
	fate	fated
	seat	seating

There are complications, of course. In American English, this rule only applies if the final syllable of the root word is accented; in British English, it applies whether or not the accent falls on the final syllable. Therefore, Americans abroad are *travelers*, while peripatetic Brits are *travellers*.

Another wrinkle involves words where the vowel-consonant pattern would normally indicate a long vowel, but the pronunciation is short, as in *head* or *come*. In this case, if we add a suffix, there is no need to protect the short vowel by doubling the consonant: *heading* rhymes with *wedding*, not with *reading*, while *coming* rhymes with *humming*, not with *homing*.

There are of course anomalies and exceptions, but following these guidelines will help you minimize your errors

Practice 19

Find the mistake(s) in the following sentences. Answers are found on page 80.

1. In fields such as human developement and family planing, it is becomming easier to find funding for basic research.

2. As the hailstorm intensified, the campers paniced and ran screamming through the grounds.

3. Effective leadership means recognizing when an objective cannot be reached without sacrificing essential resources.

Homonyms and Other Commonly Confused Words

Accept or *except*? *Alter* or *altar*? *Discrete* or *discreet*? Even if you know the difference between these words, when you're under time pressure, it's easy to type in the wrong one. Homonyms and contractions (e.g., *who's*) are especially good candidates for typos, so here's a quick review of some of the most common troublemakers.

Note: Since we reviewed contractions vs. possessives already, they aren't included in the list below. Remember that you can avoid contraction typos by simply avoiding contractions throughout your essay. (Besides, while the ETS E-rater is not programmed to grade down for the use of contractions, many professors (the sort of people who will be grading your essay!) feel strongly that contractions are not appropriate in academic prose.)

accept (v.): to take or receive. *The CEO accepted the treasurer's resignation.*
except (prep.): leave out. *The Town Council approved all elements of the proposal except the tax increase.*

adverse (adj.): unfavorable. *This plan would have an adverse impact on the environment.*
averse (adj.): opposed or reluctant. *I am averse to doing business with companies that don't treat their employees fairly.*

advice (n.): recommendation as to what should be done. *I would like your advice about how to handle this situation.*
advise (v.): to recommend what should be done. *I will be happy to advise you.*

affect (v.): to have an impact or influence on. The expansion of Pyramid Shopping Mall will certainly affect traffic on the access roads.
effect (n.): result, impact. *The proposal will have a deleterious effect on everyone's quality of life.* (v.): to cause, implement. *The engineers were able to effect a change in train's performance at high speeds.*

altar (n.): an elevated structure, typically intended for the performance of religious rituals. *The court refused to allow the construction of an altar on public property.*
alter (v.): to change. *It should be a simple matter to alter one's will.*

among (prep): used to compare three or more items or entities. *We can choose from among dozens of styles.*

between (prep): used to compare two items or entities. *We can choose between these two styles.*

amoral (adj.): neither moral nor immoral; without a sense of moral judgment. *Claire was upset with the amoral discussion of terrorist acts.*

immoral (adj.): morally wrong. *Whatever beliefs a terrorist has, terrorist acts are immoral.*

ascent (n.): climb, upward movement. *Vanessa's rapid ascent up the corporate ladder impressed us all.*

assent (n.): agreement; (v.): to agree. *Peter has given his assent to the plan.*

assure (v.): to convince or guarantee. *He has assured me that this is a safe investment.*

ensure (v.): to make certain. *Please ensure that this is a safe investment.*

insure (v.): to guard against loss. *There is no way to insure this investment.*

bazaar (n.): traditional oriental market. *I found these fantastic trinkets at the bazaar.*

bizarre (adj.): very strange, weird. *No one knew how to respond to such a bizarre question.*

cite (v.): to quote, to refer. *The article cited our annual report.*

sight (n.): something seen or visible; the faculty of seeing. *What an amazing sight!*

site (n.): location; (v.): to place or locate. *This is the perfect site for a new office.*

complement (n.): something that completes; (v.): to go with or complete. *This item really complements our product line.*

compliment (v.): to flatter; (n.): a flattering remark. *That was a sincere compliment.*

continual (adj.): repeated regularly and frequently. *Alan's continual telephone calls finally wore Rosa down and she agreed to a meeting.*

continuous (adj.): extended or prolonged without interruption. *The continuous banging from the construction site gave me a severe headache.*

decent (adj.): proper, acceptable. *You can trust Lena to do what is decent.*

descent (n.): downward movement. *The rapid descent of the balloon frightened its riders.*

discrete (adj.): separate, not connected. *These are two discrete issues.*

discreet (adj.): prudent, modest, having discretion; not allowing others to notice. *I must be very discreet about looking for a new job while I am still employed here.*

disinterested (adj.): impartial, objective. *We need a disinterested person to act as an arbitrator in this dispute.*

uninterested (adj.): not interested. *Charles is uninterested, but he'll come along anyway.*

eminent (adj.): outstanding, distinguished. *The eminent Judge Blackwell will teach a special seminar in business ethics this fall.*

imminent (adj.): about to happen, impending. *Warned of imminent layoffs, Loretta began looking for another job.*

incidence (uncountable noun: occurrence) frequency
incident *(pl.: incidents)* (countable noun: events, cases) an occurrence of an event or situation

personal (adj.): private or pertaining to the individual. *Please mark the envelope "personal and confidential."*
personnel (n.): employees. *This year we had a 5% increase in personnel.*

precede (v.): to come before. *The list of resources should precede the financial worksheet.*
proceed (v.): to go forward. *Although Jules will be absent, we will proceed with the meeting as planned.*

principal (n.): head of a school or organization, primary participant, main sum of money; (adj.): main, foremost, most important. *Joshua is one of the principals of the company.*
principle (n.): a basic truth or law. *I have always run my business based on the principle that honesty is the best policy, even in a capitalist society.*

rein (n.): a means of restraint or guidance; (v.) to restrain, control. *You need to rein in your intern, Carol—she's taking on much too much responsibility and doesn't seem to know what she's doing.*
reign *(v.)*: to exercise power; (n.): period in which a ruler exercised power or a condition prevailed. *Under the reign of King Richard, order was restored.*

than (conj.): used to compare. *I will be more successful this time because I am more experienced than before.*
then (adv.): at that time, therefore. *I was very naïve back then.*

weather (n.): climatic conditions, state of the atmosphere. *The bad weather is going to keep people away from our grand opening.*
whether (conj.): used to refer to a choice between alternatives. *I am not sure whether I will attend the grand opening or not.*

Practice 20

Find the mistake(s) in the following sentences. Answers are found on page 80.

1. Its often necessary to by more goods then can be consumed in a single day even though there likely to spoil.

2. I would of thought that journalists should avoid taking sides when they right about such controversial subjects.

3. We all here stories of people who's children refuse to accompany them on vacations.

4. Can you site three incidences in the passed in which Congress has given its ascent to such a proposal?

5. The Board of Education excepted the advise of the high school principle in chosing to altar the wording of the teachers' contracts.

6. After years of suffering under the heal of an autocrat, the citizens must steal themselves for change.

MAXIM 2: BE CLEAR

Correctness is important, but it means little if your sentences are not clear. Ambiguous, vague, and just plain confusing sentences can result from poor sentence structure or ineffective word choice.

Use Straightforward Sentence Structure

Some writers try to impress readers by writing elaborate sentences—but those sentences can often get tangled. Since the E-rater won't be able to untangle your ideas, and since clarity is essential, it's best to stick to straight-forward sentence structure: *subject, verb, indirect object, object*.

But that doesn't mean you can't write sophisticated sentences with lots of phrases and clauses. But you will need to be especially careful about where you put modifying clauses and phrases. The basic rule: Make sure your modifiers are as close as possible to the words they modify.

Modifier Placement

In English, the position of the word within a sentence often establishes the word's relationship to other words in the sentence. This is especially true with modifying phrases. Like pronouns, adjectival expressions are generally connected to the nearest word that agrees with the modifier in person and number. Likewise, when a sentence contains more than one verb or verbal element (such as an infinitive, gerund, or participial), an

KAPLAN

Test Prep and Admissions

adverbial expression will be interpreted as modifying the closest verb. The placement of prepositional phrases is particularly important, since they can modify both nouns and verbs as well as other elements.

AMBIGUOUS: The President and his closest advisors frequently discuss potential scandals behind closed doors
[Which generally occur *behind closed doors*—the *discussions* or the *scandals*?]

CLEAR: Behind closed doors, the President and his closest advisors frequently discuss potential scandals.

CLEAR: The President and his closest advisors frequently discuss potential scandals that are occurring behind closed doors.

AMBIGUOUS: A politician must consider what compensation is expected for each campaign donation at the time it is given.
[Does *at the time it is given* modify *consider* or *expected*?]

CLEAR: When accepting a campaign donation, a politician must consider what compensation is expected.

CLEAR: When a politician receives a campaign donation, he or she must consider what compensation a donor expects in return.

Many adverbial expressions can refer to words that either precede or follow them. Ambiguity can result when the modifier is squeezed between two possible referents and the reader has no way to know which is the intended referent:

AMBIGUOUS: The pharmaceutical company announced <u>suddenly</u> researchers had succeeded in identifying the neurotoxin.
[Which was *sudden—the company's announcement* or *the researchers' success*?]

CLEAR: <u>Suddenly</u>, the pharmaceutical company announced that researchers had succeeded in identifying the neurotoxin.

CLEAR: The pharmaceutical company announced that researchers had <u>suddenly</u> succeeded in identifying the neurotoxin.
[Notice how the use of *that* before the noun clause makes the sentence easier to understand.]

Avoid Vague or Ambiguous Language

Vague words are unclear; ambiguous words are words that have more than one possible meaning.

Vague Words and Phrases

Words like *lots, somewhat*, and *really* are vague. How much exactly? Your sentences will be clearer and more powerful if you use words that are more precise:

> VAGUE: We saw <u>lots of</u> improvement in employee morale over the last six months.

> MORE EXACT: We saw <u>significant</u> improvement in employee morale over the last six months.

> VAGUE: Our choices for subcontractors are <u>somewhat</u> limited.

> MORE EXACT: Our choices for subcontractors are <u>severely</u> limited.

Unclear and Ambiguous Pronoun References

A pronoun is a word that stands in for a noun (or noun expression) in a sentence. A pronoun must agree with its antecedent and must refer clearly to one and only one antecedent.

> AMBIGUOUS: No entrepreneur should tell a client that he is overly concerned with image.
> [Does *he* refer to *entrepreneur* or *client*?]

> CLEAR: No entrepreneur should accuse a client of being overly concerned with image.

> CLEAR: Being overly concerned with image is not something that an entrepreneur should admit to a client. *or* No entrepreneur should admit being overly concerned with image to a client.

Occasionally, you may have to repeat a noun, rather than rely on a pronoun that may make your sentence ambiguous.

> AMBIGUOUS: It may be cost effective to rely on subcontractors instead of company personnel, as they would certainly require extra training.
> [Who would require training—the *subcontractors* or the *company personnel*?]

> CLEAR: It may be cost effective to rely on subcontractors instead of company personnel, as the company personnel would certainly require extra training.

An antecedent must actually occur in your text. Even if you think the reader will know what you mean, do not use a pronoun without a clear and appropriate antecedent.

INCORRECT: When you are voting for a candidate, you must be sure he or she is fully qualified to undertake it.

[What does *it* refer to? The antecedent is implied but must be clearly stated.]

CORRECT: When you are voting, you must be sure the candidate you choose is fully qualified to undertake the position in question.

Avoid using *this, that, it,* or *which* to refer to a whole phrase, sentence, or idea. Even when these pronouns are placed very close to their intended antecedents, the references may still be unclear.

UNCLEAR: U.S. consumers use increasingly large amounts of non-recyclable diapers every year. Some worry that this will someday turn the Earth into a giant trash can. [What exactly is *this*? The use of diapers or the trash that results from their use?]

CLEAR: U.S. consumers use increasingly large amounts of non-recyclable diapers every year. Some worry that this ever-growing mass of waste products will someday turn the Earth into a giant trash can.

UNCLEAR: The candidate changed his position on all the key issues, which made the voters extremely nervous. [What makes the voters nervous—that the candidate changed position or the issues? *Which* could refer to either.]

CLEAR: The candidate changed his position on all the key issues, making the voters extremely nervous.

Ambiguous repetition generally involves pronouns or other words which may refer to multiple entities or concepts:

UNACCEPTABLE: They concluded that most teachers do like their students, and, while they may not clearly express their feelings, they generally do reciprocate this sympathy.

ACCEPTABLE: The researchers concluded that most teachers do like their students, and, while the children may not clearly express their feelings, they generally reciprocate their teacher's sympathy.

UNACCEPTABLE: It is well known that that problem has been the subject of a full-fledged investigation, and that will most likely yield some temporary solution that will prove acceptable to all concerned parties.

ACCEPTABLE: It is well known *that the* problem has been the subject of a full-fledged investigation, *which* will most likely yield a temporary solution acceptable to all concerned parties.

MAXIM 3: BE CONCISE

Why take 200 words to express an idea that can be conveyed in 100? Unfortunately, some of us have been "trained" to use more words than necessary because we were often under pressure to write essays of a certain length. But 100 clear and concise words are much better than 200 words of fluff. And the way to move from 100 to 200 words if so required isn't through "filler" words and phrases—it's through the development of ideas.

Unnecessary words and phrases don't improve writing; they bog it down and often irritate readers. Concise writing is clear writing; it avoids the clutter and confusion that often result from unnecessary wordiness.

Wordy Phrases

In an attempt to make their prose seem more scholarly or more formal, some test takers use phrases where single words will do: *at the present time* or *at this point in time* instead of *now,* or *take into consideration* instead of simply *consider.* Don't. Instead, use the simpler, clearer phrase. Here are some more examples of wordy phrases and their concise counterparts:

WORDY	CONCISE
along the lines of	like
as a matter of fact	in fact
at all times	always
by means of	by
because of the fact that	because
by virtue of the fact that	because
due to the fact that	because
for the reason that	because
in light of the fact that	because
in this day and age	today
in order to	to
in spite of the fact that	although, though
in the event that	if
until such a time as	until

Unnecessary Relative Clauses

Wordiness is also caused by unnecessary *that, who,* and *which* clauses and phrases. To be more concise and precise, remove the relative pronoun and verb to create an appositive or turn the phrases and clauses into adjectives:

> WORDY: The Truman Doctrine, which was established in 1947, created a "policy of containment."
>
> CONCISE: Established in 1947, the Truman Doctrine created a "policy of containment."
>
> MORE CONCISE: The 1947 Truman Doctrine created a "policy of containment."
>
> WORDY: Temporary employees who work hard and are loyal are often rewarded with full-time employment.
>
> CONCISE: Hard-working, loyal temporary employees are often rewarded with full-time employment.

Cluttered Constructions

There is, it is, and *that* often unnecessarily clutter sentences. A simple deletion or reconstruction can eliminate wordiness and create smoother sentences.

> WORDY: It is essential that all visitors and employees wear safety goggles on the production floor.
>
> CONCISE: All visitors and employees must wear safety goggles on the production floor.
>
> WORDY: There is another reason that we should switch vendors, and that is that our current vendor does not offer bulk discounts.
>
> CONCISE: We should also switch vendors because our current supplier does not offer bulk discounts.

Unnecessary Repetition

It is redundant to speak of "a beginner lacking experience": the word *beginner* in itself implies lack of experience. Yet we sometimes use repetitive phrases, especially when we are unsure that we are expressing our idea clearly or with sufficient force.

REDUNDANT	CONCISE
refer back	*refer*
few in number	*few*
small-sized	*small*
grouped together	*grouped*
in my own personal opinion	*in my opinion*
end result	*result*
serious crisis	*crisis*
new initiatives	*initiatives*
climb up	*climb*

Sometime a sentence unnecessarily "defines" a word again in an attempt to make an idea more clear:

WORDY: Jared lost a lot of business because of inflation, which drove up prices. [*Inflation* means an increase in prices, so the clause *which drove up prices* is entirely unnecessary.]

CONCISE: Jared lost a lot of business because of inflation.

WORDY: He is sad and depressed because he did not get promoted to a better position. [*Sad* and *depressed* are synonyms; *promoted* means to move up to a better position.]

CONCISE: He is depressed because he did not get the promotion.

MAXIM 4: BE EXACT

The more precise your language, the more impact your words will have. You can avoid wordiness and add power to your writing by using exact words and phrases.

IMPRECISE: Paris is a <u>very beautiful</u> city.

PRECISE: Paris is a <u>stunning</u> city.

Stunning is more precise, more concise, and more sophisticated than *very beautiful*—and thus a better word choice.

IMPRECISE: After a while, the odor disappeared into the air.

PRECISE: After a while, the odor dissipated.

IMPRECISE: The school had to close because it had many problems with safety.

PRECISE: The school was shut down because of many safety violations. [*Violations* is more specific and concrete than *problems with*; *shut down* is more exact and powerful than *had to close*.

MAXIM 5: BE APPROPRIATE

For the Analytical Writing tasks, being appropriate means writing at the appropriate level of formality. You need a style, tone, and point of view that show respect for your readers—their authority, their level of intelligence, and their time.

Of course, you know your real audience consists of a trained professor and the E-rater. But you will be expected to write for a general audience of your peers—people with a general college-level education and varied interests and backgrounds. Which is a good thing, because thinking of your audience in this way can help you write more effectively and be more relaxed during the exam.

Avoid Slang and Colloquial Expressions

There are many levels of diction, and each genre has a range of dictions generally considered appropriate. Your essays do not require the most formal diction, but an overly colloquial style will drag down your score, and slang of any kind should be strictly avoided. The E-rater won't know, for example, if you are using slang in dialogue to realistically represent how someone speaks; it will simply assume you are using inappropriate vocabulary. So remember: no slang. Zero. Zip. Zilch. Nada.

Colloquial language isn't exactly slang, but it is informal and for the most part should also be avoided. Here are some particular expressions to avoid, as well as some acceptable substitutes.

Intensifiers

Awfully, incredibly, pretty, really, totally: all these words have legitimate uses, but they should not be used as generic intensifiers. Even *very* has been so over-used that it tends to diminish rather than emphasize your point. Preferable alternatives:

absolutely	emphatically	notably	surprisingly
acutely	exceedingly	particularly	terribly
amply	excessively	positively	truly
astonishingly	extensively	powerfully	uncommonly
authentically	extraordinarily	prodigiously	unusually
certainly	extremely	profoundly	vastly
considerably	genuinely	remarkably	way
decidedly	greatly	substantially	wonderfully
deeply	highly	superlatively	
eminently	indispensably	surpassingly	

Down-toners

Kind of, sort of, pretty much—again, these expressions have legitimate uses, but not in a formal essay. Besides being too colloquial, these terms are also vague.

Instead use words such as *fairly, partially, largely, mildly, moderately, quite, rather, slightly, somewhat.*

Quantifiers

Instead of *lots, a lot of, a bunch of* and other colloquial (and vague) quantifiers, try *many, much, a number of, a substantial number of, quite a few, numerous.*

Contractions

Coulda, gonna, hafta, hadta, lotsa, oughta, shoulda, wanna, woulda: we use these all the time in speech, but these colloquial contractions are not acceptable in formal writing.

Use Sophisticated Vocabulary

An appropriate style for the GRE and GMAT essays requires a formal and somewhat sophisticated level of vocabulary. Here are a few simple substitutes to help you write on a more sophisticated level.

○ Instead of *like*, use *such as:*

> DEPRECATED: The success of a business depends on many factors, <u>like</u> convenient location, well-trained staff, and effective promotion.

> ACCEPTABLE: The success of a business depends on many factors, <u>such as</u> convenient location, well-trained staff, and effective promotion.

○ Instead of *different*, use *various.*

○ Instead of *big*, use *large, important, substantial, prestigious, significant.*

○ Instead of *okay*, use *acceptable, satisfactory, appropriate.*

○ Instead of *etc.*, use *and so on* (better yet, restructure the list and use *including* or *for example* or *include more examples*).

○ Instead of *oftentimes*, use *often.*

> UNSOPHISTICATED: For <u>different</u> reasons, I was <u>turned down</u> by <u>a lot</u> of <u>big</u> schools, <u>like</u> Harvard, Yale, Princeton, Dartmouth, <u>etc</u>.

> SOPHISTICATED: For <u>various</u> reasons, I was <u>rejected</u> by <u>many</u> <u>prestigious</u> schools, including Harvard, Yale, Princeton, and Dartmouth.

Practice 21

Find the mistake(s) in the following sentences. Answers are found on page 80.

1. Lots of people are incredibly into video games and watching the tube, and I basically feel that that's okay, although it's pretty much of a waste of time.

2. These days there're a lot of different reality shows, like Survivor, American Idol, etc., that are all kind of similar.

3. Oftentimes a perfectly good plan can be trashed by a minor oversight.

Avoid Jargon and Pretentious Language

Sophisticated does not mean *pretentious*. Pretentious texts try to impress by sounding scholarly or profound, often using over-the-top or esoteric vocabulary. You can be sophisticated without clouding meaning or annoying readers with pretentious language.

> PRETENTIOUS: Avoid periphrasis and pleonasms in your compositions.
> JUST RIGHT: Avoid wordiness and redundancy in your writing.

Jargon is technical or specialized language. Remember the rule: respect your reader. Not all of your readers will be familiar with specialized terms, and even if you think *most* of your readers are, that still leaves a few who will be confused by your word choice. So, either avoid jargon altogether and use lay terms or define any specialized language you use.

Practice 22

The following paragraph contains several examples of slang and substandard vocabulary. Rewrite the paragraph in a style more appropriate for the GRE or GMAT. Answers are found on page 81.

> It is really pretty supportable to argue that studying an academic discipline changes your view of the world. Like say if you study history, you oftentimes read about a bunch of different facts that are equally as important as the ones you learned about in school, but that totally weren't covered. Lots of big social trends and beliefs that we think shoulda been okay at this point in time turn out to be incredibly bogus. Studying a discipline like history can really change how we look at the world.

_____

_____

_____

_____

_____

_____

Use an Appropriate Point of View

Though some professors still preach "Don't use *I*," both the E-rater and the human reader are expecting you to express your opinion. So use the first person point of view, but not excessively—you don't need *I* in every sentence. Just write assertively (see Maxim 7). Use your personal experiences as examples throughout, but don't overdo it.

You can also address your readers as *you* (second person point of view), but don't address them directly (e.g., *dear reader*), and don't attribute words, ideas, or experiences to your readers. Your reader may not have seen or might not believe or might not know. Play it safe by using the generic third person (but not *one*, which often comes off sounding pretentious):.

WRONG: As you know…

WRONG: As one knows…

  RIGHT: As many people know…

WRONG: You have undoubtedly seen…

  RIGHT: As you may have seen…

MAXIM 6: BE CONSISTENT

While variety is important in some aspects of writing (see Maxim 8), **consistency** is an important element your readers will be looking for. Consistency in writing shows evidence of control over your thoughts as well as the conventions of writing. Make sure your essay is consistent in style and tone as well as point of view.

Consistent Style

Style is created primarily through word choice and sentence structure. Do you tend to write in long, descriptive sentences? In a short, bare-bones kind of style? Do you prefer words like *perambulate* and *hirsute* to *walk around* and *hairy*?

You know that the most appropriate style for the essay is formal but not stiff or pretentious (see Maxim 5). If you tend to write in a very informal style, fancy up a bit for the Analytical Writing task. Don't try to sound like someone else—stick to your natural voice—but choose words and sentence structures that are more sophisticated than normal. Whatever your natural style, start with an appropriate style and stick to it throughout your essay. A shift in style suggests an inconsistent grasp of the material, a lack of confidence in your own writing skills, or a gap in logic—all of which can be quite disconcerting to your readers.

INCONSISTENT: Lots of things can work together to create success, including education, smarts, foresight, perseverance, and sometimes plain old dumb luck.

CONSISTENT: Many factors contribute to success, including education, intelligence, foresight, perseverance, and sometimes serendipity.

INCONSISTENT: The reef is a vast ecosystem in the sea where a bunch of species live together. Lots of them are mutually dependent upon each other.

CONSISTENT: The reef is a vast ecosystem in the sea where hundreds of species live in symbiotic relationships.

Consistent Tone

Tone is the mood or attitude conveyed by writing or speech. In text, we convey tone through word choice, sentence structure, and punctuation. For example, both of the sentences below say the same thing, but the word choice and punctuation convey a different attitude towards the senator's action.

> The senator <u>evaded</u> another question.

> The senator <u>dodged</u> another question!

You might have a great sense of humor, but these essays are not the place for a light-hearted or jocular essay. The most appropriate tone is one that is serious, informative, and always respectful of readers and other points of view. Start with an appropriate tone and stick to it throughout the essay.

Consistent Point of View

It is often useful to explore contrasting points of view within your essay—in fact, consideration of other opinions is one of the hallmarks of an effective argument. But your point of view as *author* should remain consistent within your essay. It is easy, for example, to slide around from *I* to *you* to *one* to *we*. The effect can be disconcerting, to say the least. One option to avoid is the use of *one*: it is grammatically limiting and it sounds pretentious. Whatever narrative voice you choose, and whichever voices you introduce to represent other perspectives, be consistent (but avoid overuse of particular pronouns).

> TANGLED: I often feel that one has to make sacrifices to reach the goals you set for yourself, but we should always remember that life occurs in the present tense.

> STRAIGHTFORWARD: I often feel that I must make sacrifices to reach my goal, but I try to remember that life occurs in the present tense.

> STRAIGHTFORWARD: We may feel it necessary to make sacrifices in order to reach our goals, but we should always remember that life occurs in the present tense.

> STRAIGHTFORWARD: Some people feel it necessary to make sacrifices in order to reach their goals, but they should always remember that life occurs in the present tense.

> STRAIGHTFORWARD: You may feel it necessary to make sacrifices in order to reach your goals, but you should always remember that life occurs in the present tense.

MAXIM 7: BE ASSERTIVE

An assertive essay expresses confidence in its ideas, and this makes the essay far more convincing than one that is hesitant. Remember that these essays are designed in part to measure what you think and why you think it—so **state your points without hesitation**.

> HESITANT: In my humble opinion, there are few things more important to leading a relatively successful life than health and companionship.
>
> ASSERTIVE: Health and companionship are essential.
>
> HESITANT: I think maybe we could come up with some way to make chief executives more accountable for what they do.
>
> ASSERTIVE: Chief executives should be more accountable for their actions.

The more assertive sentences convey confidence, which goes a long way towards convincing readers of a particular point of view. They are also clearer and more concise than the hesitant versions.

On the other hand, there is no need to bludgeon the graders with your certitude. A few qualifiers will give the impression that you are reasonable: *fairly, rather, somewhat, relatively*, and of such expressions as *seems to be, a little,* and *a certain amount of* are good choices. But, do not overplay the modesty card.

> TOO ASSERTIVE: In light of the facts, it is absolutely certain that the election scandal could have been avoided.
>
> TOO MODEST: In light of the facts, it seems fairly reasonable that perhaps the election scandal might have been avoided. [Too wordy as well.]
>
> JUST RIGHT: In light of the facts, it seems certain that the election scandal could have been avoided.

Avoid Needless Self-Reference

Like letters to the editor of a newspaper, Analytical Writing essays are by definition expressions of your views; it is unnecessary to label every assertion as opinion. Two or three self-references may be appropriate, especially when distinguishing your point of view from another, but there is no need to draw attention to yourself. Keep your focus on the topic.

> OVERLY SELF-REFERENT: I used to believe that we should have a choice on matters of personal safety such as whether or not to wear a helmet when riding a motorcycle, but I now realize that personal safety is actually a matter of public welfare.
>
> JUST RIGHT: Personal safety is a matter of public welfare.
>
> BEST FOR AN OPENING PARAGRAPH: I believe personal safety is a matter of public welfare.

Use the Active Voice

Let's be clear: the passive voice is an extremely useful device, particularly for expressing ideas where the speaker does not know the agent or does not wish to reveal it:

> EXAMPLE: Recently, two schools in my district were vandalized.

The passive voice is also useful in manipulating sentence balance, particularly when the subject is long and involved and the predicate is brief.

> AWKWARD: Often, newspapers that are having problems with falling circulation, rising costs, and the threat of a hostile buy-out from an international publishing conglomerate hire media consultants.
>
> BETTER: Often, media consultants are hired by newspapers that are having problems with falling circulation, rising costs, and the threat of a hostile buy-out from an international publishing conglomerate.

However...the passive voice has been notoriously overused by weak writers trying to sound authoritative, to the point that graders (human as well as computerized) generally react negatively to it. Solution: **wherever possible, use the active voice**. Active sentences are more direct and more concise, conveying your ideas with more clarity and power.

> PASSIVE: The active voice should be used by essay writers.
>
> ACTIVE: Essay writers should use the active voice.

State Your Opinions

Our research indicates that the E-rater is looking for expressions of opinion in the first paragraph: *I believe, in my opinion, I think*. However, it is also looking for less obvious (but no less direct) expressions of judgment: *assume, exaggerate, fail, ignore, misconstrue, misjudge, misinterpret, misrepresent, overemphasize, overestimate, overlook, presume, underestimate, understate*, and so on. Words that indicate consideration of counterarguments or alternative points of view are also regarded as signs of engaged analysis. These expressions include *actually, admittedly, although, despite, except, even though, however, in spite of, nevertheless, nonetheless, notwithstanding, still,* and *yet*.

Practice 23

The following sentences use passive voice unnecessarily. Rewrite them in active voice. Answers are found on page 81.

1. The coolant pumps were destroyed by a surge of power.

2. The transformer was struck by a bolt of lightning.

3. The goalkeeper was too slow to stop the ball.

4. The moods of a manic-depressive are unpredictable.

5. The administrative secretary is responsible for monitoring and balancing the budgets.

6. It is important that hikers remain on marked trails.

7. All too often, athletes with marginal academic skills have been recruited by our coaches.

8. Teachers have been portrayed or stereotyped as illiterate, even though they fulfill strict requirements.

1._____

2._____

3._____

4._____

5._____

6._____

7._____

8._____

MAXIM 8: BE EXCITING

Whatever you actually *say* in your essay, *how* you say it can have a significant impact on your score. Your essay can be correct, concise, appropriate—all of the other maxims—yet still be dull and dry and at risk for a lower score. A lively and engaging essay will earn more points from both your human and computer graders. You can make your essay inviting to readers by having variety in both your sentence structure and vocabulary.

Variety in Sentence Structure

Human and mechanical graders are looking for a variety of sentence forms. What that means, specifically, is that you'll want to use a combination of simple, compound, complex, and compound-complex sentences. Here are some examples:

> **Simple** (one main clause):
> Any entrepreneur seeking a new business location should seriously consider Nashville, Tennessee.
>
> **Compound** (two or more main clauses):
> Entrepreneurs often need to select a new business location, and they should seriously consider Nashville, Tennessee.
>
> **Complex** (one main clause, one subordinate clause):
> If any entrepreneurs are looking for a new business location, they should seriously consider Nashville, Tennessee.
>
> **Compound-complex** (two or more main clauses, plus at least one subordinate clause):
> Entrepreneurs often need to select a new business location, and when they do, they should seriously consider Nashville, Tennessee.

In addition to using a variety of these basic sentence forms, you can enliven your sentences by placing "interrupters," phrases and clauses in various places:

> X is unlike Y because of Z.
> Because of Z, X is unlike Y.
> However, X is unlike Y because of Z.
> X, however, is unlike Y because of Z.
> However, because of Z, X is unlike Y.

Practice 24

Fill in the table below. Each sentence is provided in either simple, compound, complex, or compound-complex form. Rewrite each given example in the three other forms. Answers are found on pages 81–83.

Simple	Sometimes the fresh perspective of a non-expert can be valuable in the consideration of a subject.
Compound	
Complex	
Compound-Complex	

Simple	
Compound	The feeling of having fulfilled a personal goal is important, but the tangible rewards of society are at least as important.
Complex	
Compound-Complex	

Simple	
Compound	
Complex	Even though Company B is more expensive, the important question is whether the combined cost of pest-control and savings in product damage are greater with Company B.
Compound-Complex	

Simple	
Compound	
Complex	
Compound-Complex	Different academic communities have different traditions, and while these differences may be significant, it is an oversimplification to say that there can be no meaningful interaction between them.

Simple	It is reasonable to argue that a cheaper brand of sunscreen might encourage people to have a false sense of security.
Compound	
Complex	
Compound-Complex	

Length

The scorers are also looking for a variety of sentence lengths. A short sentence (four to eight words) can effectively emphasize a simple point; a long sentence (30–45 words) might be necessary to present a relatively complicated idea. Varying sentence length throughout also creates a more pleasing rhythm for your readers—too many short sentences are likely to sound monotonous while too many long sentences may be difficult on your reader.

> EXAMPLE: Entrepreneurs often need to select a new business location, and when they do, they should seriously consider Nashville, Tennessee. This southern city has a great deal to offer.

Sentence Openers

How you *start* your sentences should vary, too. If all of your sentences start with the subject, even if the sentence lengths and forms vary, it can sound awfully monotonous (*unless* you are purposely using parallel construction).

> MONOTONOUS: Nashville was founded in 1779. Tenessee became the sixteenth state of the union in 1796. Nashville became the state's capital in 1812.

> EXCITING: Founded in 1779, Nashville became the capital of Tennessee in 1812, sixteen years after Tennessee became the sixteenth state of the union.

To add variety, combine sentences as in the example above and start some sentences with introductory clauses and phrases rather than the subject. But keep the basic order for sentence structure for your core clause (subject, verb, indirect object, object).

> NEEDS VARIETY: Nashville was founded in 1779. It became the state capital in 1812.

> HAS VARIETY: Founded in 1779, Nashville became the state capital in 1812.

A Varied Vocabulary

Repetition is one of our most effective rhetorical devices. As we have already pointed out, the E-rater cannot measure the quality of essay content directly. Instead, it focuses on surface characteristics that ETS researchers believe are statistically symptomatic of good or bad writing. Not only does it look for and penalize excessive repetition, but the E-rater also compares the diversity of vocabulary of each submitted essay with prompt-specific vocabulary lists as well as essay-type vocabulary lists. Thus, one of our most important sentence-level strategies is to use synonyms instead if relying on a few key words throughout your essay.

REPETITIVE VOCABULARY: <u>Business</u> is not an occupation for the faint of heart. Every <u>businessperson</u> should be aware that nearly 50% of <u>businesses</u> fail in their first year, while 75% of <u>businesses</u> go under within three years. Our first order of <u>business</u> in this essay is to consider the question, "What are the causes of <u>business</u> failure?"

SYNONYM-ENRICHED: <u>Business</u> is not an occupation for the faint of heart. Every <u>entrepreneur</u> should be aware that nearly 50% of new <u>ventures</u> fail in their first year, while 75% go under within three years. Our first <u>concern</u> in this essay is to consider the question, "What are the causes of <u>commercial</u> failure?"

An effective way to avoid repetition is to make lists of terms pertinent to the various prompt topics. For example, here is a clustered list of nouns that might be useful in answering a question about higher education.

- facilities, campus, library, dormitory, laboratory, location, faculty-to-student ratio, sports
- recruitment, scholarship, financial aid, stipend, assistance, promotional material, catalogue, publication, publicity, public relations
- admissions, requirements, standards, entrance, application
- administration, administrator, dean, official, board of trustees, committee
- faculty, professor, advisor, candidate, academic, researcher, lecturer, teaching assistant, educator
- student, applicant, candidate, alumnus, registrant, freshman, sophomore, junior, senior, undergraduate, graduate, scholar, researcher
- field, major, research, study, discipline, program
- instruction, courses, curriculum, elective, required course, lecture, seminar, workshop, lab, syllabus, assigned readings, assignments, homework
- grades, marks, scores, average, points, GPA
- test, competition, examination, quiz, midterm, final
- college, university, institution, higher education, academia, school, junior college,
- goals, objectives, degree, graduation, commencement, employment, career, job, placement, opportunity

Practice 25

The following paragraph contains examples of overly repetitive word use. Correct the problems by rewriting the paragraph with appropriate synonyms in place of the repetitive words and phrases. Answers are found on page 83.

Courses that focus on intellectual development are more important than courses that contribute to professional development. Courses focused on professional development assume that these courses will still be relevant to the future job market, while in fact the constant changes in the job market might make such courses obsolete. In contrast, courses that work toward intellectual development are courses that train a person for a variety of job market roles, so that even if the job market changes, the work done in the courses remains relevant. This is not to say that many courses cannot do both: preparing a person for the job market while also preparing her for a variety of different job market possibilities. But, while courses on professional development have their place in the realm of university courses, they should not be allowed to supersede courses that train the intellect for a changing job market.

_____

_____

_____

_____

_____

_____

_____

_____

_____

_____

_____

EIGHT MAXIMS, REDUX

Here's a quick recap of our Eight Maxims of Effective Writing:

Be correct.

Be clear.

Be concise.

Be exact.

Be appropriate.

Be consistent.

Be assertive.

Be exciting.

Check your answers to the practice exercises from this chapter on the following page. To learn about writing strong paragraphs and essays, turn to chapter four.

PRACTICE ANSWERS AND EXPLANATIONS

Practice 1

1. Most of us wish that our parents <u>were</u> better prepared to face retirement.

2. While we may wish that our physical conditioning <u>were</u> better, few of us are pre-pared to invest the time and effort in the kind of exercise and diet that might help us achieve it.

3. No mistake.

4. Although it is simple to mouth words of support for the work of others, it is prefer-able that they <u>be</u> given negative feedback where it applies.

5. No mistake.

6. Judging from recent pricing patterns, it is imperative that the American government <u>begin</u> to regulate retail milk prices

Practice 2

1. **Many** people in New York **travel** by subway.

   Many is a singular indefinite pronoun.

2. **Workers** in New York often **commute** a long way to work.

   The prepositional phrase *in New York* interferes with the connection between the plural subject, *workers* and the plural verb *commute*.

3. **Tourists** in New York **expect** to see the subway.

   The prepositional phrase *in New York* separates the plural subject *tourists* and the plural verb *expect*.

4. The "redbird" subway **cars** with a red body **have** been a common sight in New York until recently.

   The prepositional phrase *with a red body* might mislead you about the connection between the plural subject *cars* and the plural verb *have been*.

5. The **streets** of large cities such as New York **are** undercut by complex networks of subway tunnels.

   The long-distance phrases *of large cities such as New York* interferes with your per-ception of the relationship between the plural subject *streets* and the plural verb *are*.

6. Today, the **economy** of New York and other large cities **is** booming.

   The word *cities* next to the verb can interfere with your sense that the subject *econ-omy* matches the singular verb *is*.

7. **New Yorkers** with a good income **are** less likely to commute by subway.

   The prepositional phrase *with a good income* might confuse the relationship between the plural subject *New Yorkers* and the plural verb *are*.

8. A **worker** with a long commute **does** not want to spend hours on the subway.

   The singular subject *worker* takes the singular verb form *does*.

9. A **private car**, although convenient, **pollutes** the air.

   The subject *car* is singular, so it takes the singular verb form *pollutes*.

10. **Parking** in one of New York's many overcrowded garages **is** also a problem.

    The singular subject *parking* requires the singular verb *is*. Don't be misled by the plural word *garages* because it is part of a prepositional phrase, not the subject of the sentence.

11. Every day, **Joe and Carla ride** the subway to work.

    A compound subject joined by *and* is plural.

12. Every day, Joe **or Carla rides** the subway to work.

    In a compound subject joined by *or*, the verb matches the closer part of the subject. *Carla* is singular, so use the singular verb *rides*.

13. Every day, Joe's sisters **or Carla's sisters ride** the subway to work.

    In a compound subject joined by *or*, the verb matches the closer part of the subject. *Carla's sisters* is plural, so use the plural verb *ride*.

14. Every day, Joe's sisters **or Carla rides** the subway to work.

    In a compound subject joined by *or*, the verb matches the closer part of the subject. *Carla* is singular, so use the singular verb *rides.*

15. Every day, Carla **or Joe's sisters** from Long Island **ride** the subway to work.

    In a compound subject joined by *or*, the verb matches the closer part of the subject. Don't be thrown by the prepositional phrase *from Long Island*. Since *Joe's sisters* is plural, use the plural verb *ride*.

16. **Everyone enjoys** a summer vacation.

    Most indefinite pronouns, including *everyone*, are singular.

17. **Nobody has** fun when the Cyclones lose a game.

    Most indefinite pronouns, including *nobody*, are singular.

18. **Either** of the answers **is** valid in response to that question.

    Either is a singular indefinite pronoun. Disregard the prepositional phrase *of the answers* when figuring out the proper verb form.

19. **Each** of the students **brings** a book to class every day.

    Each is a singular indefinite pronoun. Disregard the prepositional phrase *of the students* when working out subject-verb agreement for this sentence.

20. Many **are** obsessed with reality television these days.

    Many is one of a very few plural indefinite pronouns in English.

Practice 3

1. The installation of video cameras in public areas certainly <u>adds</u> a measure of security but may eventually erode our right to privacy.

2. Competition for grades, jobs, and mates ultimately <u>benefits</u> society.

3. The main flaw in most of these arguments <u>is</u> the reliance upon unsupported infer-ences. *or* In most of these arguments, the main flaw <u>is</u> the reliance upon unsupported inferences.

Practice 4

1. The entire team of scientists <u>was</u> allergic to the very chemicals they were studying

2. No mistake.

3. A number of Internet companies <u>are</u> doubtless preparing to challenge Google for dominance of the search engine market.

Practice 5

1. The CEO, along with the Board of Directors, <u>is</u> responsible for any infraction of the corporation's environmental protection policy.

2. Either the Attorney General or his senior assistants <u>have</u> the option of prosecuting such violations.

3. No mistake.

Practice 6

1. Looking at the data carefully, <u>we see that</u> the premises simply will not support the conclusion.

2. Having selected an appropriate brand name, <u>the entrepreneur still faces</u> many obsta-cles to successful marketing of the new product.

3. In this argument, an essential inference is that to pass the course <u>one must take the exam</u>.

Practice 7

1. For example, I would say that my roommate could be characterized as a poor stu-dent because he waited until the last minute to study for exams, wrote his lab reports without completing the assigned experiments, and <u>lacked motivation</u>.

2. It is reasonable for a Kravis Software sales representative to expect that he will have an opportunity to introduce his products at the meeting, that there will be a projector for his slide presentation, and <u>that</u> prospective buyers will ask questions about the product.

3. We would like to hire someone who is eager, responsible, and <u>hardworking</u>.

Practice 8

Sentence fragments are underlined in the paragraph below:

> Everyone feels shy. <u>At some point in life</u>. It is perfectly normal to be concerned about how strangers might view you in an unfamiliar situation. <u>For example, a social gathering or new job</u>. However, shyness can sometimes become a major difficulty. <u>If a person feels overpowering anxiety about common situations such as going to the store, attending classes at school or even walking down the street.</u> That anxiety can interfere with the person's ability to carry on a normal life. A few shy people develop a serious fear of strangers. <u>Forcing them to restrict or avoid contact with people most of us interact with daily</u>. <u>Such as the mail carrier, co-workers or teachers</u>. <u>These people who feel overwhelmed by the mere thought of contact with a stranger</u>. Such people may have agoraphobia.

One suggested way to fix the fragments in this paragraph is to connect sentences and drop words that make sentences into subordinate clauses:

> Everyone feels shy at some point in life. It is perfectly normal to be concerned about how strangers might view you in an unfamiliar situation, for example, a social gathering or new job. However, shyness can sometimes become a major difficulty. If a person feels overpowering anxiety about common situations such as going to the store, attending classes at school or even walking down the street, that anxiety can interfere with the person's ability to carry on a normal life. A few shy people develop a serious fear of strangers, forcing them to restrict or avoid contact with people most of us interact with daily, such as the mail carrier, co-workers or teachers. These people feel overwhelmed by the mere thought of contact with a stranger. Such people may have agoraphobia.

Practice 9

1. Elementary schools must impart the tools <u>necessary to</u> teach the basic skills.

   A restrictive element ("to teach the basic skills") should not be set off by a comma.

2. The <u>role of</u> providing lifelong assistance to disabled <u>people belongs</u> to the <u>government,</u> which can muster the vast resources needed to properly care for the ill.

   The prepositional phrase "of providing…" is not parenthetic, so it doesn't need commas. But the nonrestrictive phrase "which can muster…" does need to be set off by a comma. Nonessential phrases, which begin with the word "which," are nonrestrictive.

3. Advocates of the proposed <u>law, however,</u> will most likely insist on the need to forestall improper sharing of intellectual <u>property and</u> classified information.

   The word "however," in this case, is parenthetic, so set it off with commas.

4. All the support for this argument is either <u>flawed</u>, superfluous or irrelevant.
   OR
   All the support for this argument is either <u>flawed</u>, <u>superfluous</u>, or irrelevant.

   Items in a series should be separated by commas. Although current usage favors omitting the last comma just before the conjunction ("or" in this case), either method is correct.

5. In fact it is just as likely that some other cause can explain why the products at the uptown factory are cheaper to produce.
   OR
   <u>In fact</u>, it is just as likely that some other cause can explain why the products at the uptown factory are cheaper to produce.

   The introductory clause "in fact" is short and is unlikely to cause any confusion in this sentence. Although current usage favors omitting the comma that sets off a short introductory clause, either usage is correct.

6. Although <u>discounted</u>, the evidence of the second survey is actually more informative to this argument.

   In this case, the comma is required even though the introductory clause is short. Without the comma, the clause "Although discounted" is likely to cause confusion as the word "discounted" runs into the first part of the subject "the evidence," that immediately follows it, so the comma is required to prevent confusion.

Practice 10

1. We may well ask ourselves what colleges can possibly do to prevent <u>cheating.</u>

2. No mistake.

3. For years, the largest contingents of international peacekeepers have come from the <u>U.K.</u> and the <u>U.S.A.</u>

Practice 11

1. When a society is in agreement on the need to meet social objectives, government generally takes on a powerful <u>role; in such cases,</u> taxation, rather than simply raising money, becomes, in addition, a means of implementing those goals.

2. The assets of such an enterprise might include, for example, $30 million in real estate, equipment and <u>infrastructure; $20</u> million in cash, investments, and accounts <u>receivable; and</u> $10 million in inventory.

3. No mistake.

Practice 12

1. No mistake.

2. No mistake.

3. No mistake.

Practice 13

1. Three <u>principles</u> are at issue in this case.

2. Ultimately, a leader must be guided by her <u>people's</u> wishes.

3. With very few exceptions, <u>women's</u> rights have been adjudicated by the courts over the past few <u>decades</u>.

4. Many Princes of Wales have served long terms as the heir to the crown of Great Britain, and Prince Charles is no exception.

Practice 14

1. In most developing <u>countries</u>, up to 80% of the population lives in rural <u>communities</u>.

2. No mistake.

3. <u>Humans</u> are not the only <u>primates</u> that have been known to murder their own kind: infanticide is well-documented among <u>chimpanzees</u>, <u>baboons</u>, and several species of monkeys.

Practice 15

1. In the age of electronic media, reading <u>books and magazines</u> is not as important as it once was.

2. Consumers must have the confidence that they have an option to get a <u>refund or to exchange</u> any online purchase that does not meet with their satisfaction.

3. Statistics for <u>births per year per capita</u> can give a useful measure of a nation's reproductive status.

Practice 16

Below is the corrected paragraph. Explanations are found on the following page.

(1) Abraham Lincoln described the U.S. government as being, as he said in the Gettysburg Address, "of the people, by the people, and for the people." (2) This notion, I believe, puts the priorities between the achievements of institutions and the achievements of governments in proper perspective. (3) It is not a question of the achievements of individuals vs. the achievements of the government; that contrast is a false dilemma. (4) Rather, it is the achievements of individuals, which make up the achievements of a government, that determine the greatness of a nation. (5) This is what Lincoln meant when he referred to the nation's "unfinished work": that each of us has a task to perform, and those tasks determine what kind of nation we will live in. (6) With this fundamental argument in mind, how can we not join with Lincoln in wishing that such a nation "shall not perish from the earth?"

Explanations

(1) The expression *as he said in the Gettysburg Address* is a parenthetic, and so is enclosed in commas. The quotation beginning *of the people* is a direct quotation, so it is introduced by a comma. The three items in the quote are in a series, so they should be separated by commas. Note that the comma before the conjunction in the last item *and for the people* is technically optional, although Lincoln included it in the written version of his speech so in this case it is probably best not to omit it. Also, omit the extra space between the initials of the abbreviation U.S.

(2) The phrase *I believe* is parenthetic, and so should be set off with commas. The phrase *and the achievements of government* is not parenthetic (and not in a series) so it should not be set off by commas. Omit the apostrophe on the simple plural *priorities*.

(3) This sentence is a run-on, having two independent clauses joined by a comma with no conjunction. Probably the best way to fix the run-on here is to replace the comma with a semicolon as shown (a period and new sentence would also work). Also, there's an incorrect abbreviation (with an extra space) for *versus*. Finally, omit the slash from Analytical Writing essays.

(4) The comma after the short introductory *rather* is not absolutely vital, but probably contributes to avoiding misunderstanding in this case. The nonrestrictive clause *which make up...government* must be set off with commas.

(5) The "unfinished work" belongs to the nation, so *nation's* takes a possessive apostrophe. The terminal colon goes outside the quotation marks. The part of the sentence after the colon consists of two independent clauses joined by a conjunction, so the clauses must be separated by a comma.

(6) The first part of this sentence, *With this fundamental...mind*, is a long introductory prepositional phrase, so set it off with a comma. The sentence itself is a question (beginning with *how*) so it must end with a question mark—which goes inside the quotation marks. Finally, the quote is run into the sentence, so it doesn't take an introductory comma.

Practice 17

1. During the Middle Ages and the most of the Renaissance, <u>philosophy</u> was hardly distinct from <u>theology</u>.

2. By the end of <u>spring</u>, <u>American</u> and <u>Canadian</u> <u>university</u> students have been enjoying their <u>summer</u> <u>vacation</u> for well over a month.

3. Widely regarded as the most important <u>U.S.</u> <u>trade</u> <u>agreement</u> in the past two decades, the U.S.-Canada Free Trade Agreement phased out all tariffs and quotas between the two countries by the end of the <u>twentieth century</u>.

4. Last year, <u>Doctor Sanford</u> was elected president of the <u>Brooklyn Council</u>. The president of the council meets regularly with the <u>Dean of Students</u>.

5. <u>American Independence Day</u> and <u>Memorial Day</u> occur during the summer, but Labor Day is in the fall.

6. The novels of <u>William Faulkner</u> are set in the <u>American South</u>, and the author himself lived most of his life south of the <u>Mason-Dixon Line</u>.

Practice 18

Many people think it is **all right** to **accept** charitable assistance **regardless** of their ability to secure financial **independence** for themselves. Other people think it **cannot affect** them, or that they do not **lose** money, if these **professional** charity cases force the government to **accommodate their** free **rein**. I would not be **exaggerating** if I said that **no one** lives in a **vacuum**, and all **decent** people need to be **responsible** for **their** own welfare **too**. I **wonder** if it would **have** ever **occurred to** these folks to **assent** to **buy** food, clothing and shelter firsthand for people who will not **alter** their **indiscreet** financial habits. I think **it's** unlikely. When **you're** looking **past** the question of **who's** paying for these goods and services, **then you're accepting their** right to **steal** from **your** pocket **every day**.

Practice 19

1. In fields such as human <u>development</u> and family <u>planning</u>, it is <u>becoming</u> easier to find funding for basic research.
2. As the hailstorm intensified, the campers <u>panicked</u> and ran <u>screaming</u> through the grounds.
3. No mistake.

Practice 20

1. <u>It's [or: It is]</u> often necessary to <u>buy</u> more goods <u>than</u> can be consumed in a single day even though <u>they're [they are]</u> likely to spoil.
2. I would <u>have</u> thought that journalists should avoid taking sides when they <u>write</u> about such controversial subjects.
3. We all <u>hear</u> stories of people <u>whose</u> children refuse to accompany them on vacations.
4. Can you <u>cite</u> three <u>incidents</u> in the <u>past</u> in which Congress has given its <u>assent</u> to such a proposal?
5. The Board of Education <u>accepted</u> the <u>advice</u> of the high school <u>principal</u> in <u>choosing</u> to <u>alter</u> the wording of the teachers' contracts.
6. After years of suffering under the <u>heel</u> of an autocrat, the citizens must <u>steel</u> themselves for change.

Practice 21

1. <u>Many people</u> are <u>obsessed with</u> video games and <u>television, which I believe are relatively harmless wastes of time.</u>
2. These days there are many reality shows, <u>such as *Survivor* and *American Idol*, that are all essentially similar.</u>
3. <u>Often</u> a perfectly good plan can be <u>ruined</u> by a minor oversight.

Practice 22

Your version may vary.

It is supportable to argue that studying an academic discipline changes your view of the world. For example, if you study history, you often read about many facts that are as important as the ones you learned about in school, but which weren't covered. Many large social trends and beliefs that we think are valid today turn out to be wrong. Studying a discipline such as history can change how we look at the world.

Practice 23

1. A surge of power destroyed the coolant pumps.
2. A bolt of lightning struck the transformer.
3. The slow goalkeeper failed to stop the ball.
4. Manic-depressives experience unpredictable moods.
5. The administrative secretary monitors and balances the budgets.
6. Hikers must remain on marked trails.
7. All too often, our coaches have recruited athletes with marginal academic skills.
8. The media portrays or stereotypes teachers as illiterate, even though they fulfill strict requirements.

Practice 24

Simple	Sometimes the fresh perspective of a non-expert can be valuable in the consideration of a subject.
Compound	Experts often have the best advice about a subject, but some times the fresh perspective of a non-expert can be valuable too.
Complex	Although experts often have the best advice about a subject, sometimes the fresh perspective of a non-expert can be valuable too.
Compound-Complex	Because experts typically have the most information about a subject, they often have the best advice about that subject, but sometimes the fresh perspective of a non-expert can be valuable too.

Simple	The tangible rewards of society are at least as important as the feeling of having fulfilled a personal goal.
Compound	The feeling of having fulfilled a personal goal is important, but the tangible rewards of society are at least as important.
Complex	Although the feeling of having fulfilled a personal goal is important, the tangible rewards of society are at least as important.
Compound-Complex	Rewards are important, and although the feeling of having fulfilled a personal goal is important, the tangible rewards of society are at least as important.

Simple	The important question is whether the combined cost of pest-control and savings in product damage are greater with Company B.
Compound	The important question is not which pest-control company is cheaper, but rather which company provides the best combination of cost and savings in product damage.
Complex	Even though Company B is more expensive, the important question is whether the combined cost of pest-control and savings in product damage are greater with Company B.
Compound-Complex	Even though Company B is more expensive, if the combined cost of pest-control and savings due to product damage is greater, then Company B is a better deal overall.

Simple	It is an oversimplification to say that there can be no meaningful interaction between academic communities with different traditions.
Compound	Different academic communities have different traditions, but it is an oversimplification to say that these differences preclude meaningful interaction between them.
Complex	Even though different academic communities may have different traditions, it is an oversimplification to say that there can be no meaningful interaction between them.
Compound-Complex	Different academic communities have different traditions, and while these differences may be significant, it is an oversimplification to say that there can be no meaningful interaction between them.

Simple	It is reasonable to argue that a cheaper brand of sunscreen might encourage people to have a false sense of security.
Compound	The cheaper brand of sunscreen is less effective, and so the sense of security it gives is false.
Complex	Because the cheaper brand of sunscreen is less effective, it is certainly reasonable to say that it encourages a false sense of security.
Compound-Complex	Because the cheaper brand of sunscreen is less effective, and because it encourages people to stay in the sun longer, it is fair to say that it encourages a false sense of security.

Practice 25

Answers will vary slightly.

Repetitive words and phrases in this paragraph: *courses, development, job market*

Synonyms for "courses": *lessons, classes, curricula, programs, learning, education*

Synonyms for "development": *improvement, training, education, advancement, enhancement*

Synonyms for "job market": *employment, professional setting, occupation, trade, the world of work*

Sample rewrite using these synonyms:

A curriculum that focuses on intellectual improvement is more important than a curriculum that contributes to professional training. An educational program that emphasizes professional advancement assumes that this education will still be relevant to the future occupation of the student, while in fact the constant changes in the job market might make such learning obsolete. In contrast, a course of study that works toward intellectual growth trains a person for a variety of occupational roles, so that even if the demands of employers change, the educational program remains relevant. This is not to say that many curricula cannot do both: preparing a person for employment in a specific field while also preparing her for a variety of potential vocations. But, while classes that provide professional training have their place in the realm of university curricula, they should not be allowed to supersede education that trains the intellect for the ever-changing world of work.

Chapter Four: **Writing Strong Paragraphs and Essays**

Your goal is to write a 6-point essay. Our goal is to show you exactly how to do that. In this chapter, we'll review the writing process and the steps you need to take to write an essay that earns a top score. We'll also review the logic skills you need to effectively analyze and present arguments. Finally, we'll show you the Kaplan Five-Step method for writing as well as versatile sample templates to use on test day.

PART ONE: THE WRITING PROCESS

You probably know by now that a good written *product* comes from a good writing *process*. Whether you tend to brainstorm and organize in your head or put everything down on paper, whether you like to write one draft or ten, your writing will come out stronger when you start with a **plan**, **write** out your ideas, and then **revise** and **edit** your work.

In most real-life writing situations, you have plenty of time to work through each of these writing stages. But, except for the GRE Issue essay, you have only 30 minutes each, so you should forget about the planning stage and jump right in, right? Emphatically, NO. Even though your time is limited, even if you tend to write well under pressure, you're far more likely to earn a higher score if you work through each stage of the writing process (especially the planning stage). A few minutes of brainstorming can help you come up with powerful examples to support your assertions; a few minutes of revising and editing can help you catch and correct errors that would otherwise reduce your score. So here's a review of the writing process as it specifically applies to writing a top-scoring essay for the GRE or GMAT.

Planning Your Essay

This first step in the writing process is also perhaps the most essential for a timed essay exam. Planning (also called **prewriting**) should take about 1/4 of your test time (save half for the actual writing, and another 1/4 for revising and editing). So for a 30-minute essay, spend about 7 minutes planning your essay before you begin to write.

Understanding the Writing Task

Before brainstorming, before outlining, before you do anything else, make sure you understand the writing task. Exactly what is it that you are being asked to do?

The Issue Stimulus. The Issue stimulus is intended to provoke. Most stimuli present two sharply contrasting points of view on an issue and invite you to take a stance. Some appear to present only one point of view, but in fact there is an implied alternative. Sometimes it will seem to you that the question is a no-brainer, that you simply must take one particular point of view. This is a mistake. The scoring protocol places a premium on a *critical response* to the stimulus itself. That is, you must choose a side, but you must also *analyze* your choice and how it compares to other alternatives. If you simply choose a side and launch into a recitation of supporting arguments, you will not get a top score.

For example, let's look at the following Issue stimulus:

> Some people think a college education should be available to every citizen. Others think that only the most talented students should be offered this opportunity. Which viewpoint do you agree with?

Before you take a side, consider all of the possible positions. The stimulus only lays out two possibilities—that college education be available to everyone and that it only be available to the most talented students. Clearly there are other alternatives, not just theoretically but in reality. For example, some of our institutions are highly selective, while others are open to anyone who completes a high school education. Yet even the most selective universities espouse a policy of inclusiveness, with admissions policies that take into account a variety of non-academic factors. And even those public colleges with the most lenient admissions policies still have academic standards that effectively prevent the least talented students from obtaining a diploma.

Whatever side you choose (or whether you take a middle ground), to earn a top score, you must both take a position *and* show that you have carefully considered a whole range of possibilities, not just an automatic yes/no or either/or response. (This stimulus is an example of a **false dilemma**, covered in more detail later in this chapter.)

The Argument Stimulus. While the Issue essay gives you the opportunity to *make* an argument, the Argument essay is designed to see how well you can *assess* an argument. Although you may be tempted to offer your opinion on the topic or issue in the argument, **don't**. Your job is not to argue your position but to *analyze* the argument on three levels:

1. expose its structure
2. highlight its weaknesses, including
   a. the assumptions upon which the argument is based
   b. poorly defined terms
   c. logical fallacies
3. suggest ways to make it more logical and compelling

For example, here's a typical Argument stimulus about education:

> The following appeared in a memo from an admissions officer at Brandywine University:
>
> Experts agree that to an overwhelming extent, perceived job prospects determine undergraduates' choice of field of study. Currently, the most popular major at Brandywine is computer technology, which must be due to the success of our recent graduates in finding good jobs. Clearly our recruitment efforts would be much more successful if we drew attention to our eminent professors in the field of computer technology, and publicized the successes of our recent graduates in landing high-paying jobs.

Your response to this stimulus should not discuss whether Brandywine should use a different recruitment strategy or why computer technology is such a popular major. Your task is to analyze the logic of this proposal. Is "perceived job prospects" indeed the key factor in determining a field of study? (Says who?) Is the popularity of computer technology most likely due to graduate job success rates, or are there other reasons? Is it therefore logical to draw attention to professors in that field and publicize the success of graduates to recruit new students? As you prepare to write, you need to consider these and other questions and look for the flaws in the argument—and there will be several. Knowing that analysis is your task, you can begin to brainstorm ideas for your response.

Brainstorm Ideas

Now that your task is clear, it's time to start brainstorming ideas. Do you know what position you want to take from the get-go, or do you need to think about it? Think it through on paper.

Brainstorming Techniques. *Brainstorming* simply refers to the technique of focusing on a particular problem or issue to come up with ideas. For an essay, you can try **listing**, **mapping**, or **freewriting**. Write down whatever comes to your mind about the topic. Remember that in a brainstorm, *anything goes*. Don't discount any ideas yet—you're still in the planning stage, and an idea that doesn't seem relevant now can lead you to another that may form the crux of your argument. Forget about grammar, sentence structure, or anything else that might hinder your thoughts. Just get your ideas down on paper. If you don't know where to start, try writing the main issue or question and answering it or addressing the first assertion in the Argument stimulus.

For the Issue stimulus, if you don't know which position you will take, first brainstorm to determine your thesis. If you know as soon as you read the stimulus what position you would like to argue, then jump right into the second step: brainstorming support for your argument. It's particularly important to brainstorm ideas for opposing points of view so you can address counterarguments in your essay.

Argument Stimulus Topics

Most of the Argument stimuli in ETS's current published pool for the GRE and GMAT are mini-proposals based on two to four pieces of evidence. In 40 percent of the GRE Argument stimuli, the evidence includes results of a "recent study," most often a survey. The topics can be roughly sorted out as follows (percentages are approximate):

Business: recommendations to improve profits, generally through of choice of products or services offered, absenteeism, and worker productivity (GRE: 30–35% of the pool; GMAT: 60%)

Health and Safety: findings and recommendations focusing on diet, nutrition, exercise, safety equipment (GRE: 20–25%; GMAT: 10%)

Community Planning: proposals to increase revenues and improve services, generally through modifications in land use, infrastructure, and utilities contracts (GRE: 19%; GMAT: 10%)

Education: recommendations to adjust course offering or other policies so as to improve revenues, recruit more students, create more job opportunities for graduates (GRE: 15%; GMAT: 10%)

Scholarly Research: findings in a variety of fields, but primarily archaeology and Earth history (GRE: 5%)

Ecology: findings and recommendations related to endangered species (GRE: 5%)

Public Policy: how to deal with crime, trade deficit, other national problems; improve services; political campaign strategies (GMAT: 10%)

This list of topic categories is not comprehensive, and the categories are not mutually exclusive. Many health and safety stimuli as well as education stimuli, for instance, are essentially commercial in focus.

Below are examples of three brainstorming techniques for the sample Issue and Argument stimuli:

> **ISSUE:** Some people think a college education should be available to every citizen. Others think that only the most talented students should be offered this opportunity. Which viewpoint do you agree with?
>
> **ARGUMENT:** Experts agree that to an overwhelming extent, perceived job prospects determine undergraduates' choice of field of study. Currently, the most popular major at Brandywine is computer technology, which must be due to the success of our recent graduates in finding good jobs. Clearly our recruitment efforts would be much more successful if we drew attention to our eminent professors in the field of computer technology, and publicized the successes of our recent graduates in landing high-paying jobs.

Listing means just that—simply list whatever ideas come to mind. In the sample list below, the author starts with a series of questions that leads him to more concrete ideas he can use as the base of his essay.

Is education a right or privilege? BOTH
  Right: To what level?
          Why cut off at high school? (Cost prohibitive?)

  Privilege: Must be earned—but how?
              Who earns that privilege?
              Who decides who's earned it?

What kind of talent? Not just academic, also dedication

Problem: how to define talent

*Democracy vs. meritocracy

More educated populace = good for EVERYONE
          Less ignorance (thus more tolerance, better health care, etc.)
          More skilled work force
          Less poverty
          More active in community and politics

Mapping takes a more spatial approach than the linear list. Use a map to lay out relationships between ideas as you brainstorm.

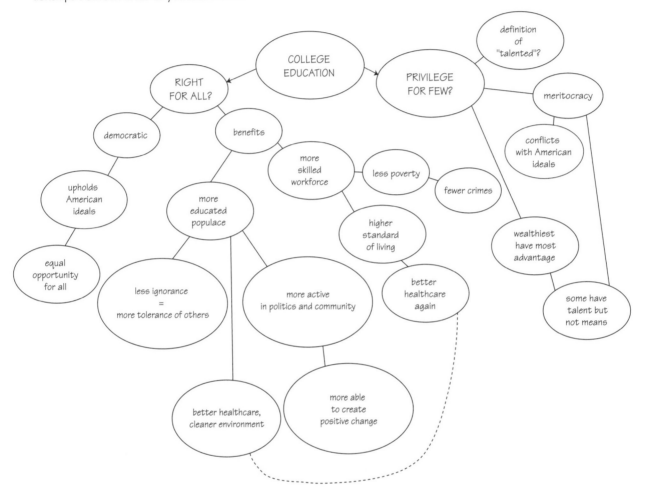

Freewriting is exactly that—a free narrative response to develop ideas unencumbered by the conventions of essay writing (no worries about grammar, paragraphing, cohesion, etc.).

OK, perceived job prospects are important but my initial reaction is they put too much weight on this. Most people I know didn't choose their major because of potential jobs but because they like the field, or if they did choose because of a specific job its because they think they'll like that career, of course if there's a high demand for a particular career that does make it more appealing, but for example I'd never switch from biology to computer technology simply because there's a lot of highpaying jobs waiting for me upon graduation. I think comp tech is so popular because kids like computers, not <u>just</u> because those undergrads want good jobs. Another prob: doubt that it's the most popular major because of the success of recent grads. That's *always a boost, because it's evidents of a good program. But is that what recruiting should focus on? Yes, eminent profs and grad success rates are important but recruitment should also focus on solidity of program. And what about the other programs at B? What's not said here is what % of students are comp tech majors and how that fits into the overall mission/departmts/programs at the school. (BTW who are those experts? Memo doesn't say.)*

Outlining Your Essay

Once you've brainstormed ideas, it's time to put them—quickly—into a logical order. It might be tempting to just jump in and write, but resist that temptation. A good outline will make the actual writing of your essay much easier and help minimize revising needs.

The goal of an outline is two-fold: (1) to put the ideas you brainstormed into a logical order and (2) to help ensure that you have enough support for each of the assertions you plan to make in your essay. By laying everything out before you write, you can see if you have any gaps in support or logic in your argument. If so, you can fix those problems before it's too late. You can also map out a logical sequence of ideas so that your argument or analysis flows smoothly from one paragraph to another.

A Well-Organized Outline = A Well-Organized Essay. You may tend to resist writing outlines for your normal writing tasks, but it's too important a step to ignore on this exam. After all, brilliant analysis alone will not earn you a top score on your essay. ETS graders are looking for logical organization at every level of the essay, from the broad structure down to the individual sentence.

At the broadest level, the essay must have a beginning, a middle, and an end. The introductory paragraph must engage the stimulus, state the thesis, and lay out the plan for the body of the essay. The body of the essay must present two to four well-developed points in support of the claim staked out in the introduction. The conclusion should summarize the essay as a whole.

Too often, though, this three-part structure becomes something of a "list sandwich": the introduction and conclusion are just there to hold an undifferentiated list of points. As a result, the reader has no idea where the argument is going, and feels jerked along, rather than feeling like a paying customer on a guided tour. While it is not necessary to declare explicitly the rationale behind your organization, you should definitely lay out your points in a clear trajectory. That is, your supporting ideas must be arranged in some logical sequence, even if there is no logical necessity to that sequence. Here are some of the possibilities:

- If your points respond to a series of fallacies in an argument, you might organize them in the same sequence as they appear in the stimulus.

- You might follow the structure of a logical argument and organize your points according to the parts of an argument: problems with premises, problems with assumptions, and (therefore) problems with the conclusion.

- You might deploy your arguments in order of importance, or in order of accessibility or complexity (most obvious to most subtle, least complicated to most intricate).

Or you can let the subject matter be your guide and arrange your points by

- **chronology**
- **cause** and **effect**
- **comparison** and **contrast**
- **analysis** or **classification**
- **problem-solution**
- **scale**

Scale can be perceived along many gradients. Here are just a few examples:

- local, regional, national, global
- individual, family, neighborhood, community, society
- microscopic, organic, systemic
- employee, department, division, corporation

Once you've determined your overall organizing principle, outline your major supporting points and the specific evidence and examples you can use to support each of those main points. Here's an example:

1. Intro: *College education is a right, not just a privilege. It should be available to every citizen, and those with talent should be offered extra opportunities.*
2. Why it's a right: democracy not meritocracy
    a. Country founded on democratic principle, all created equal, equal opportunity
        i. Principle used throughout primary and secondary schooling
        ii. Used in work force, government, law enforcement
        iii. Why not higher ed?
        iv. Counterargument: high school should be enough to satisfy equality for all principle
            1. rebuttal: lack of college education limits a whole segment of population, keeps them at lower wages, lower socio-economic status (transition to next para)
3. Why meritocracy is a problem
    a. Few in control of many (who decides who can go to college?)
    b. How do you define "talented"?
    c. Ripe for corruption
4. Benefits of equal opportunity
    a. Less ignorance (thus more tolerance, better health care, less drugs/violence, etc.)
    b. More skilled workforce
    c. Less poverty
    d. More involvement in community and politics
5. Conclusion (restate thesis)

A Well-Developed Outline = A Well-Developed Essay. Why is *development* an issue in the outlining stage? Because your outline can show you which paragraphs need more support. Now's the time to review your outline for completeness. Do you have enough ideas and information to cover each topic thoroughly? Do you cover everything you need to cover, including counterarguments (in the Issue essay) and suggested improvements for the proposal (in the Argument essay)? For example, in the previous outline, the author does not address counterarguments in paragraphs 3 and 4, and paragraph 3 in general could use more development/support.

Writing Your Essay

Now that you have a detailed outline, the actual writing of your essay should go rather smoothly. You know what you want to say and the order in which you want to say it.

Introductions: Get Off to a Strong Start

In regular academic writing, your essay introductions typically have two main goals: (1) to grab the reader's attention and (2) to clearly state your thesis. On the Analytical Writing tasks, however, your focus should emphatically be on the latter. Right from the start, readers (both human and computer) need to know the main idea of your essay.

What about grabbing the reader's attention with a catchy introduction? A real attention-grabber might impress your human reader, but it won't make a whit of difference to the E-rater. In fact, depending upon your approach, the E-rater may interpret such an introduction as a bit off topic. Our advice: if you can *immediately* think of a catchy introduction *with a highly relevant word base* (the E-rater is programmed to look for a list of topic-related words), then by all means, use it. However, you don't have time to waste thinking of a good attention-grabber, so if it doesn't come to you right away, stick to a standard introduction.

Template for a Standard Introduction

1. Begin by briefly paraphrasing the issue or summarizing the argument.
2. State your thesis.
3. Outline the main points to be covered in your essay (in the order in which you will cover them).

Example:

> Is higher education something that should be available just to the most talented students, or should it be available to everyone? I firmly believe the latter. Limiting access to higher education to a small percentage of our population undermines our democracy and hurts our society on many levels—socially, economically, and even morally. It also creates a host of problems in selecting those who are "most talented." Academic talent does deserve to be rewarded—but not at the expense of everyone else.

Now here's the same introduction with a catchy sentence added to the beginning to grab the reader's attention:

> If, as the Declaration of Independence states, our country is founded on the belief that "all men are created equal," then why should only the most talented students be allowed the chance to attend college? This opportunity should be available to all citizens, not just the academic elite. Limiting access to higher education to a small percentage of our population undermines our democracy and hurts our society on many levels—socially, economically, and even morally. It also creates a host of problems in selecting those who are "most talented." Academic talent does deserve to be rewarded—but not at the expense of everyone else.

Writing a Strong Thesis Statement. Before we go any further, it's time to review the definition of a *thesis statement*. First, here's what a thesis statement is *not*:

- A thesis statement is not a question: *Is higher education a right or a privilege?*

- A thesis statement is not a paraphrase of the stimulus: *Some argue that higher education is a right; others that it is a privilege.*

- A thesis statement is not a general statement about the topic: *There is much debate about whether higher education is a right or a privilege.*

- A thesis statement is not a general statement about how other people feel about the topic: *Many people believe that higher education is a right, not just a privilege.*

Now here's what a thesis statement *is*:

A sentence that makes an assertion about the topic and clearly expresses the main idea of the essay: *Access to higher education is a right, not a privilege.*

For your essay, a **good** thesis statement:

- Issue essay: Clearly states your position on the issue (what you think and why you think it).

- Argument essay: Clearly states the main flaws in the argument (summarizes what's wrong with the stimulus).

Writing Strong Paragraphs

A paragraph by definition is a group of sentences about a single idea. Make sure your paragraphs have clear topic sentences stating that main idea of each paragraph. In your regular writing you may be more subtle, but for the Analytical Writing task—given your readers (a tired human and a computer program) you want to be as clear and obvious as possible.

Developing Ideas. There's no magic number for how many sentences should be in a paragraph, because this depends upon the length of sentences and the purpose of the paragraph. For example, there are times when a short, one-sentence paragraph is rhetorically effective. But the Analytical Writing task is no such place, because the E-rater is likely to consider your rhetorical technique an underdeveloped paragraph. Likewise, there are times when a seven or eight sentence paragraph is appropriate—but not on the Analytical Writing task.

To play it safe on the exam, aim for 4–5 sentence paragraphs throughout your essay. In general, that's about what it takes, given average sentence lengths, to fully develop an idea: one topic sentence, two or three sentences with specific examples or evidence, and a sentence or two acknowledging and refuting counterarguments or providing a transition into the next paragraph.

The only exception to this guideline for paragraph length might be the conclusion, which is likely to be more concise than other paragraphs because there isn't a new idea to develop.

Organizing Ideas. You've already decided upon your overall principle of organization in your outline. But ETS graders will be looking not just for macro-organization (overall organizing principle of the essay), but also for meso- (intermediate, paragraph level) and micro- (sentence level) organization as well. At the meso-scale, there are three issues:

1. **Paragraph unity.** Does each paragraph deal with a single coherent idea? Do any extraneous ideas creep in to distract the reader's attention? The E-rater cannot directly evaluate content, but it does analyze the vocabulary used in each paragraph in order to assess the likelihood that a single point is presented and developed, without extraneous ideas. (And your human reader will catch an off-topic sentence no matter how quickly he or she reads through your essay.)

2. **Topic sentences.** Does each paragraph have one main idea clearly stated in a topic sentence? We all know that the topic sentence can occur anywhere in the paragraph. Perfectly good paragraphs may even lack a topic sentence. But on the exam, play it safe. If at all possible, deploy a fully-developed topic sentence at the opening of each paragraph.

3. **Transitional phrases.** Are there smooth and effective transitions between and within paragraphs? Your entire essay should be stitched together with transitional phrases. From the second paragraph to the conclusion, each topic sentence should begin with a conspicuous signpost marking the trajectory of your argument: *the first problem, first of all, second, furthermore, one additional factor, in conclusion,* etc. Within each paragraph, use signals that will draw the reader's attention to what you are doing: *such as, for example, an alternative explanation, on the one hand/on the other, by contrast, however, nonetheless, consequently, therefore,* and so on.

Here's a more complete list of some of the most useful transitional words and phrases for your essays:

Purpose	Transitions
Show addition	and, also, again, in addition, furthermore, moreover, besides, next, too
Introduce an example	for example, for instance, such as, in particular, in fact, in other words, that is, specifically, on the one hand/other, to illustrate
Indicate the passage of time	before, after, afterward, next, during, meanwhile, later, eventually, in the meantime, immediately, suddenly, finally
Indicate rank	first, second, third, etc. (of all); first and foremost; most important; more importantly; above all
Indicate cause	because, since, for this reason
Indicate effect	as a result, consequently, therefore, hence
Indicate comparison	similarly, likewise, like, just as, in the same manner
Indicate contrast	but, however, on the other hand, on the contrary, conversely, in contrast, yet, whereas, instead, rather, while, although, though, despite
Add emphasis	in fact, indeed, certainly, above all
Summarize or conclude	in sum, in summary, in short, in conclusion, to conclude, to sum up, that is, therefore

Wrapping It All Up: Writing Your Conclusion

Think for a moment about the last movie you saw. What's the first scene that comes to mind? Chances are you best remember the beginning or the end of the film. For better or for worse, first and final impressions do count, and this is especially true in writing. Indeed, conclusions often have the power to make or break an essay. A weary human reader, for example, might be well satisfied throughout your essay only to be disappointed by a weak conclusion, turning your 6 into a 5—or worse.

As we've said many times now, your best bet is to play it safe throughout your essay, and this includes the conclusion. You want your ending to have impact, but you don't have the time or the rhetorical freedom to do anything fancy with your conclusion. (Remember, the E-rater won't pick up on any sophisticated rhetorical techniques.) Instead, stick to a standard conclusion that:

1. restates your main idea *and*
2. *briefly* summarizes your main support.

Development and Organization

A well-developed essay:

- has at least four full paragraphs. Five or six are even better.

- has at least three sentences in each paragraph, with the possible exception of a concise conclusion. Four to six sentences are even better.

- provides specific examples, details, or evidence for the main idea of each paragraph.

A well-organized essay:

- has an overall organizing principle for the essay.

- has an organizing principle for each paragraph.

- has only one main idea per paragraph.

- clearly states the main idea of each paragraph.

- has strong transitions between sentences and between paragraphs.

In the Argument essay, you should also:

3. point out ways in which the argument could be improved and/or what additional information you need to more accurately assess the argument (*unless* you have addressed these issues in a separate, fully-developed paragraph).

Your conclusion should *not*:

• Repeat the thesis statement in exactly the same words. Your essay is too short for direct repetition. When you restate your main idea, make sure it's an effective paraphrase.

• Open a new can of worms. A good conclusion will always provide a sense of closure for readers so that they feel as if the topic has been covered completely. If you introduce a new topic, readers will feel cheated because your essay is over and you have no place to develop this new idea.

Revising and Editing Your Essay

The difference between *revising* and *editing* is simple: revising refers to any changes you make above and beyond the level of grammar and usage, mechanics, or formatting, as these fall within the realm of editing. Typically writers are advised to revise first, as revision addresses big-picture issues such as organization and development and sentence-level issues such as structure and word choice. But your time on the Analytical Writing tasks is limited, and if you used your time effectively, you will only have about 7 or 8 minutes left to review your essay. So you will have to revise and edit simultaneously.

Big Picture Checklist

As you revise, check for the following "big picture" issues. Your essay should:

• **State ideas assertively and clearly.** Do you have a clear thesis statement at the beginning of your essay? Do you have clear topic sentences in each paragraph?

• **Develop ideas fully.** Do you explain your ideas clearly and completely? Do you provide strong and specific support for your assertions?

• **Organize ideas logically.** Do you have an effective organizing principle for your essay? Within your paragraphs? Have you paragraphed effectively?

• **Stay focused.** Does your essay stick to one main idea? Is all of your support relevant? Are your paragraphs free from any sentences that digress off-topic?

• **Signpost constantly.** Do you use strong transitions within and between paragraphs?

Sentence-Level Checklist

On the sentence level, check for the Eight Maxims of Effective Writing:

- Are your sentences **correct**? Can you find and correct any errors in grammar or mechanics?
- Are your sentences **clear**? Are there any ambiguous or vague sentences because of poor sentence structure or word choice?
- Are your sentences **concise**? Can you eliminate any unnecessary repetition or wordiness?
- Are your sentences **exact**? Have you used exact words and phrases as well as specific details?
- Are your sentences **assertive**? Do you state your points without hesitation?
- Are your sentences **appropriate**? Do you use the right level of formality throughout your essay?
- Are your sentences **consistent**? Do you maintain an appropriate style, tone, and point of view throughout your essay?
- Are your sentences **exciting**? Do you have variety in sentence structure and vocabulary?

Practice 1

Directions: Each of the following is a paragraph similar to those that might appear in a typical GRE or GMAT essay. Each paragraph includes numerous errors. Practice proofreading by locating and correcting all the errors in each paragraph. Compare your answers to the answers found on pages 153–156.

Paragraph 1

(1) The advise given to the company managers that hiring more additional workers will result in a larger number of houses being built contain a fallacy of exclusion. (2) Several pieces of extremely vital information are not taken into consideration in the reasoning that more workers means more houses built, a moments reasoning reveals that many factors other then merely the number of workers determines the answer to the question of how many houses will be built? (3) For example, if the construction company doesn't have enough construction equipment/tools to equip more worker's, then extra workers won't help irregardless. (4) If there aren't enough building sights available,

a raw materials shortage, or sufficient infrastructure to support additional workers, then hiring more workers might well been just a waste of money. (5) The whole question of diminishing returns is not considered by this line of reasoning at all in increasing staff size.

Paragraph 2

(1) While the School Boards argument that eating breakfast is related to a reduction of absenteeism in the school breakfast program may be convincing. (2) The conclusion that forcing more students to eat breakfast on the school program will cause a decreasing drop in absences is unwarranted. (3) The statistic's show a correspondance that is far from clear enough to assume causation. (4) The attendance of students at the school-sponsored breakfast program and at subsequent classes maybe both result from a third, unexamined cause that creates the observed affect. (5) For example, students who eat school breakfasts everyday might just happen to be the ones who go to bed early, and therefore are up in time for both the breakfast and for classes. (6) Or maybe the students with better attendance experience a different kind of parent supervision that contributes to both one's better diet and their improved attendance.

Paragraph 3

(1) In surveying their customers and found that they prefer games with lifelike graphics, the computer game company has correctly identified a cause for an increase in the popularity of particular game types. (2) From the evidence presented it seems okay to think that certain customers might maybe buy the more lifelike games in preference to games with worse graphics. (3) However, the conclusion that game sales will rise as an end result of this action neglects to take

into account the evidence. (4) That the more lifelike games require the latest new computer hardware. (5) The argument presents no evidence to show the fact that the target audience is undergoing a transition to this more advanced and more expensive type of computer platform. On the contrary common sense seems perhaps to suggest that, since the target audience tends to be young, that their earning power would not allow them to acquire the equipment necessary to accomodate the games in question, and thus it would not necessarily result in increased sales of those games. (7) If the company was to invest in developement of these games, they might waste money in the end.

PART TWO: A BRIEF LOGIC PRIMER

Logic is a key factor in the scoring of both the Issue and Argument essays. ETS graders are, of course, looking for logical organization in your essays. Equally important, they are looking for logic in your analysis of the essay stimulus. This requirement is clearer in an Argument task, since you are specifically asked to critique a line of thinking. The Issue task, on the other hand, *seems* to be rather straightforward: you are told to take a stance on the given issue and support that position. In actuality, however, you are expected to *engage the issue*, to consider the complexities not only of the general idea behind the prompt but also of the specific wording of the prompt itself. That confrontation must be founded on logic, and it must be presented as part of the essay.

The study of logic is a field in itself, one that is central to philosophy, mathematics, and other fields. You are not expected to have any formal training in logic or in any other field that is covered in the Argument stimuli. However, a primer in some of the basics of critical thinking, including the basic structure of arguments and common logical fallacies, will give you an edge in analyzing your Argument stimulus and writing an effective essay.

Basic Argument Structure

First, some terms. In logic, an **argument** is not a quarrel, dispute, or verbal disagreement. Rather, it is a persuasive appeal involving two or more statements, including a **conclusion** and at least one **premise** (evidence to support that conclusion). A conclusion is the main claim of the argument. The conclusion of an argument may take the form of a declarative statement, but it may also be embedded in a proposal, recommendation, plan, or prediction. It is only a conclusion *as part of* an argument; without the premise(s) to support it, it is simply an **assertion** or **claim** that lacks support. That's

Logic Terms

Claim: an assertion that is either true or false

Argument: a set of claims with a premise(s) and conclusion

Conclusion: the main claim of the argument

Premise: claims that support the conclusion

essentially what differentiates Issue stimuli from Argument stimuli—the former are assertions while the latter are arguments (however problematic).

Premises and Conclusions

In approaching an Argument stimulus, your first task will be to identify the conclusion and the premises. The conclusion is not necessarily the last point presented. It could just as well appear in the guise of a topic sentence, at the beginning of a passage, or in the middle of the passage, after a sentence or two of background exposition.

Common indicators of the **conclusion** include:

therefore	this proves/shows/suggests/implies that
so	we can infer that
hence	which implies that
thus	should
accordingly	must
consequently	may be inferred from
it follows that	

Common verbal indicators of a **premise** include:

because
since
in as much as
given that
for the following reasons
in view of the fact that

In the recruitment memo Argument stimulus, the conclusion is marked by the less obvious indicator *clearly*. But many other conclusion indicators could easily be inserted before the final sentence:

> [**Premise**] Experts agree that to an overwhelming extent, perceived job prospects determine undergraduates' choice of field of study. [**Premise**] Currently, the most popular major at Brandywine is computer technology, which must be due to the success of our recent graduates in finding good jobs. [**Conclusion**] *This proves that/Thereofre/Accordingly/It follows that/Clearly our recruitment efforts would be much more successful if we drew attention to our eminent professors in the field of computer technology, and publicized the successes of our recent graduates in landing high-paying jobs.*

All claims have a truth value; they are either true or false. In a **valid** argument, the conclusion must be true if all of the premises are true. *But no Argument stimuli are valid.* They are all rather weak **invalid** arguments in which the conclusion is not necessarily true even if the premises are all true. In most cases, one or more of the premises will be false, so even if the conclusion is true, the argument will still be **unsound** because it is based on one or more false premises.

On the other hand, it is important to bear in mind that even though an argument is defective, the conclusion may still be true; it is simply the *argument* that is invalid. Similarly, the fact that a conclusion is clearly true does not mean that the argument is strong or cogent because the premises may be problematic.

Logical Fallacies

Your task on the essay is to show the weaknesses in the Argument stimulus and to critically engage the Issue stimulus. Often there are leaps in logic, erroneous assumptions, and vague or otherwise problematic terms. Common sense alone will often be enough to identify these faults, but many arguments and issues also rely on a number of logical fallacies with which you may not be so familiar. Thus, we provide a brief review of the most common of those fallacies.

False Dilemma

False dilemma is one of the fundamental fallacies in logic. A familiar example of this fallacy is "America: love it or leave it." This statement assumes that there are only two options: love America or leave it—and we must choose only between these two courses of action. Obviously, there are other options: we might love some things about America, but not everything; we might not love it, but choose to stay anyway; and so on. Hence the false dilemma, because there are more than two options from which to choose. These are very common in Issue stimuli such as the following:

1. The key to success is not competition but cooperation.
2. The goal of an educational system must be to instill values, not to provide vocational training.

The first presents a false choice between competition and cooperation, when in fact competition and cooperation are not mutually exclusive and there are many other possible keys to success. The second presents a false choice between the goal of instilling values and providing training. But educational systems have many goals; instilling values and providing job training are both important. A good response might discuss some of the other goals and how to balance those with instilling values and job training.

Practice 2

Each of the following presents a false dilemma. Prove that the dilemma is false by listing alternatives in the space provided. Answers are found on page 156.

1. The key to success is not competition but cooperation.

   _____

   _____

2. The goal of an educational system must be to instill values, not to provide vocational training.

   _____

   _____

3. Government needs to provide social services instead of wasting money on the arts.

   _____

   _____

4. If you're not going to work hard at your job, you should quit.

   _____

   _____

5. Anybody who supported that bill in the Senate either didn't understand the issue or was trying to ruin America.

   _____

   _____

   _____

6. The challenger is so unskilled in chess that the champion will either lose the game and be humiliated, or win and feel really guilty.

   _____

   _____

Overstated Generalization

Another common Issue stimulus format is the overstated generalization, which can also make its way in to the Argument stimulus. Often such propositions make a broad statement about a specific group or institution:

> Professional athletes must take their responsibility as role models more seriously.
>
> Government cannot support the arts without undermining them.
>
> It is not the place of schools to provide health education.

Other signs of the overstated generalization are superlatives (*the most important*), and extreme adverbs (*never, always, rarely, only, everything, nothing, impossible,* and of course *extremely*):

> The chief lesson of history is that we have nothing to learn from it.
>
> Progress arises only out of disagreement and discontent.

In terms of both form and content, these stimuli are frequently aphoristic: like proverbs, they are rhetorically balanced, morally instructive, and somewhat paradoxical. Here's a perfect example:

> Success is easy to achieve but difficult to enjoy.

Statements like this often *sound* sound. But the problem is that they make assumptions about the whole when there is at least one possible exception to the statement. For example, don't some people enjoy their success? Don't some people (in fact, probably many) have a difficult time achieving success? In reality, these overstated generalizations are much like false dilemmas—they assume only X is true and don't consider alternatives. False dilemmas present you with two choices; you have to think of the in-betweens. Overstated generalizations state one point of view; again, you have to think of the alternatives.

Some stimuli may also present false dilemmas embedded *within* overstated generalizations:

> An individual's attitudes are primarily determined by his or her character rather than by the particular situation in which they are evoked.

Practice 3

Each of the following presents an overstated generalization. Prove that the generalization is overstated by listing exceptions in the space provided. Answers are found on page 157.

1. Government should never seek to restrict the rights of individuals.

2. In business, the most important secret to success is originality.

3. In leadership, no skill is so rare and yet so vital as the ability to make decisions.

4. Any person who thinks schoolteachers have an easy job wouldn't last a day in most public schools.

5. The main goal of research should be practical technology that makes life more enjoyable for people in general.

6. In today's society, everyone thinks that style is more important than substance.

Appeal to Authority

In making an argument, it is frequently legitimate to invoke the views of authorities. The argument might be strong if the authorities have pertinent expertise and credibility. The argument will be less strong if it cites "experts" without establishing their credentials or if there is substantial disagreement among experts as to the point in question. An argument based on anonymous authority (like one based on hearsay) is extremely weak, since the expertise of the authority cannot be verified.

For example, the sample argument on page 87 begins with an appeal to authority:

> Experts agree that to an overwhelming extent…

Who are these experts? A serious flaw in this argument is that it doesn't provide credentials for these authorities. The evidence attributed to anonymous experts may seem unobjectionable, but the appeal to authority is itself a weakness in the argument and should be cited in your critique of the stimulus.

Inductive Fallacies

All of the Argument stimuli will be inductive arguments, which means the conclusion is drawn from the evidence that is presented (the premises). Inductive reasoning frequently involves drawing inferences about a population as a whole based on information about a sample. Inductive fallacies arise from inappropriate reliance on a sample. That is, the conclusion is drawn from a sample that is too small (hasty generalization), unrepresentative of the target population (unrepresentative sample), or not analogous to the target population (false analogy).

Practice 4

The following is an example of inductive reasoning. Identify the conclusion and premises. Is the conclusion valid? Is it true? Answers are found on page 157.

The following appeared in a memo from a member of the school board in the town of Delos.

"For the past five years, Mr. Evan Brockhoff has been the head football coach at Central High School. During that time the varsity football team from Central High has won three state championships. In addition, the quality of the gymnasium and the athletic equipment at Central High has improved significantly over the past five years. Because of the outstanding achievements of Central High, the Delos school board should hire Mr. Brockoff as the general director in charge of athletic programs for the entire Delos school system."

Conclusion:

_____

_____

Premises:

_____

_____

_____

_____

_____

_____

_____

_____

_____

Hasty Generalization. A hasty generalization occurs when the size of the sample is too small to serve as a basis for the conclusion. We make hasty generalizations all the time. Eat at a restaurant once, for example, and say the food is lousy—hasty generalization. Eat at it two or three times, trying different dishes each time, and you have a better sample upon which to make your judgment.

GMAT hasty generalizations are apt to look like the following stimulus:

> Surveillance cameras installed in two of the town's ten municipal parking lots show that the lots are overcrowded, particularly between 8:30–10:00, 11:30–1:00, and 4:00–5:30. Overcrowded lots during these periods create hazards to drivers and pedestrians and increase congestion in nearby streets. Therefore, to alleviate congestion and improve safety, the township needs to build a new, multi-level municipal parking garage.

Common sense should tell you that two out of ten is not a large enough sample to come to the conclusion about all the parking lots in this argument. These two lots may be busier than the other eight—we don't know—and we can't rely on the information from this small a sample.

Unrepresentative Sample. An unrepresentative sample is one that differs in significant ways from the population as a whole. For example, if a study of sleep disorders is conducted on teenagers, but the results are projected on the entire population (including children and the elderly), the argument is invalid because the conclusions is based on an unrepresentative sample. Teenagers are a specific group within the population with specific characteristics that are not shared by other segments of the population. Likewise, the two parking lots in the hasty generalization sample stimulus might not be representative of the parking lots as a group. They may be much busier, or significantly smaller, or differ in other important ways from the other eight lots.

Practice 5

In what way is the sample in this stimulus unrepresentative of the population about which the claim is made? Answers are found on page 158.

> Typically, as people age, the fatty deposits in their blood vessels (atherosclerosis) increase in size and number, making people more vulnerable to blood clots and blockages. A recent study concludes an effective way to reduce the risk of blockages in later life is to take aspirin daily. The four-year study followed a group of Belgian women in their eighties who were residents of assisted care facilities. The women were given daily dosages of aspirin. In addition, the women participated in an aquatic aerobics program. After three years, these women showed a much lower rate of atherosclerosis than is average for their age.

Ways the sample is unrepresentative:

_____

_____

_____

_____

_____

False Analogy. In making an analogy, one first establishes that two entities, processes, or situations are similar; then one infers that since the first term of comparison has a certain property, that property must also occur in the second term. A false analogy (comparing apples to oranges) occurs when the two terms of comparison differ in such a way as to invalidate the inferred commonality.

For example:

> Our mall franchise has 30% less seating than our downtown franchise, yet it produces nearly twice the daily revenue. The lack of seating often creates a crowded condition in the store. This gives passersby the impression that our products are highly desirable. If we want to increase in our downtown franchise, we should cut back on seating.

There are many problems with the logic in this argument, but the most fundamental is that the two franchises are not directly comparable because of their locations. Mall traffic is likely to be heavier and steadier than a typical downtown location.

Practice 6

Identify the analogy and explain its weakness. Answers are found on page 158.

> When Stuckley's Family Buffet first opened, it was the largest, most heavily attended restaurant in town. It is still the largest restaurant, but it is no longer heavily used. A tally of table receipts last month revealed the restaurant's drop in popularity: the receipts showed an average of only 50 parties of diners per day. In contrast, tiny Javamunch Cafe in the heart of the business district is visited by more than 150 people on a typical weekday. An obvious difference is that Javamunch Café, unlike Stuckley's Buffet, provides full table service instead of buffet-style dining. Thus, if Stuckley's is ever to be as popular as Javamunch, the management will obviously need to provide full table service, thereby providing what customers want.

Analogy: _____

_____

Weaknesses: _____

_____

_____

_____

Causal Fallacies

Many Argument stimuli include causal arguments. Here are two key causal fallacies likely to appear.

Post Hoc, Ergo Propter Hoc

The easiest causal fallacy to identify is probably *post hoc, ergo propter hoc* ("after this, therefore because of this"). The fallacious assumption is that because X came before Y, it *caused* Y. However, there are three other important possibilities:

X and Y might have independent causes

X and Y might have the same cause

X might have been only one of several causes.

Here's an example:

> Our mall franchise put a new coat of paint on the walls, purchased potted plants, and put fresh flowers on the tables to coincide with the launch of our new value menu. In the first week of the new menu, its sales were 20% higher than all other franchises, and on many customer satisfaction surveys, clients specifically mentioned the new décor. To increase business at our other franchises, we should similarly upgrade the décor.

Of course, the improved décor came before the launch of the new menu, but it's not likely the décor alone is responsible for the significantly higher percentage of sales. It certainly may be a factor, but there are too many other possible factors, including the knowns—the new value menu and the high-traffic location—and possible unknowns, such as advertising.

Indeed, in any causal argument, it's important to consider whether X caused Y, or whether W caused both X and Y, or whether X and Y were both caused by independent factors, including the possibility of multiple causes.

Practice 7

Identify the weakness in the causal argument embedded in this stimulus. Answers are found on page 158.

> The following appeared in a newspaper article published in the country of Saludia:
>
> "Ten years ago, one half of all citizens in Saludia met the standards for healthy height-to-weight ratios as then defined by the ministry of health and fitness. Today, the ministry says that only one quarter of all citizens meet the standards and suggests that the increasing prevalence of office jobs may be the reason. But since healthy height-to-weight levels are highest in regions of Saludia where levels of office employment are also highest, it is clear that working in offices has not made citizens less physically fit. Instead, as shown by this year's unusually low expenditures on fitness-related products and services, the recent decline in the economy is most likely the cause, and healthy weight levels will improve when the economy does."

Weaknesses:

_____

_____

_____

_____

Genuine but Insignificant Cause. Finally, there's the causal fallacy of putting too much weight on a real but insignificant cause. In such an argument, a cause is correctly identified as such, but the argument neglects other pertinent and much more significant causes. Again, the mall franchise stimulus provides a good example. Sure, the new décor may have helped, but it is a far less significant factor than the new value menu. Other more significant causes could include advertising and the business's location.

Suppressed Information

The **fallacy of exclusion** applies when there is a violation of the "principle of total evidence": a valid argument must consider all relevant information. This fallacy applies to the majority of Argument stimuli. In many cases, a precedent or supposedly analogous case is introduced as evidence, but we cannot evaluate its relevance without pertinent data. The trick is to determine if essential information is missing or whether conclusions were drawn based on only part of the story.

The surveillance camera stimulus is a good example of the fallacy of exclusion. We cannot legitimately accept or reject the conclusion without knowing how representative the two parking lots are of the other eight. We also need more information on the impact such a project would have on the community as well as how such a project would be funded.

Slippery Slope

This fallacy is aptly named, because it's easy to fall into the slippery trap set by the if/then scenario it presents. The slippery slope argues that if X happens, then Y will definitely follow. In some cases, there is a logical and definite causal relationship. But when X doesn't necessarily lead to Y, then you have slippery slope reasoning, as in the following example:

> Many companies these days have "casual Fridays" when employees have the opportunity to "dress down" and come to work in polos and slacks rather than suits and ties. But casual dress leads to a casual work ethic. People feel more professional when they are dressed professionally; thus they will feel less professional when they dress casually. In addition, one day of casual attire will affect professionalism throughout the week, and employees will attempt to wear more casual attire Monday through Thursday as well. Therefore, if we implement casual Fridays, we can expect to have a less productive and less professional workforce.

There are two slippery slopes in this argument: that casual Fridays will reduce profession-alism throughout the week and that casual Fridays will result in a "less productive and less professional workforce." There may indeed be a relationship between attire and pro-fessionalism, but not necessarily of the sort predicted here. In fact, casual clothes might help people feel more relaxed and comfortable at work, which may in turn *boost* pro-ductivity (not to mention employee satisfaction).

To summarize: We have reviewed the basic logical concepts as well as several specific types of fallacies that regularly appear in the stimuli. Familiarize yourself with these logi-cal tools. They will equip you to quickly dismantle the reasoning behind the essay stim-uli, saving you those precious minutes that can make the difference between a powerful, well-written essay and one that is merely acceptable.

PART THREE: THE KAPLAN FIVE-STEP METHOD FOR GRE AND GMAT ANALYTICAL WRITING

As you know, you have a limited amount of time to show the graduate school admis-sions people that you can think logically and express yourself in clearly written English. They don't care how many syllables you can cram into a sentence or how fancy your phrases are. They care that you're making sense. Whatever you do, don't try to hide beneath a lot of hefty words and abstractions. Just make sure that everything you say is clearly written and relevant to the topic. Get in there, state your main points, back them up, and get out. Here's our five-step plan to do just that.

1. Take the Issue/Argument Apart

- Identify the topic (the broad subject), the scope (the specific aspect of the topic you'll be dealing with), and the conclusion (the main idea the author wanted to establish in the prompt).
- Locate the evidence used to support the conclusion.
- Look for assumptions (pieces of evidence that are not explicitly stated, but that must be true in order for the argument to be valid).
- Note any terms that are ambiguous and need defining.

2. Select the Points You Will Make

- In the Issue essay, think of the arguments for both sides and make a decision as to which side you will support or the exact extent to which you agree with the stated position.
- In the Argument essay, identify all the important gaps between the evidence and the conclusion. Think of remedies for the problems you discovered when taking apart the argument.

3. Organize Your Thoughts

- Outline what you want to say in the introduction, in the middle paragraphs (one main idea per paragraph), and in your final paragraph.
- Lead with your best arguments.
- Think about how the essay as a whole will flow.

4. Write Your Essay

- Start out and conclude with strong statements.
- Be assertive.
- Make transitions, link related ideas; it will help your writing flow.

5. Proofread

- Save enough time to read through the entire essay.
- Have a sense of the errors you are liable to make.

APPLYING THE KAPLAN FIVE-STEP METHOD TO THE ISSUE ESSAY

Let's use the Kaplan Five-Step method on this sample Issue prompt:

> The drawbacks to the use of nuclear power mean that it is not a long-term solution to the problem of meeting ever-increasing energy needs.

1. Take the Issue Apart

Topic: Energy sources

Scope: Whether or not nuclear power is a suitable replacement for other forms of energy

Conclusion: Nuclear power is not a solution to the problem of meeting ever-increasing energy needs

Evidence: Unnamed drawbacks

Assumptions:

- Nuclear power has the potential to meet long-term energy needs.
- Nuclear power is not our only energy option.

2. Select the Points You Will Make

Your job, as stated in the directions, is to decide whether or not you agree and explain your decision. Some would argue that the use of nuclear power is too dangerous, while others would say that we can't afford not to use it. So which side do you take? (Remember that you need to take a position, but you aren't limited to just one or two options as presented in the stimulus. For example, you don't have to argue that nuclear power is too dangerous or that it is the solution to our energy needs. Your side could present a third, "in between" position.)

Remember, the essay isn't about showing the admissions people what your deep-seated beliefs about the environment are—it's about showing that you can formulate an argument and write it down. Quickly think through the pros and cons of each major point of view, and choose the side for which you have the most relevant and substantial support. For this topic, that process might go something like this:

Arguments for the use of nuclear power:

- Inexpensive compared to other forms of energy
- Fossil fuels will eventually be depleted
- Solar power still too problematic and expensive

Arguments against the use of nuclear power:

- Harmful to the environment
- Dangerous to mankind
- Safer alternatives already exist
- Better alternatives may lie undiscovered

Again, it doesn't really matter which side you take. Let's say that in this case you decide to argue against nuclear power. Remember, the question is asking you to argue why the cons of nuclear power outweigh the pros—the inadequacy of this power source is the end you're arguing toward, so don't list it as a supporting argument.

3. Organize Your Argument

You've already begun to think out your arguments—that's why you picked the side you did in the first place. Now's the time to write them all out, including ones that weaken the opposing side. Here's where you spell out your specific support for your thesis.

Nuclear power is not a viable alternative to other sources of energy because:

- Radioactive, spent fuel has leaked from storage sites (too dangerous)
- Reactor accidents can be catastrophic—Three Mile Island, Chernobyl (too dangerous)
- More research into solar power will bring down its cost (weakens opposing argument)

- Solar-powered homes and cars already exist (alternatives proven viable)
- Renewable resources require money only for the materials needed to harvest them (alternatives are cheaper in the long run)
- Energy companies don't spend money on alternatives; no vested interest (better alternatives lie undiscovered)

4. Write Your Essay

Remember, open up with a general statement and then assert your position. From there, get down your main points.

Sample Essay

Proponents of nuclear energy as "the power source for the future" have long touted its relative economy, "clean burning" technology, and virtually inexhaustible fuel supply. However, a close examination of the issue reveals that nuclear energy proves more problematic and dangerous than other forms of energy production and thus is not an acceptable solution to the problem of meeting ever-increasing energy needs.

First and foremost, nuclear power production presents the problem of radioactive waste storage. Fuel byproducts from nuclear fission remain toxic for thousands of years, and the spills and leaks from existing storage sites have been hazardous and costly to clean up. This remains true despite careful regulation and even under the best of circumstances. Even more appalling is the looming threat of accidents at the reactor itself: Incidents at the Three Mile Island and Chernobyl power plants and at other production sites have warned us that the consequences of a nuclear meltdown can be catastrophic and felt worldwide.

But beyond the enormous long-term environmental problems and short-term health risks, the bottom line issue for the production of energy is one of economics. Power production in our society is a business just like any other, and the large companies that produce this country's electricity and gas claim they are unable to make alternatives such as solar power affordable.

Yet—largely due to incentives from the federal government—there already exist homes heated by solar power, and cars fueled by the sun. If the limited resources devoted to date to such energy alternatives have already produced working models, a more intensive, broadly based, and supported effort is likely to make those alternatives less expensive and problematic.

Besides the benefits in terms of both of cost and safety, renewable resources such as solar and hydroelectric power represent far better options in the long run for development: They require money only for the materials needed to harvest them. While sunlight and water are free, the innovative technologies and industrial strategies devised to harness them have created a geometric progression of spin-offs affecting fields as diverse as agriculture, real estate, space exploration, and social policy. They have also repeatedly produced secondary economic and social benefits, such as the large recreational and irrigation reservoirs created in the American Southwest behind large hydro-electric dams like the Hoover and Grand Coullee.

While it may now be clear that the drawbacks to the use of nuclear power are too great, it should also be apparent that the long-term benefits of renewable resources would reward investment. If these alternatives are explored more seriously than they have been in the past, safer and less expensive sources of power will undoubtedly live up to their promise. With limited resources at our disposal and a burgeoning global population to consider, further investment in nuclear power would mark an unconscionable and unnecessary waste of time and money.

5. Proofread Your Work

Take that last couple of minutes to catch any glaring errors.

APPLYING THE KAPLAN FIVE-STEP METHOD TO THE ARGUMENT ESSAY

Let's use the Kaplan Five-Step Method on an Argument topic:

> The problem of poorly trained teachers that has plagued the state public school system is bound to become a good deal less serious in the future. The state has initiated comprehensive guidelines that oblige state teachers to complete a number of required credits in education and educational psychology at the graduate level before being certified.

Explain how logically persuasive you find this argument. In discussing your viewpoint, analyze the argument's line of reasoning and its use of evidence. Also explain what, if anything, would make the argument more valid and convincing or help you to better evaluate its conclusion.

1. Take the argument apart.

First, identify the conclusion—the point the argument's trying to make. Here, the conclusion is:

> The problem of poorly trained teachers that has plagued the state public school system is bound to become a good deal less serious in the future.

Next, identify the evidence—the basis for the conclusion. Here, the evidence is:

> *The state has initiated comprehensive guidelines that oblige state teachers to complete a number of required credits in education and educational psychology at the graduate level before being certified.*

Finally, sum up the argument in your own words:

> *The problem of badly trained teachers will become less serious because they'll be getting better training.*

Explain how logically persuasive you find this argument. In explaining your viewpoint, analyze the argument's line of reasoning and its use of evidence. Also explain what, if anything, would make the argument more valid and convincing or would help you to better evaluate its conclusion.

- Credits in education will improve teachers' classroom performance.
- Present bad teachers haven't already met this standard of training.
- Current poor teachers will not still be teaching in the future, or will have to be trained, too.

2. Select the points you will make.

Analyze the use of evidence in the argument.

Determine whether there's anything relevant that's not discussed.

- Whether the training will actually address the cause of the problems
- How to either improve or remove the poor teachers now teaching

Also determine what types of evidence would make the argument stronger or more logically sound. In this case, we need some new evidence supporting the assumptions.

- Evidence verifying that this training will make better teachers
- Evidence making it clear that present bad teachers haven't already had this training
- Evidence suggesting why all or many bad teachers won't still be teaching in the future (or why they'll be better trained)

3. Organize.

For an essay on this topic, your opening sentence might look like this:

> *The writer concludes that the present problem of poorly trained teachers will become less severe in the future because of required course work in education and psychology.*

Then use your notes as a working outline. Remember to lead with your best arguments. You might also recommend new evidence you'd like to see and explain why.

The argument says that:

The problem of poorly trained teachers will become less serious with better training.

It assumes that:

- Course work in education will improve teachers' classroom performance.
- Present bad teachers haven't already met this standard of classroom training.
- Current poor teachers will not be teaching in the future or will get training, too.

4. Write your essay.

Keep in mind the basic principles of writing and remember the following issues:
What assumptions are made by the author?

- Are these assumptions valid? Why or why not?
- What additional information or evidence would make the argument stronger?

Your essay might look something like this:

Sample Essay

The writer concludes that the present problem of poorly trained teachers will become less severe in the future because of required credits in education and psychology. However, the conclusion relies on assumptions for which there is no clear evidence.

First, the writer assumes that the required courses will make better teachers. In fact, the courses might be entirely irrelevant to the teachers' failings. If, for example, the prevalent problem is cultural and linguistic gaps between teacher and student, graduate level courses that do not address these specific issues probably won't do much good. The argument that the courses will improve teachers would be strengthened if the writer provided evidence that the training will be relevant to the problems.

In addition, the writer assumes that current poor teachers have not already had this training. In fact, the writer doesn't mention whether or not some or all of the poor teachers have had similar training. The argument would be strengthened considerably if the writer provided evidence that current poor teachers have not had training comparable to the new requirements.

Finally, the writer assumes that poor teachers currently working will either stop teaching in the future or will have received training. The writer provides no evidence, though, to indicate that this is the case. As the argument stands, it's highly possible that only brand-new teachers will receive the training, and the bright future to which the writer refers is decades away. Only if the writer provides evidence that all teachers in the system will receive training—and will then change their teaching methods accordingly—does the argument hold.

5. Proofread.

Save a few minutes to go back over your essay and catch any obvious errors.

PART FOUR: PREPARE YOUR TEMPLATES

On test day, you will be facing two writing assignments that you must complete quickly and effectively. You will be under pressure: little time is allotted for each task. Your best strategy is to do as much advance preparation as possible, and that means arming yourself with a pair of flexible and logically robust templates that will guide you in your analyses and assist you in formulating your essays.

Sample Template for an Issue Essay

Introduction

Objectives: Restate the issue; take a stand. Make your position clear in a strong thesis statement at the end of your first paragraph.

Body (3+ paragraphs)

Objective: In each paragraph, develop one of the reasons for your position. Provide concrete support for that reason using empirical evidence, expert testimony, or anecdotes. Acknowledge and refute counterarguments.

Conclusion

Objective: Reaffirm your position and summarize main points of support.

Sample Template for an Argument Essay

Introduction

Objective: Rephrase the argument. Briefly identify its main flaws in the order in which you will discuss them.

1) Paraphrase the argument. If the stimulus includes an attribution of the argument, you should incorporate it into your opening paraphrase (e.g., *"The Clairville Township Planning Board proposes to [accomplish X] by [doing Y]. The Board supports this proposal by [such-and-such evidence or rationale]. "*). If the stimulus is presented without such attribution, you can simply refer to it as "the given argument" or "the given proposal."

2) Acknowledge the appeal of the argument.

3) Catalog the weaknesses of the argument or defects in the plan.

4) Allude to other evidence that might have been introduced to strengthen the argument or proposal.

Body (3+ paragraphs)

Objective: Explain in detail the weaknesses cited in your introductory paragraph. Use one paragraph per weakness (two if the weakness requires lengthy discussion).

Conclusion

Objectives: Summarize the weaknesses and suggest ways to strengthen the argument or proposal.

PART FIVE: ISSUE AND ARGUMENT PRACTICE EXERCISES

Issue Task Exercises

Directions: The following is a series of prompts of the sort that you might encounter on the GRE or GMAT. Using the methods of logical analysis and organization you have learned in this chapter, practice planning an essay for each sample prompt. For each stimulus,

1. Read the stimulus.

2. Use the questions below the stimulus as a guide to approach organizing an answer. The questions guide you through one of the essay templates discussed earlier in this chapter.

3. Briefly list or draft out the paragraphs of an essay that takes a stand on the issue described by the stimulus in the spaces provided. Don't worry about form, language or mechanics at this point: you just want to get the key ideas down.

A detailed discussion of each stimulus with sample answers is found at the end of the chapter. Although the exact content of answers will vary, the example of discussion and analysis will give you a good idea of whether or not you are on the right track in your own analysis.

1. "Many people believe that the people in their early environment (for example parents, family, teachers, friends) have caused them to think and behave in the way
they do. Yet, in fact, it is primarily the nature of our innate and inherited personality
characteristics that mainly define who we are as individuals."

Describe the false dilemma and/or overstated generalization contained in the stimulus:

_____

_____

1) Briefly paraphrase the point of the proposition as you believe it was intended to be
understood:

_____

_____

2) Point out words and phrases that are imprecise and mention the complexities they
entail.

_____

_____

3) For a false dilemma, suggest a range of potential alternatives to the extreme positions
cited.

_____

_____

4) Allude to and address the potential objections to your position.

_____

_____

5) Argue in support of your position.

_____

_____

2. "Science tends to contribute to the stability of society. Art tends to destabilize society. This complementary relationship embodies their value."

Describe the false dilemma and/or overstated generalization contained in the stimulus:

_____

_____

_____

_____

_____

Paragraph 1: restate the issue, explain the complications, take a stand.

_____

_____

_____

_____

_____

Paragraphs 2, 3, etc.: elaborate on your position using empirical evidence, expert testimony, or anecdotes.

_____

_____

_____

_____

_____

Last Paragraph: Conclude your essay.

_____

_____

_____

_____

_____

_____

3. "The ease of communication common in today's electronic media environment promotes a habit of hasty, ill-conceived thinking instead of thoughtful, well-reasoned
   judgment."

   Describe the false dilemma and/or overstated generalization contained in the stimulus:

_____

_____

_____

_____

_____

_____

Paragraph 1: Restate the Issue, explain the complications, take a stand and characterize
(without elaborating) the arguments that you will present.

_____

_____

_____

_____

_____

_____

Paragraphs 2, 3, etc.: Elaborate on your position, using empirical evidence, expert testimony, or anecdotes.

_____

_____

_____

_____

_____

_____

Paragraph next-to-last: Develop and then refute the alternative position.

_____

_____

_____

_____

_____

_____

Final Paragraph: Conclude your essay.

_____

_____

_____

_____

_____

_____

4. "Colleges should emphasize general intellectual development as the primary goal for students rather than focusing on career preparation."

Describe the false dilemma and/or overstated generalization contained in the stimulus:

_____

_____

_____

_____

_____

_____

_____

Paragraph 1: Restate the Issue, explain the complications, take a stand and characterize (without elaborating) the arguments that you will present.

_____

_____

_____

_____

_____

_____

Paragraphs 2, 3, etc.: Elaborate on your position, using empirical evidence, expert testimony, or anecdotes.

_____

_____

_____

_____

_____

_____

Paragraph next-to-last: Develop and then refute the alternative position.

_____

_____

_____

_____

_____

_____

Final Paragraph: Conclude your essay.

_____

_____

_____

_____

_____

_____

_____

Argument Task Exercises

Directions: The following is a series of prompts of the sort that you might encounter on the GRE or GMAT. Using the methods of logical analysis and organization you have learned in this chapter, practice planning an essay for each sample prompt. For each stimulus,

1. Read the stimulus.

2. Analyze the argument and fill in the blanks provided for the conclusion and premises of each argument.

3. Use the questions below the stimulus as a guide to approach organizing an answer. The questions guide you through one of the essay templates discussed earlier in this chapter.

4. Briefly list or draft out the paragraphs of an essay that appropriately analyzes the argument described by the stimulus in the spaces provided. Don't worry about form, language or mechanics at this point: you just want to get the key ideas down.

A detailed discussion of each stimulus with sample answers is found at the end of the chapter. Although the exact content of answers will vary, the example of discussion and analysis will give you a good idea of whether or not you are on the right track in your own analysis.

1. The following appeared in a memo from the general director of marketing for Never-Stick, Inc.

"A recent study of cooks who use the Never-Stick frying pan shows that our company is wasting the money it spends on its exclusive 'Bondure' process, which ensures that our non-stick coating will last for five years. Never-Stick has made the Bondure process a centerpiece of its advertising for ten years, but the new study shows that the average Never-Stick owner replaces used frying pans every three or four years. Furthermore, Never-Stick owners surveyed in the Southwestern states, where many Never-Stick customers live, value the unique Cool-Grip handle and fashion enamel colors more than the durability of the Bondure coating. This study suggests that Never-Stick can boost profits by discontinuing the use of the Bondure process."

What conclusion does this stimulus draw?

_____

_____

_____

_____

_____

_____

List the premises in this stimulus that lead to its conclusion:

_____

_____

_____

_____

_____

_____

List the fallacies that make the argument weak:
Paragraph 1
1) Paraphrase the argument:

_____

_____

_____

_____

_____

_____

2) Acknowledge the appeal of the argument:

_____

_____

_____

_____

_____

_____

_____

3) Catalog the weaknesses of the argument:

_____

_____

_____

_____

_____

_____

_____

4) Allude to other evidence that might have been introduced to strengthen the argument:

_____

_____

_____

_____

_____

_____

_____

Paragraph 2, 3, etc.
Explain in detail the weaknesses alluded to in your introduction:

_____

_____

_____

_____

_____

_____

Final Paragraph
Summarize the weaknesses and suggest ways to strengthen the argument:

_____

_____

_____

_____

_____

_____

_____

Test Prep and Admissions

2. The following appeared as part of a memorandum issued by the managing editor of Deceus, a large publishing house.

    "Our least-successful line of books over the past three years has been the Angelus line of romance thriller novels. The covers of books in the Angelus line feature the main characters depicted in an action pose. Over the same period, competing publishing houses have noticeably decreased their offerings in the genre of romance thrillers and have moved away from picturing main characters on book covers. Furthermore, the cost of advances and royalties to authors who write romance thrillers has been steadily increasing. Therefore, Deceus Publishing should eliminate the Angelus line of romance thriller novels."

What conclusion does this stimulus draw?

_____

_____

_____

_____

_____

_____

List the premises in this stimulus that lead to its conclusion:

_____

_____

_____

_____

_____

_____

List the fallacies that make the argument weak:
Paragraph 1
1) Paraphrase the argument:

_____

_____

_____

_____

_____

2) Acknowledge the appeal of the argument:

_____

_____

_____

_____

_____

3) Catalog the weaknesses of the argument:

_____

_____

_____

_____

_____

_____

4) Allude to other evidence that might have been introduced to strengthen the argument:

_____

_____

_____

_____

_____

_____

_____

Paragraph 2, 3, etc.
Explain in detail the weaknesses alluded to in your introduction:

_____

_____

_____

_____

_____

_____

_____

Final Paragraph
Summarize the weaknesses and suggest ways to strengthen the argument:

_____

_____

_____

_____

_____

_____

_____

3. The following recommendation was made in a letter from the board of trustees of Plum Island College, a private educational institution, and presented to the governing committee of the college.

   "We recommend that Plum Island College remain at its traditional 150 year-old campus site off the coast of Baytown rather than moving to the site available on the mainland. True, the majority of the faculty members voted in favor of relocating the college, pointing out that the proposed site allows for greater expansion and growth. But a survey conducted by the Student Congress showed that seventy-five percent of the students who responded preferred that the school stay at its original site, and a majority of the alumni who responded to a second survey also opposed relocation. Keeping the college at its original location, therefore, will maintain student morale and preserve the financial support provided by alumni."

What conclusion does this stimulus draw?

_____

_____

_____

_____

_____

_____

List the premises in this stimulus that lead to its conclusion:

_____

_____

_____

_____

_____

_____

List the fallacies that make the argument weak:
Paragraph 1
1) Paraphrase the argument:

_____

_____

_____

_____

_____

_____

2) Acknowledge the appeal of the argument:

_____

_____

_____

_____

_____

_____

3) Catalog the weaknesses of the argument:

_____

_____

_____

_____

_____

_____

4) Allude to other evidence that might have been introduced to strengthen the argument:

_____

_____

_____

_____

_____

_____

Paragraph 2, 3, etc.
Explain in detail the weaknesses alluded to in your introduction:

_____

_____

_____

_____

_____

_____

Final Paragraph
Summarize the weaknesses and suggest ways to strengthen the argument:

_____

_____

_____

_____

_____

_____

4. The following appeared in a letter addressed to the superintendent of schools for the Smalltown Independent School District

"All students should be required to take a course in advanced algebra at Smalltown High School. In the past three years, Western Community College has complained that first-year students entering from Smalltown High are very poorly prepared to deal with their required first-year college mathematics courses. Since a number of parents in the Smalltown area have pointed out that they are too busy to provide additional help for their children, alternative instruction is needed to ensure that these students are prepared with the skills they need. Although there is an after school tutoring center available in Smalltown, not all parents have the financial means necessary to afford to send their teenage children there. Therefore an effective and required advanced algebra course provided by Smalltown High School is the only solution to this dilemma."

What conclusion does this stimulus draw?

_____

_____

_____

_____

_____

_____

List the premises in this stimulus that lead to its conclusion:

_____

_____

_____

_____

_____

_____

List the fallacies that make the argument weak:
Paragraph 1
1) Paraphrase the argument:

_____

_____

_____

_____

_____

2) Acknowledge the appeal of the argument:

_____

_____

_____

_____

_____

3) Catalog the weaknesses of the argument:

_____

_____

_____

_____

_____

_____

4) Allude to other evidence that might have been introduced to strengthen the argument:

_____

_____

_____

_____

_____

_____

Paragraph 2, 3, etc.
Explain in detail the weaknesses alluded to in your introduction:

_____

_____

_____

_____

_____

_____

Final Paragraph
Summarize the weaknesses and suggest ways to strengthen the argument:

_____

_____

_____

_____

_____

_____

ISSUE AND ARGUMENT ANSWERS AND EXPLANATIONS

Issue Tasks

1. **This issue prompt is the old nature vs. nurture argument recast in slightly different words.** By now you should be able to recognize this issue as a false dilemma. No one is a product exclusively of either their environment or of their genetics. The challenge of this prompt is to move systematically through the issue when you write your essay without getting bogged down or carried away in tangents. If you have some additional information that can be used as support, such as knowledge of studies of identical twins, that can help you in your argument. But even if you don't have any background in the psychology of the issue, you can still argue from a logical standpoint that the prompt is an oversimplification of a complex situation, and that your own position is better.

   1) Briefly paraphrase the point of the proposition as you believe it was intended to be understood.

      "The contention that inherited factors, rather than environmental influences, are primarily responsible for the formation of the personality is an enticing argument..."

   2) Point out the words and phrases that are imprecise, and mention the complexities they entail.

      "Such a contention is more complex than it seems on the surface. For example, the position statement mentions 'personality' as though it were a well-defined and static phenomenon, when in fact it is difficult even for experts to define exactly what constitutes personality..."

   3) For a false dilemma, suggest a range of potential alternatives to the extreme positions cited.

      It may be more accurate to say, not that people inherit particular personality traits, but rather that people inherit a range of potentials for emotional traits. Environmental factors contribute to whether or not these potentials are expressed—or perhaps even if some of them are expressed at all. For example, genetically identical twins who are separated at birth ..."

   4) Allude to and address the potential objections to your position.

      "Some may wish to object to my position by making the argument either that a person's personality results completely from that person's environment, or that personality results completely from inborn factors. Such arguments become suspect when viewed in light of a few simple examples. For instance, people obviously sometimes make rational decisions that go against the values of their upbringing. By the same token, people do apparently inherit some mental traits from their families. But the big picture is not that simple. The primary

flaw of the argument that inheritance is more important than environment in shaping personality is that it oversimplifies a complex issue into an illusory false dilemma. I believe that a combination of nature and nurture goes into the personality makeup of each individual… "

5) Argue in support of your position.

"For example, my sister and I couldn't be less alike. Even though we are close in age and grew up in essentially the same environment, she is a world traveler and adventurer who always disliked school whereas I am … Yet we also share some similar traits with our parents, such as … These examples illustrate how environmental and inherited factors all contribute to a mix of elements that go into personality….

"Both the argument that my sister is very different from me because she must have inherited different traits and the argument that she is different because she was subject to a different environment are arguments that contain causal fallacies… The fact that both arguments can be made with roughly the same level of merit (i.e., very little) demonstrates that they are equally specious…"

2. **This assertion takes two overstated generalizations (one about art and one about science) and combines them into a third overstated generalization (that the contrast is the source of their value).**

As always, attack the generalizations by pointing out exceptions. In planning this essay, brainstorm a list of examples of cases where science destabilizes society and cases where art stabilizes. Then generate examples of cases where science and art have value independent of each other. Arrange these examples into a coherent position.

Paragraph 1: restate the issue, explain the complications, take a stand.

"Art and science both have their respective places in society, and both are important. To say, however, that science tends to make society more stable while art tends to make it less stable is an overstated generalization that doesn't account for the complexities of those roles…I believe that, while art and science both contribute in important ways to society, those contributions are more rich and varied than the statements imply.

Paragraphs 2, 3, etc.: elaborate on your position using empirical evidence, expert testimony, or anecdotes.

"It's often easier to think of examples of artistic works that destabilize society. For instance, the symphonies of Beethoven made people question the scope and emotional pitch of what a symphony should be … However, there are many cases in which artistic works actually contribute to the stability of society. An extreme example might be the propagandistic painting and sculpture of Stalinist era Russia, but a milder example is Rudyard Kipling's stories, poems and novels, which were designed to perpetuate the status quo of Victorian Imperial England…"

"Also, while it is tempting to think of science as mainly a stabilizing force in society, in many cases science can be the source of destabilization. We think of helpful inventions such as penicillin, steam power and flight as things that contribute to stable society, but in fact these inventions cause great long-term upheavals … Furthermore, some of the advances of science, for example atomic weapons, can be a source of massive social change…"

"Finally, it is hard to say with absolute certainty how much the interaction between science and art influences the stability of society. There are even areas in which the two overlap so much as to become nearly indistinguishable…"

Last paragraph: conclude your essay

"Ultimately, the role of science and art in society is much more complex than an essay of this scope can encapsulate. But an examination of the examples outlined above does illuminate the intricacy of the issue…"

3. **This essay prompt is built on a false dilemma:** the contrast between the hasty, off-the-cuff thinking encouraged by electronic media (presumably such as the Internet, email and so forth) as opposed to the supposedly well-reasoned thinking habits of the past (presumably the paper-and-pencil or typewriter environment). Always attack a false dilemma by pointing out exceptions to its extremes. Simply because a document or idea is recorded in an electronic medium does not mean that it cannot be well-thought-out. By the same token, much of the writing done in the paper and typewriter era was just as hasty and ill-advised as anything ever put into an email.

While it is possible to write an essay that agrees with the assertion of this stimulus and supports its ideas with appropriate evidence, it is probably easier to defend the position that the idea in the stimulus is a false dilemma and instead support a position that a shift in the style and care of thinking has not automatically resulted from the change to electronic media.

Paragraph 1: Restate the Issue, explain the complications, take a stand and characterize (without elaborating) the arguments that you will present.

"If it is true that the medium in which an idea is recorded reflects something about the way that idea was generated, then the advent of the electronic age can arguably have been said to have had an impact on how thoughts are generated. The idea that speedier communication is a two-edged sword that allows people to bring thoughts to the public before they've had time for review and consideration is an interesting potential result of this change. But to assert categorically that electronic communication necessarily results in a sloppier style of thinking than other, less ephemeral forms of communication is, itself, not a very well-thought-out idea. In the broader scope, the question of the relationship between the medium and the amount of thinking behind an idea is more complex than that. In fact, the assertion sets up a false dilemma between two contrasting extremes that are not mutually exclusive..."

Paragraphs 2, 3, etc.: Elaborate on your position, using empirical evidence, expert testimony, or anecdotes.

"One good example of an exception to the idea that communication in the pre-electronic era was more well-reasoned is the voluminous mail systems of the 19th century world. In the days before telephones, many educated people were prolific letter writers, as anyone who has ever had to search through the letters of a famous historical figure can attest. In London in the 19th century, mail was delivered 12 times a day, and telegrams were delivered continuously. One need only glance at a novel such as Bram Stoker's *Dracula* to see that written communication in the pre-electronic era was often just as hasty and sloppy as the most hurried email of the 21st century..."

"Although the example of emails tends to make people think of the rapid communication involved in different kinds of instant messaging, work written on electronic devices and then published on paper or the Internet also constitutes electronic communication. There is no evidence to support the idea that work written on a word processor is any less well-developed in its thinking than work written on a piece of parchment with a quill pen. Indeed, because word processing allows authors and editors to change things more easily, it may actually contribute to more developed thoughts making it into the final version..."

Paragraph next-to-last: Develop and then refute the alternative position.

"Opponents of my position will point to the worst instances of verbal incontinency available in electronic media: self-indulgent blogs, off-the-cuff editorials, hurried commercial sites and documents published without reliable review. But these abuses of the forums of public communication are not new to the electronic media: examples of similar types of publications have been common at least since the invention of the printing press..."

Final Paragraph: Conclude your essay

"The examples outlined above show that the electronic medium is a tool, like the printing press or the pen, that doesn't inherently reflect the depth and complexity of the thought behind it...

4. **This essay prompt sets up a false dilemma** between "intellectual development" (whatever that is) and career preparation as student goals emphasized by colleges. The more complex view is that it is possible for colleges to perform both functions at the same time, to a greater or lesser extent. Also, the assertion that "colleges should" is an overstated generalization. It is possible to imagine a lot of scenarios with different types of colleges and different student bodies that have different curricular needs. The term "colleges" itself is ill-defined here, as is "general intellectual development."

Whichever side of the issue you come down on in writing your response to this prompt, it is important to remember that the readers are looking for how well you respond, not for a "correct" response. The example answers below include samples of arguments from both sides of the issue.

Paragraph 1: Restate the Issue, explain the complications, take a stand and characterize (without elaborating) the arguments that you will present.

"From their earliest days, institutions of higher education have always served a dual purpose: nurturing the intellectual development of the young and preparing them for future careers. From Plato's academy preparing young men for their lives of aristocratic citizenship, to the mediaeval European universities training future clergymen, to the modern array of colleges and universities training aspiring doctors, lawyers and rocket scientists, most higher education institutions have sought to straddle the fence between training the person and the professional. While the situation is more complex than the either/or false dilemma of the topic would have one believe, I generally ..."

Example of agreement

"... agree that colleges and other undergraduate institutions should focus primarily on intellectual development rather than career preparation. My stance on this issue is based on the idea that intellectual development creates mental flexibility and professional adaptability. These qualities are far more important in today's changing marketplace than a fixed and limited curriculum of career preparation."

Example of disagreement

"... disagree that colleges and other undergraduate institutions should focus primarily on intellectual development rather than career preparation. My stance on this issue is based on the idea that today's marketplace is so competitive and the career skills needed—especially in particular fields—are so extensive that specialization and focus are more necessary than ever if students are to achieve their career goals. Many students are aware of this need, and will rightfully demand the career preparation that their institutions should be prepared to give."

Example of middle-of-the-road position

"... feel that colleges should do their best to provide both intellectual development and career preparation together. The versatility and cultural literacy of a general intellectual education is a perfect compliment to the focused career skills required by students going into particular fields, and a blending of the two provides the best of both worlds without losing any of the important aspects of either."

Paragraphs 2, 3, etc.: Elaborate on your position, using empirical evidence, expert testimony, or anecdotes.

(Agreement) *"Overspecialization has proven to be the undoing of many laid-off workers in today's job market. Witness the plunge in employment among high-tech workers last decade. Overnight, thousands of highly-trained Web designers, software engineers and computer experts found themselves displaced with no jobs available and inadequate training for an alternate career. How might they have been better off if they had undergone a general curriculum that prepared them for success in a variety of fields and careers..."*

(Disagreement) *"Gone are the days when a general education in arts and literature was adequate for anyone (usually any man) to acquire the career of his choice. In today's world, corporate employers and post-graduate professional schools require an intensive range of specialized skills before they will even consider a candidate seriously. By not providing them with the necessary training, colleges are setting their students up for failure..."*

(Middle of the road) *"The key idea underlying my position is the idea that general intellectual development is career preparation. The patterns and methods of critical thinking that are taught in a good general curriculum are the essential tools used to approach and understand the information relevant to preparation in a particular career. The old adage about giving a man a fish versus teaching a man to fish applies here as well. Career preparation gives students the tools they need to succeed in their chosen career, and general intellectual education gives students the tools they need to succeed in career preparation..."*

Argument Tasks

1. Conclusion: Discontinuing the Bondure process will increase profits.

Premises:

- Most customers replace their frying pans before they benefit from the special process.
- A sample of customers valued other features of the product over the special process.

Discussion:

When you extract the premises and conclusion from this stimulus, the logical disconnect should become clear: the premises do not support the conclusion about higher profits. The premises do support the idea that discontinuing the Bondure process will not hurt sales. Customers are either not concerned with the process or are not using the benefits of it, so they are unlikely to make purchase decisions based on the presence or absence of the bonding process. But that evidence does not necessarily translate into higher profits.

In order to make a strong argument for the higher profits conclusion, the stimulus needs to extend the preliminary conclusion (that ceasing the process will not hurt sales) with additional evidence (for example, that it is cheaper to make frying pans without the Bondure process).

1) Paraphrase the argument:

> "The marketing director of Never-Stick proposes to increase profits by ceasing use of the Bondure process…As evidence, the director cites the customer pattern of replacing frying pans every three years, thus depriving them of …Also, the director points to a recent study that shows …"

2) Acknowledge the appeal of the argument:

For this prompt, one of the appealing things about its argument is that the evidence does support a conclusion: that sales will not be hurt by ceasing the process. There are other possibilities, but this one stands out:

> "At first, this argument seems well-constructed. The study and the survey do certainly support the conclusion that sales will not decrease because of …"

3) Catalog the weaknesses of the argument:

The main weakness is the logical leap from the conclusion that sales will not decrease to the increase in profits. Also there is a possible causal fallacy in premise one: just because people don't use the whole five-year lifespan of the nonstick coating doesn't mean that they don't make buying decisions based on it being there. Finally, there is a hasty generalization embedded in the limited sample size of the survey mentioned in premise two.

> "However, this argument is weakened by serious flaws. First of all, the conclusion does not follow logically from the premises. The argument that ceasing the process will not hurt sales does not necessarily lead to higher profits because … Secondly, the argument shows a possible causal fallacy in assuming that customers don't buy frying pans on the basis of the special process … Finally, the cited study may be based on an inappropriate sample…"

4) Allude to other evidence that might have been introduced to strengthen the argument:

In this case, in order to make sure the conclusion follows from the premise, we need evidence that connects the Bondure process with the bottom line:

> "The argument would have been more compelling if the director of marketing had direct evidence that an appropriate sampling of customers don't purchase frying pans on the basis of the process … More importantly, though, the argument should show evidence that Never-Stick Inc. can lower costs by eliminating the process, and that those lower costs translate to higher profits…"

5) Summarize the weaknesses and suggest ways to strengthen the argument:

Briefly go back over the main points that you've elaborated.

> *"Given the weaknesses inherent in this argument, it is not sur-prising that its conclusion is less than compelling. The argument might have been somewhat stronger if the marketing director had been able to show a relevant connection between ... "*

2. Conclusion: Deceus publishing should eliminate the Angelus line.

Premises:

1) The Angelus line has not been selling as well as other Deceus lines of books.

2) The covers of Angelus books feature the main characters.

3) Other publishers have decreased their offerings in this genre and have not fea-tured main characters on the book covers.

4) The cost of producing Angelus books has gone up.

Discussion:

Again, as with all Analytical Writing prompts, the argument here is invalid—the premises do not lead logically to the conclusion. Premise one contains a fallacy of exclusion: we know from the stimulus that Angelus is the "least-successful" book line at the company, but we don't know whether or not that means it is unprofitable. Premise four has a simi-lar problem, still failing to connect the rising costs with any mention of profit. Premise two and three set up a false analogy, comparing Deceus to other companies about which we know nothing at all.

In order to be strengthened, this argument needs development along two major lines. First, it needs some evidence one way or another about whether or not the Angelus line is making a profit. Then it needs evidence to connect the analogous situation of other companies to the situation of Deceus.

Sample Outline:

Paragraph 1

1) Paraphrase the argument:

> *"...that the lack of success of the Angelus line and the actions of other publishers mean that Deceus should discontinue ..."*

2) Acknowledge the appeal of the argument

> *"...it may seem reasonable, at first glance, that a company should withdraw its faltering products from the market. But that is not, in fact, the conclusion supported by the evidence presented here..."*

3) Catalog the weaknesses of the argument or defects in the plan

> *" ... fails to connect the lack of success of the Angelus line with any mention of profitability. Furthermore, the information on book cov-ers and the withdrawal of similar books by other publishers is not related by any clear evidence to the situation at Deceus..."*

4) Allude to other evidence that might have been introduced to strengthen the argument or proposal

" *…argument would be strengthened by a clear connection between the Angelus line and evidence about its present and future profitability …*"

Paragraphs 2, 3, 4 …

Explain the argument's weaknesses in detail

"*First of all, the proposal tells us that Angelus is the company's 'least-successful' line of products. 'Least-successful' is a relative term that is not related to the question of whether or not the line makes a profit. Deceus's 'Least-successful' product may be immensely successful compared with the products of other companies, for all we know…*"

"*In a related vein, the proposal makes no mention of the impact of the rising costs of the Angelus line on the profitability of the product…*"

"*The information on the actions of other companies sets up a false analogy…this information is only pertinent to the argument if there is further information that the other companies, who are discontinuing their romance thriller lines, have some connection with the situation of Deceus. If we know, for example, that there is evidence to indicate a loss of consumer interest in the genre of romance thrillers … even then, it may be that the actions of other companies in discontinuing their romance thrillers will give a boost to the Angelus line by reducing supply in a market where demand is constant…*"

"*Finally, the point about the book cover is largely irrelevant. In the absence of clear evidence of a connection between consumer buying decisions and the design of book covers, the information has no bearing on the argument. The proposal may be attempting to use the similarity as part of the premise supporting the false analogy above, but a similarity in book jacket designs is hardly evidence of an analogous situation…*"

Final Paragraph

Summarize the weaknesses and suggest ways to strengthen the argument

"*In sum, the weaknesses inherent in the logic of this proposal make it less convincing than it could be…*"

3. Conclusion: Plum Island College should remain at its original site rather than moving to the mainland.

Preliminary conclusion:

Keeping the college where it is will maintain student morale and keep alumni donating.

Premises:

A survey showed that most students prefer that the college remain where it is.

Another survey showed that alumni prefer that the college stay off the mainland.

Discussion:

This argument has a series of major flaws. First, its two major pieces of evidence, the student survey and the alumni survey, are used to support a preliminary conclusion in what may be a hasty generalization: we have no way of knowing if the survey sample is appropriate to support the idea that students and alumni might actually withdraw support if the college moved. Second, even if the preliminary conclusion is true, what about that faculty survey? The proposal merely asserts that the views of students and alumni are more important than the views of faculty without offering any evidence why this is so. Finally, the stimulus does not deal effectively with the counter-argument that the move would be a benefit for growth and expansion of the college. Also—and this is a small thing but worth mentioning—the description of the original college site as "traditional" constitutes an improper appeal to authority. Just because something is old or traditional doesn't necessarily mean it's the best thing.

This argument would be strengthened by direct evidence that student morale and a drop in alumni support would constitute a real threat to the existence of the college. Then, the argument needs an effective counter for the faculty survey and the possible need for expansion space that the original site does not have.

Paragraph 1

> 1) Paraphrase the argument that the college should remain where it is in order to maintain student morale and alumni support.
>
> > "...the trustees argue that the college should remain at its current site based on the views expressed in two surveys ..."
>
> 2) Acknowledge the appeal of the argument
>
> > "The morale of students and the support of alumni are definitely two important factors in the prosperity of a private college, and on that basis this argument has a certain appeal."
>
> 3) Catalog the weaknesses of the argument or defects in the plan
>
> > "Using the results of these two surveys, which are potentially problematic to begin with, as the only criterion for deciding the future location of the college shows itself under close examination to be less-than-convincing."

4) Allude to other evidence that might have been introduced to strengthen the argument or proposal

"If there were some evidence that the views expressed by the faculty about the need for expansion space are invalid, along with a direct indication that student morale and alumni support are vital for the continuation of the college... However, as the argument stands, it is weak."

Paragraphs 2, 3, etc.: Explain the argument's weaknesses in detail

"To begin with, the surveys mentioned in the trustees' letter are problematic. The letter gives us no evidence that the size and selection of the samples was appropriate to the issue being surveyed, creating the possibility of a hasty generalization... The fact that the views expressed in the student and alumni survey are so divergent from the views expressed in the faculty survey is, in itself, an inconsistency that suggests some inadequacy in the methodology."

"Beyond the design of the surveys, the trustees' use of the survey results as premises to support their conclusion is unwarranted. The letter summarizes the results of three surveys, then disregards the evidence suggested by the faculty survey without comment and jumps to the conclusion that the student and alumni views are more important. There is no effective counter-argument against the view that the school may need expansion room..."

"Finally, and this may seem like a small point, but worth mentioning, the characterization of the school's current site as 'traditional' constitutes an improper appeal to authority..."

Final Paragraph: Summarize the weaknesses and suggest ways to strengthen the argument

"In spite of these weaknesses in the areas of survey design, application of survey evidence and fallacious arguments, the trustees' proposal can be made stronger by the inclusion of additional evidence. If there were some reliable indication that student morale and alumni support are vital to the continuation ... If there were information on the validity of the survey design... If the letter contained a counter-argument that clearly showed the faculty concerns about the need for expansion were unfounded, and that no serious negative consequences would result from overriding the views of the faculty... And, finally, if the word 'traditional' were removed from the first sentence..."

4. **Conclusion: A required advanced algebra course for every student is the only solution to the problem of students' lack of preparedness for freshman math at Western CC.**

Premises:

The college has complained that Smalltown High students are not prepared.

Smalltown parents are too busy to help their kids learn more math.

Not all parents can afford tutoring.

Discussion:

There are really two parts to the conclusion here, both flawed in slightly different ways. One part of the conclusion is that the advanced algebra course should be mandatory for all students. The second part is that the only solution is a course taught by the school, not provided by other means. In your essay, you can criticize both these parts of the argument.

The problem with insisting that the course be mandatory for all students is that not all students will be going to Western Community College—or even intending to go to college at all—so many of them will not need an advanced algebra course. The problem with insisting that only the school can provide such a course is that it sets up a false dilemma. Parent tutoring, use of the tutoring center, and the high school are not the only choices available for students to get the preparation they need.

Finally, the letter also makes an unfounded assumption when it jumps from the problem of the students' lack of math knowledge to the solution of a high school course. A school course is not a magic bullet for solving a problem with deficiencies in students' math knowledge.

Paragraph 1:

    1) Paraphrase the argument

        "…the author of this letter argues that the complaints of a local college constitute grounds for the institution of a mandatory advanced algebra course for all students at Smalltown High."

    2) Acknowledge the appeal of the argument

        "While advanced algebra may be desirable and useful, and it is important for local educational institutions to collaborate on curriculum, the evidence presented hardly warrants the implementation of a mandatory course."

    3) Catalog the weaknesses of the argument or defects in the plan

        "…feedback from a single community college cannot be taken as representative of the level of preparedness of all students. More important, though, are the two major flawed lines of argument in this letter: (1) that the course should be mandatory for all students and (2) that the high school is the only possible means of providing the course."

    4) Allude to other evidence that might have been introduced to strengthen the argument or proposal

        "If there were some evidence that the complaints of Western Community College are more general, or other information about how these complaints are symptomatic of a larger need, that would strengthen the argument for making the course mandatory. Furthermore, if the letter specified further evidence about why the high school is the best forum for providing …"

Paragraphs 2, 3, etc.: Explain the argument's weaknesses in detail

"The connecting of the criticism from Western Community College with the need for a course for all students is unfounded. Presumably many of the students at Smalltown high will not attend this particular college—or may not attend college at all—and therefore won't need this advanced algebra course."

"Furthermore, the letter's insistence that the course be taught by the high school creates a false dilemma. The parents, the local tutoring center, and the school are not the only possibilities for providing the needed education to Smalltown students. For example, Western Community College itself might be interested in offering high school enrichment courses or remedial courses for entering freshmen…"

"Finally, although it would be nice to believe that a course in the high school would solve the problem of students not knowing advanced algebra, in fact this is an unwarranted assumption. If students have undergone twelve years of schooling without—as Western Community College claims—acquiring the math skills they need for freshman math classes, how will yet another course help? The letter offers no evidence for why a course at the high school is a solution at all…"

Final Paragraph: Summarize the weaknesses and suggest ways to strengthen the argument

"In the form presented by this letter, the argument for a mandatory advanced algebra course at the high school has little merit… Evidence that the deficiencies seen by Western CC represent a more general lack of preparedness in math for all students, along with evidence that such courses had been successful in the past or at other schools, would tend to support the argument for the merits of the course…"

PRACTICE ANSWERS AND EXPLANATIONS

Practice 1

Paragraph 1

(1) The advice given to the company managers that hiring additional workers will result in a larger number of houses being built contains a fallacy of exclusion. (2) Several pieces of vital information are not taken into consideration in the reasoning that more workers means more houses built, and a moment's thought reveals that many factors other than merely the number of workers determines the answer to the question of how many houses will be built. (3) For example, if the construction company doesn't have enough construction equipment or tools to equip more workers, then extra workers won't help regardless. (4) If there aren't enough building sites available, enough raw materials, or sufficient infrastructure to support additional workers, then hiring more workers might well be just a waste of money. (5) The whole question of diminishing returns in increasing staff size is not considered by this line of reasoning at all.

(1) Advice is the noun; advise is a verb.

More additional is an example of pleonasm (redundancy).

Advice is the singular subject of the sentence, so it takes the singular verb form, *contains*.

(2) *Extremely vital* is redundant.

This sentence is a run-on—two independent clauses joined by a comma with no conjunction. Fix it by either adding a conjunction or by making it into two sentences (or possibly by swapping the comma for a semicolon).

Moment's is possessive here, so takes an apostrophe.

Reasoning is repetitive with the preceding clause, so swap it out for another term such as *thought*.

The sentence compares the number of workers with the other factors, so the comparative *than* is required.

The final question is embedded, so it takes a period rather than a question mark.

(3) Omit the slash as a substitute for the conjunction *or* in essays.

Workers is a simple plural here, so no apostrophe is necessary.

Always use *regardless* rather than *irregardless*.

(4) The sentence here refers to building locations (sites), not things seen (sights).

  The middle term in this series violates parallelism in the original, creating confusion.

  The future conditional subjunctive here takes the verb be rather than been.

(5) The phrase *in increasing staff size* modifies the question of diminishing returns, so put the modifier next to the thing it modifies in order to avoid confusion.

Paragraph 2

   (1) While the school board's argument that eating breakfast in the school breakfast program is related to a reduction of absenteeism may be convincing, (2) the conclusion that forcing more students to eat breakfast on the school program will cause a decrease in absences is unwarranted. (3) The statistics show a correspondence that is far from clear enough to assume causation. (4) The attendance of students at the school-sponsored breakfast program and at subsequent classes might both result from a third, unexamined cause that creates the observed effect. (5) For example, students who eat school breakfasts every day might just happen to be the ones who go to bed early [no comma] and therefore are up in time for both the breakfast and for classes. (6) Or perhaps the students with better attendance experience a different kind of parent supervision that contributes to both their better diet and their improved attendance.

(1) *School board* is a common noun, so no capitals. If it were the name of a specific school board, for example the Shelby County School Board, then it would be capitalized.

  In the school breakfast program modifies *eating breakfast*, so it should go closer to what it modifies in order to avoid confusion about what exactly is in the program.

  This sentence is a fragment because of the subordinate while at the beginning. One easy way to fix this problem is to join it to the next sentence by changing the period to a comma and eliminating the capital letter at the beginning of the next sentence as shown.

(2) *Decreasing drop* is redundant.

(3) *Statistics* is a simple plural, not a possessive, so no apostrophe is needed.

  Correspondence is misspelled.

(4) *Maybe* is a lowbrow qualifier; prefer *might* or *perhaps*.

  Effect is the noun that describes an influence or outcome. The noun *affect* is psychological jargon for "emotion."

(5) The word *everyday* means "ordinary." The phrase *every day* means "happening on each day."

> The phrase that follows the conjunction *and* is not an independent clause (it shares its subject with the clause before the conjunction) so the comma is omitted in this case.

(6) *Maybe* is a lowbrow qualifier; prefer *might* or *perhaps*.

> Keep the perspective consistent, and try to avoid the use of *one* as a pronoun.

Paragraph 3

> (1) In surveying their customers and finding that most prefer games with lifelike graphics, the computer game company has correctly identified a cause for an increase in the popularity of particular game types. (2) From the evidence presented, it seems reasonable that certain customers buy the more lifelike games in preference to games with inferior graphics. (3) However, the conclusion that game sales will rise as a result of this action neglects to take into account the evidence (4) that the more lifelike games require the latest computer hardware. (5) The argument presents no evidence that the target audience is undergoing a transition to this more advanced, and more expensive, type of computer platform. (6) On the contrary, common sense seems to suggest that, since the target audience tends to be young, that their earning power would not allow them to acquire the equipment necessary to accommodate the games in question, and thus the change in emphasis would not necessarily result in increased sales of those games. (7) If the company were to invest in development of these games, it might waste money in the end.

(1) The company has been *surveying* and *finding*. Changing the verb form to *found* in the original version violates parallelism and creates confusion.

> It's not clear in the original version who *they* refers to: it could be the customers or the company. Changing the pronoun clarifies that it is the customers who prefer lifelike games.

(2) *Okay* is a lowbrow modifier; *reasonable* is more appropriate.

> The comma after the introductory clause *From the evidence presented* is technically optional, but probably helps prevent possible confusion in this case.
>
> *Might maybe* is too tentative.
>
> *Worse* is too lowbrow to be consistent with the tone of the rest of the paragraph; prefer *inferior*.

(3) *End result* is redundant.

(4) This sentence is a fragment. One easy way to fix the problem is to join this sentence to the previous one. Since it is a restrictive clause (beginning with *that*) it doesn't need a comma or conjunction—just remove the period and the initial capital letter.

> *New* and *latest* together are redundant.

(5) Omit the wordy filler phrase *to show the fact that*

> *And more expensive* is a parenthetic phrase, so it should be set off by commas.

(6) Add a comma after the introductory phrase *On the contrary*.

> Omit the qualifier *perhaps* in this case because, in combination with the verb *suggests*, it comes across as overly tentative.
>
> *Accommodate* is misspelled in the original.
>
> The referent of the pronoun *it* is unclear in the original version. Specify what *it* is with a specific phrase such as *the change in emphasis* as shown.

(7) The subjunctive conditional in this sentence takes the *were* form of the verb.

> *Development* is misspelled in the original.

Practice 2

1. Competition and cooperation are not mutually exclusive: think of team sports or corporate business ventures.

2. Educational systems have many goals; instilling values and providing job training are both important. Other goals include recreation, fitness training, and public service.

3. Government spending is more complicated than a choice between the arts and social services: a way can be found to afford both. Or, what about arts institutions such as museums, artists' colonies and grant programs that provide social services (employment, daycare, support) and advance the arts at the same time?

4. It might show good work ethics to quit a job that you're not enthusiastic about, but it is a false dilemma. Other alternatives include staying at your job but not working hard, or working hard and then quitting anyway.

5. Alternatives to this false dilemma include the possibility that some supporters of the bill understood it and thought that it would be good for America anyway, or that they didn't understand it but weren't thinking about the good of America at all—among others.

6. Or maybe the chess champion will win and feel great anyway, or he'll lose and be impressed, pleased or relieved.

Practice 3

1. Any of the many cases where the rights of individuals come into conflict with each other is a good exception to this generalization. For example, a restaurant owner's right to try and make a profit doesn't supersede his/her customer's right to healthy food: that's why we have health department regulations.

2. There are many factors that contribute to commercial success: efficiency and quality are obviously important, for instance. Originality may be useful, but imitation can certainly be profitable.

3. There are many "vital" qualities for a leader. For example the ability to get other people to follow must be just as important as the ability to make decisions.

4. This generalization suggests that the only way to understand the difficulties that face public school teachers is to be one. That's not necessarily true: the difficulties can be understood by observation or study, or a person could be a teacher and still not think that it was difficult.

5. The generalization here lies in connecting "practical research" (whatever that is) with enjoyable life. A lot of technologies that make life more enjoyable—for example the Graphite materials used in different kinds of sporting equipment—comes from general or abstract research.

6. This statement contains a false dilemma (style and substance are not mutually exclusive) but it also contains an overstated generalization in the assertion that "everyone thinks" style is more important. Any example of a person or group that values substance over style is a good example for attacking this generalization.

Practice 4

Conclusion: Brockhoff should become the athletic director of the district.

Premises:

- Mr. Brockhoff began as the head coach five years ago.
- In the last five years, the team has won three championships.
- In the last five years, the quality of athletic facilities has improved.
- As with all inductive arguments, the conclusion here is invalid. The premises show that Mr. Brockhoff's tenure coincides with an improvement in the athletics program of the school, so you can infer a relationship. But there's not necessarily a relationship: it might just be a coincidence, or there may be a confusion between causes and effects here. For example, an improvement in the athletic equipment may have caused the championships without any contribution from the coach. Furthermore, there's no evidence to suggest that Mr. Brockhoff's ability as a football coach necessarily makes him a good general director. It's impossible to know whether the conclusion is true or not, but it isn't necessarily false either.

Practice 5

In this stimulus, the conclusion implicitly bears on *all people of all ages*. Yet the study group is extremely limited. Any of the distinguishing characteristics of the sample group (that the subjects were women, that they were Belgian, that they were over eighty years old, that they lived in assisted care, and that they exercised) could have introduced factors that do not apply to the population as a whole.

Practice 6

In this instance, the differences in size and location between the two restaurants invalidate any inference you could make about the impact of table service on their relative popularity.

Practice 7

In this example, the drop in physical fitness is attributed to the economic recession on the grounds that expenditures on fitness-related products and services have dropped recently. Common sense should tell us that, at the national level, physical fitness is not determined by the amount spent on fitness products and services: in the best of times, the proportion of Saludians who even try to stay fit through such devices would probably not be enough to impact 25% of the population, and of those who tried, even fewer would have seen significant results. It is much more likely that the correlation is coincidental than causal.

Chapter Five: **GRE Essay Prompts**

PRESENT YOUR PERSPECTIVE ON AN ISSUE PROMPTS

This chapter contains 25 sample prompts for the Issue task and 25 sample prompts for the Argument task. For your convenience, blank space is provided for you to plan your essays. Please use extra paper if necessary, or practice typing your essay on a computer. Prompts that are marked by an asterisk (✱) are those for which sample essays are found in the following chapter.

Present your perspective on the issue below, using relevant reasons and/or examples to support your views.

> "Competitive athletics have a negative effect on student athletes because sports engender an environment where students learn to win by any means necessary."✱

_____

_____

_____

_____

_____

_____

_____

_____

_____

_____

Present your perspective on the issue below, using relevant reasons and/or examples to support your views.

"Society does not place enough emphasis on the traditional arts, such as painting, sculpting, and drawing."

_____

_____

_____

_____

_____

_____

_____

Present your perspective on the issue below, using relevant reasons and/or examples to support your views.

"Children do not receive the same high level of education that they could expect 50 years ago."

_____

_____

_____

_____

_____

_____

_____

_____

Present your perspective on the issue below, using relevant reasons and/or examples to support your views.

"The knowledge that is developed through direct experience far outstrips anything that can be gleaned from a book."

_____

_____

_____

_____

_____

_____

_____

_____

Present your perspective on the issue below, using relevant reasons and/or examples to support your views.

"Without spending significant time studying him or herself, a person cannot ever truly understand anyone else."

_____

_____

_____

_____

_____

_____

_____

_____

_____

Present your perspective on the issue below, using relevant reasons and/or examples to support your views.

"The mission of any government is to improve the everyday lives of its people."

_____

_____

_____

_____

_____

_____

_____

Present your perspective on the issue below, using relevant reasons and/or examples to support your views.

"Scholars spend too much time on philosophical, ethereal debates. The public would be better served if these scholars spent more of their time on more practical matters."

_____

_____

_____

_____

_____

_____

_____

_____

Present your perspective on the issue below, using relevant reasons and/or examples to support your views.

> "The perceived greatness of any political leader has more to do with the challenges faced by that leader than with any of his or her inherent skills and abilities."*

_____

_____

_____

_____

_____

_____

_____

_____

Present your perspective on the issue below, using relevant reasons and/or examples to support your views.

> "Parents should encourage their children to pursue careers that are reasonably achievable, rather than those that have stronger barriers to entry."

_____

_____

_____

_____

_____

_____

_____

_____

Present your perspective on the issue below, using relevant reasons and/or examples to support your views.

"People should ignore the opinions of professional critics, who are all too often out of touch with the common citizen. Everyone would be better off if they chose movies, restaurants, or bottles of wine based on the recommendations of friends and family members."

_____

_____

_____

_____

_____

_____

_____

Present your perspective on the issue below, using relevant reasons and/or examples to support your views.

"College students should be required to take a course in public speaking, even if taking such a course lessens the amount of time a student would spend on more academic subjects."*

_____

_____

_____

_____

_____

_____

_____

Present your perspective on the issue below, using relevant reasons and/or examples to support your views.

"It is preferable to imagine the future rather than to consider the past."

_____

_____

_____

_____

_____

_____

_____

_____

_____

Present your perspective on the issue below, using relevant reasons and/or examples to support your views.

"Society would be better served by instilling a healthy dose of skepticism into young people, rather than training them simply to follow orders."

_____

_____

_____

_____

_____

_____

_____

_____

_____

Present your perspective on the issue below, using relevant reasons and/or examples to support your views.

"A person should never criticize the work of someone else unless he or she has a better way of accomplishing the task."

_____

_____

_____

_____

_____

_____

Present your perspective on the issue below, using relevant reasons and/or examples to support your views.

"Progress should be the aim of any great society. People too often cling unnecessarily to obsolete ways of thinking and acting because of both a high comfort level and a fear of the unknown."*

_____

_____

_____

_____

_____

_____

_____

_____

Present your perspective on the issue below, using relevant reasons and/or examples to support your views.

"History books should focus more on the daily lives of the common people than on the actions of their leaders."

_____

_____

_____

_____

_____

_____

_____

_____

Present your perspective on the issue below, using relevant reasons and/or examples to support your views.

"The primary concern of the government should be the safety of its citizens."

_____

_____

_____

_____

_____

_____

_____

_____

Present your perspective on the issue below, using relevant reasons and/or examples to support your views.

"To achieve success, a person should set goals at an early age and continually measure himself against those goals."*

_____

_____

_____

_____

_____

_____

_____

Present your perspective on the issue below, using relevant reasons and/or examples to support your views.

"You can learn more about a person by observing them away from work than you can by observing them in their place of business."

_____

_____

_____

_____

_____

_____

_____

_____

Present your perspective on the issue below, using relevant reasons and/or examples to support your views.

"Technology does as much to impair quality of life as it does to improve it."

_____

_____

_____

_____

_____

_____

_____

_____

Present your perspective on the issue below, using relevant reasons and/or examples to support your views.

"The availability of 24-hour news coverage of major global events has caused the average person today to be better informed about the world around him or her than the average person was 30 years ago."

_____

_____

_____

_____

_____

_____

_____

_____

Present your perspective on the issue below, using relevant reasons and/or examples to support your views.

"People have become too focused on technological progress. Because of this, other aspects of society—such as the arts—have suffered."

_____

_____

_____

_____

_____

_____

_____

Present your perspective on the issue below, using relevant reasons and/or examples to support your views.

"In order to become successful, one must make mistakes and learn from one's failures."

_____

_____

_____

_____

_____

_____

_____

_____

KAPLAN
Test Prep and Admissions

Present your perspective on the issue below, using relevant reasons and/or examples to support your views.

> "A person should not take a job if he or she knows that the work will not be personally fulfilling."

_____

_____

_____

_____

_____

_____

_____

_____

Present your perspective on the issue below, using relevant reasons and/or examples to support your views.

> "People take too much pleasure from personal achievement, and not enough from the successes of society."

_____

_____

_____

_____

_____

_____

_____

_____

ANALYZE AN ARGUMENT PROMPTS

Discuss how well reasoned you find the following argument.

Recent studies have shown that the senior citizen population of Desert City is growing faster that that of any other major city in the country. It has also been shown by medical researchers that 70% of seniors suffer from at least mild arthritis pain and that living in a warm, dry environment, like that of Desert City, can help to alleviate the pain of arthritis. In fact, more seniors suffer from arthritis than from any other single affliction. Therefore, seniors must be moving to Desert City in large numbers in order to enjoy relief from arthritis pain.*

Discuss how well reasoned you find the following argument.

For years, archaeologists have noted the existence of wheels on small toys used by children in Central Apria over two thousand years ago. This fact is not striking by itself, since many civilizations throughout the world had developed the wheel by 1 A.D. What is perplexing is that wheels appear in the archaeological record as part of children's toys and do not appear as part of carts or other tools of agriculture or commerce. Dr. Chevanik of Central Aprian University has concluded that the wheel was not used for agricultural or commercial purposes because Central Apria is almost devoid of trees today, indicating that there may not have been enough timber to create large wheels two thousand years ago.

Discuss how well reasoned you find the following argument.

The following appeared in a memo to the superintendent of schools in Bridgetown:

"Recent studies on the health effects of leafy greens, such as broccoli, suggest an interesting solution to our school attendance problems. A nationwide survey on eating leafy greens found that adults who eat at least one serving per day of leafy greens report fewer stomach aches and digestion problems than a control group. Since the most noted reason for an absence from our elementary schools is an upset stomach, serving leafy greens for lunch in our cafeterias every day will improve attendance."

Discuss how well reasoned you find the following argument.

The following appeared in a letter to the editor of the Sun City Post newspaper:

"The tourism tax revenues of Sun City will continue to fall unless the city government takes action to bring our health resort industry up to the standard of other tourist destinations in our region. Our main competitor for tourists, Warm Springs City, completed two state-of-the-art spa complexes last year, and their level of tourism increased by over 20%; Sun City's tourist level actually declined for the fifth year in a row. If the city government does not sponsor the construction of a spa in Sun City, there is no chance that these trends will reverse."*

Discuss how well reasoned you find the following argument.

The following appeared in an editorial in the Hermosa Beach Gazette, a local newspaper:

"In a fitness journal report, Hermosa Beach recently ranked third in a listing of the most physically fit cities in our state. People moving to our state can now know with confidence that our city will provide them the ability to pursue an active outdoor lifestyle. Hermosa Beach is a place where swimming, jogging, and team sports thrive. We will certainly see a surge in new residents because of this fitness journal article."

Discuss how well reasoned you find the following argument.

Harp seals live primarily on the Atlantic coast of Canada. Female seals give birth to their pups during the spring on sheet ice that forms during the winter. If the sheet ice is too thick from a cold winter, many pups will die because they cannot reach the sea. If the ice is too thin, it will also cause many pups to die because they are forced into the sea before they are ready to fend for themselves. A recent census by the Canadian government has found a dramatic increase in the number of harp seals on the Atlantic coast. Clearly, this shows that global warming is not affecting harp seal populations by reducing the thickness of sheet ice.

Discuss how well reasoned you find the following argument.

The following appeared in a memo from the president of Whack-A-Weed International, the maker of lawn care machinery:

"Whack-A-Weed International has decided to discontinue sales of our original product, the Weed Destroyer, in an effort to improve the profits of our company. By halting production of the Weed Destroyer, we will be able to shut our Machine City production plant, which has been our least efficient plant over the last 3 years. Moreover, 40% of our advertising budget has been devoted to the Weed Destroyer, so now Whack-A-Weed can devote more money to promote our other product lines."

Discuss how well reasoned you find the following argument.

The following appeared in a memo from the Beach City office of the National Environment Protection Agency to the Director of the Agency:

"The amount of pollution in Beach City Harbor is staggering. This year alone 500 used car tires, 40,000 aluminum cans, 60,000 cigarette butts, and 75,000 glass bottles have been picked up from the city's beaches by our sanitation patrols. Additionally, the number of tourists visiting Beach City has grown by over 10% for each of the last 7 years, giving us reason to believe that levels of pollution will only grow in the future. If we cannot find a way to discourage the growth in tourism here, there is no chance of survival for the marine life in our harbor."*

Discuss how well reasoned you find the following argument.

The following appeared in an editorial in the Windy Valley Post, a local newspaper:

"As the population of Windy Valley has increased, the graduation rate from our city's high schools has fallen precipitously. In nearby Sunny Valley, the city has opened two new high schools to accommodate a similar increase in population and has seen no decline in graduation rate. Clearly, Windy Valley needs to invest more in new schools to keep class sizes down and graduation rates up."

_____

_____

_____

_____

_____

_____

_____

_____

_____

_____

_____

_____

_____

_____

_____

_____

_____

_____

_____

Discuss how well reasoned you find the following argument.

The following is a recommendation from the business manager of Quality Hardware Store:

"Quality Hardware should open a coffee shop inside the store to attract more customers and increase sales. Quality Hardware is known throughout the region as a place to find the widest possible variety of home improvement supplies, but lacks the ability to offer refreshment to its patrons. A coffee shop would also attract more female customers, something the store has been lacking. A recent survey found that over 80% of females drink coffee on a regular basis. I suggest that we create room for the coffee shop by reducing the size of our lumberyard. This is not likely to hurt sales since fewer homes are being built in our region these days."

Discuss how well reasoned you find the following argument.

The following is a recommendation from the manager of Family Friendly Restaurant:

"Family Friendly Restaurant needs to improve its facility to remain competitive in our city's restaurant market. Mega-Family Restaurant, recently opened in a suburb of our city, offers a video arcade, fine wood furniture, and 7 big-screen televisions. Due to a recession in our town, people report having less discretionary income for eating out. Therefore, if we are to hold our share of a shrinking restaurant market, we need to offer at least all the features of Mega-Family Restaurant."*

Discuss how well reasoned you find the following argument.

The following appeared in a letter to the editor of a newsletter on health issues:

"For years, doctors have been recommending that parents limit the number of sweets and candies they feed to their children, in order to reduce hyperactivity. However, the number of recorded cases of hyperactivity has actually increased over the last 10 years. Furthermore, a recent medical survey of 50 children with hyperactivity problems found that reducing sugar intake by 50% had little effect on hyperactivity. Therefore, doctors should stop giving advice on this matter, since reducing sweets has little effect on hyperactivity."

Discuss how well reasoned you find the following argument.

The following appeared in a letter to the editor of the Sam's Town Post, a local newspaper:

"The level of juvenile crime in our city has grown by 15% per year over the last decade. The citizens of Sam's Town are outraged and have asked that the police step up enforcement of curfews for juveniles, since most of these crimes occur after the curfew hour. This plan will not work, however, because our city's youth commit crimes when they do not have other options to fill their time. Our city would benefit more from creating late-night programs, such as basketball camps, that will occupy our youth and keep them out of trouble."

_____

_____

_____

_____

_____

_____

_____

_____

_____

_____

_____

_____

_____

_____

_____

_____

_____

_____

_____

Discuss how well reasoned you find the following argument.

The following appeared in an advertisement for Mighty Toothpaste:

"Using Mighty Toothpaste is a great way to improve tooth and gum health. In a trial, 500 dentists recommended that their patients use Mighty Toothpaste. These dentists reported that their patients had 25% fewer cavities than before the switch to Mighty Toothpaste. Moreover, 80% of the patients reported that their mouths felt cleaner when using Mighty Toothpaste than when using their normal toothpaste."

Discuss how well reasoned you find the following argument.

The following appeared in a newsletter on nutrition and health:

"Brighton Mineral Water was first bottled by the town of Brighton because of its fresh, clean taste. However, a study of people who suffer from kidney stones shows that those who drink 8 glasses a day of Brighton water had a much lower rate of kidney stone recurrence than those who did not drink Brighton water. Brighton Mineral Water should change its advertising campaign to emphasize the benefits to sufferers of kidney stones. Not only will this drive additional sales of Brighton water, but also it will cause fewer people to develop kidney stones."

Discuss how well reasoned you find the following argument.

The following appeared as part of a recommendation to the administration of Sandy Beach University:

"Applications and admissions to Sandy Beach University have fallen by 5% in each of the last 5 years. In order to learn more about the reasons for this decline, our admissions office administered a survey to nearby high school seniors about their impressions of Sandy Beach University. The results showed that prospective students felt that Sandy Beach's dorms and cafeteria were below average. If Sandy Beach is to reverse its negative trend of enrollment, it must invest heavily in a new cafeteria and improved dorm rooms."

Discuss how well reasoned you find the following argument.

The towns of West Charleston and East Charleston lie on either side of the flood-prone Charleston River. To avoid future flood damage, both cities passed an ordinance in 1978 banning the construction of new buildings along the waterfront or other low-lying areas. Many buildings were already built in the low-lying areas, but were largely abandoned in favor of new construction in East Charleston. In 1999, a large flood afflicted the area, and more inhabited buildings were damaged in West Charleston than in East Charleston. Clearly, the people of West Charleston did not abandon their homes along the waterfront at as great a rate as the people of East Charleston did.

_____

_____

_____

_____

_____

_____

_____

_____

_____

_____

_____

_____

_____

_____

_____

_____

_____

Discuss how well reasoned you find the following argument.

The following appeared in a memo to the Mayor of Norchester from the School Board:

"The city of Norchester has a student-to-teacher ratio of 25:1 in its elementary schools, a ratio in line with the national average. Recent research by educational leaders, however, indicates that the highest acceptable ratio for optimal child learning is 22:1. While the city's ratio is slightly higher than the guideline, our town's population has been shrinking. Therefore, Norchester can respond to its current budget deficit by putting in place a teacher hiring freeze for the next 3 school years and still have a student-to-teacher ratio that is acceptable for child development."*

_____

_____

_____

_____

_____

_____

_____

_____

_____

_____

_____

_____

_____

_____

_____

_____

_____

_____

_____

_____

Discuss how well reasoned you find the following argument.

Tuberculosis is an infectious disease that usually attacks the lungs of an infected person and kills an estimated 2 million people per year. Ten years ago, the World Health League started a program to detect and eradicate the disease worldwide. These efforts, however, appear to be failing. Since the League started working in third-world countries, the number of deaths from tuberculosis in those countries has actually increased 15% per year. The World Health League clearly needs to develop a whole new plan to stop the spread of this deadly disease.

_____

_____

_____

_____

_____

_____

_____

_____

_____

_____

_____

_____

_____

_____

_____

_____

_____

Discuss how well reasoned you find the following argument.

The following appeared in the editorial section of a local paper:

"Many people believe that public radio is a waste of taxpayer money because it is only listened to by a small subsection of the community. This view is clearly false. A recent questionnaire administered to guests of our city's finest hotels found that 62% of the nearly 500 respondents listen to public radio at least two hours a week."

Discuss how well reasoned you find the following argument.

The children living in the city of Melody Beach have fitness levels that exceed those of all other cities in the state. Sports medicine experts have concluded that this is because of the large number of parks in the city. In fact, Melody Beach has 5 full acres devoted to park space within the confines of the city. Melody Beach parents are known to take their children to the park as many as 10 times per week.

_____

_____

_____

_____

_____

_____

_____

_____

_____

_____

_____

_____

_____

_____

_____

_____

_____

_____

_____

Discuss how well reasoned you find the following argument.

The following appeared in a memo to the President of KRXW Radio:

"Our most recent market data shows that 65% of male listeners nationwide enjoy listening to 'Shock Jock' radio shows, where a DJ expresses outlandish views and pokes fun at a variety of people. Our main competitor KWXR radio recently switched their morning programming to a 'Shock Jock' show and their ratings among men doubled. We should change our current morning show to a 'Shock Jock' show in order to improve our profits."

Discuss how well reasoned you find the following argument.

The following appeared in a memo from FoodMart's regional manager:

"Our newest store in Hodge City, located near the growing Warm Springs housing development, advertises sales mostly on television instead of in the newspaper. This new store has seen customer and sales growth of over 10% per month for the last year since it opened. The unprecedented success of this store indicates that we should switch all our advertising dollars to television commercials in order to improve our profits."

_____

_____

_____

_____

_____

_____

_____

_____

_____

_____

_____

_____

_____

_____

_____

_____

_____

_____

_____

_____

Discuss how well reasoned you find the following argument.

The following appeared in a memo from the Vice President of Sales for Atta-Boy Dog Products:

"Our regional sales manager for the Sun Valley area conducted a survey of dog owners in his region, and he found that 78% of respondents prefer to bathe their dogs outside. The other 22% prefer to wash their dogs indoors in a bathtub. We need to develop a soap that people can use to wash their dogs outside, in order to capture this untapped market."

Discuss how well reasoned you find the following argument.

The following appeared in a memo to the new Secretary of the Department of Transportation:

"For many years, the Department of Transportation has collected and published data on the number of traffic accidents and the percentage of people who wear seatbelts or drive cars with airbags. The percentage of people using safety equipment such as seatbelts or airbags has increased from 30% to 85% in the last twenty years. However, the number of traffic accidents has doubled in the same time period. Clearly, people feel more comfortable when they use safety equipment and therefore pay less attention to the road. In order to reverse this trend, the Department of Transportation should begin a new advertising campaign advising drivers to pay more attention when they drive."

_____

_____

_____

_____

_____

_____

_____

_____

_____

_____

_____

_____

_____

_____

Chapter Six: **GRE Sample Essays**

Here are sample top scoring essays to five of the sample Issue prompts and five of the sample Argument prompts found in the previous chapter. Remember that an essay does not have to be perfect to receive a top score. Review these essays and note which qualities earned them a score of 6.

PRESENT YOUR PERSPECTIVE ON AN ISSUE ESSAYS

Present your perspective on the issue below, using relevant reasons and/or examples to support your views.

> "Competitive athletics have a negative effect on student athletes, because sports engender an environment where students learn to win by any means necessary."

The author of the prompt believes that students are worse off if they participate in competitive athletics because they learn to be cutthroat and to adopt a "win at all costs" mentality. However, there are also many benefits of competitive athletics that are not addressed: students athletes learn important physical and social skills; students athletes benefit from the mental refreshment that physical activity allows; students participating in team sports learn cooperative skills; and student athletes also enjoy significant health benefits. While it may be true that competitive athletics at times put too much emphasis on winning, the many benefits of competitive athletics far outweigh any negative effects such programs may produce.

Interscholastic and intramural sports offer students training in both physical and social skills that can be used throughout life. Programs such as AYSO soccer or Little League baseball teach grammar school aged children to enjoy outdoor, physical activities. At the same time, these programs allow these young students to interact and socialize several hours a week. Many people retain these tendencies their entire lives. Adults continue to enjoy the physical and social benefits of competitive athletics far beyond their student days. For example, the local newspaper devotes an entire page of the sports section to the many adult volleyball, softball, and basketball leagues in town; these leagues continue to entertain thousands.

Student athletes may also benefit from a clearer, more focused mind after participating in competitive athletics. On my college water polo team, the team GPA was much higher in season than out of season. When I mentioned this to a psychology professor, he noted that many studies show that the human mind can perform better, and thus learn better, after physical activity. If these studies are true, then competitive athletics actually produce better students.

While not every competitive sport is a team sport, the majority is. At my college, a full three quarters of the college-sanctioned sports are team sports such as football or lacrosse, rather than individual sports such as tennis or track and field. Any participant in a competitive team sport learns important lessons in teamwork and sacrifice for a common goal. These lessons are often applicable to future endeavors in life. For example, someone who learns to play selflessly on the basketball court to win more games will be a better team player when they move on to the professional ranks of business, law, medicine or other job. Even in the traditionally individual sports, many of these lessons can be learned. A close friend gave up the individual glory he might have attained as a singles tennis player because his college tennis team needed a strong doubles player. He did what was needed for his overall team to win and has carried those same skills into his career in strategic planning for a Fortune 500 company.

The health benefits of physical activity are a strong endorsement of competitive athletics. Numerous studies have shown that aerobic activity found in most team sports helps to improve circulation, reduce cholesterol and blood pressure, and build a metabolism that burns fat more quickly. Many people would not enjoy these health benefits if they did not participate in competitive athletics. Personally, I stopped most physical activity for a few years after I graduated from college and left my water polo team. Only by joining an adult water polo league have I been able to get back into shape.

Many would argue that the negative effect of a 'win at all costs' attitude would outweigh the benefits listed above. However, these people ignore the fact that many competitive athletics do not engender such an environment. When I was a high-school swimmer, I learned from my coaches to try to beat my best time, not the person in the next lane. Because of this, I never felt the need to cheat or do anything immoral to win. Other sports, such as Ultimate Frisbee, put more of an emphasis on spirit and moral than on winning at all costs. All disputes are settled on the field and awards are given to teams with the best spirit. All this coexists with the competitive aspects of the game.

It is not true that competitive athletics have a negative impact on student athletes because of a win at all costs environment. In fact, students gain important benefits from competitive athletics, such as better health; physical, social and team skills; and more focused minds. Also, many competitive student athletes are never subjected to a win at all costs environment—many of the best coaches and sports put more emphasis on personal betterment than on cheating to win.

Present your perspective on the issue below, using relevant reasons and/or examples to support your views.

"The perceived greatness of any political leader has more to do with the challenges faced by that leader than with any of his or her inherent skills and abilities."

Perceptions of greatness in national and political leaders are largely determined by the seriousness of the problems that they face during their terms in office. Most national histories principally highlight individuals in the context of significant events in which the leaders played important roles. Most political leaders need to have large stores of inherent skill and ability just in order to become a political leader. However, history remembers those who lived in great times more fondly than those who did not. Examples of this are numerous and include the histories of Abraham Lincoln, Woodrow Wilson, and Winston Churchill—all men who are perceived as great leaders largely because of the times in which they lived.

Abraham Lincoln is often considered the greatest of all the American Presidents. He graces two units of the currency and has one of the largest monuments built in his honor in Washington D.C. However, Lincoln is considered great largely because he faced a great challenge—the civil war between the North and the South in the 1860s. Lincoln led the United States to victory over the rebels and reunited the country and is therefore considered great. This is not to say that Lincoln was not skilled. Many know that he was born in a log cabin and progressed to law school and eventually to the presidency. He was also a skilled orator. However another man, James Buchanon, also was born in a log cabin, went to law school, gave good speeches and ascended to the presidency. However there are no monuments to Buchanon in the capital or pictures of his face on the five-dollar bill.

Woodrow Wilson was another talented man who ascended to the presidency of the United States. However his talents are not what make his perceived greatness. In this age, few remember if Wilson was particularly smart, a very good speechmaker, or a good arbitrator. Most remember that he led the United States to victory in the first World War and therefore perceive him as great. At the time, however, Wilson was rather unpopular. In fact, he had so little sway with Congress that he was unable to get the United States to join the League of Nations—a fact that many claim helped lead to the second World War.

Winston Churchill was another man that history views favorably because of the incredible challenges that he faced. However, Churchill was not very popular before the war. When Franklin Roosevelt first met Churchill before either was the leader of his respective country, Roosevelt wrote in his diary that Churchill was full of himself and far too talkative. Early in his term as Prime Minister, Churchill even faced a no-confidence vote in Parliament. However, the events of World War II gave him the perception of greatness.

Many might argue that these men and other men and women were already great before history gave them great challenges. While it is impossible to definitely disprove this assertion and it may be true that they had great skill and ability, otherwise they would not have been political leaders, most examples point to the fact that the times make the man or woman. If the presidencies of Buchanon and Lincoln were switched, we would very likely have the Buchanon memorial instead.

In summary, it is true that the perceived greatness of a political leader is more due to great challenges than great inherent ability. The historical examples of Lincoln, Wilson, and Churchill bear this out. All were talented, but so too are all political leaders. Only the leaders that live in eventful times are remembered as great.

Present your perspective on the issue below, using relevant reasons and/or examples to support your views.

"College students should be required to take a course in public speaking, even if taking such a course lessens the amount of time a student would spend on more academic subjects."

While the ability to speak comfortably before a group of people can be a valuable skill, colleges should not require students to take a separate course in public speaking, especially if taking such a class comes at the exclusion of more academic subjects. Since public speaking is a valuable skill for some students, public speaking classes should be offered as electives. However, colleges should not make the classes a requirement because students should have the ability to choose their course loads for themselves, students pursuing careers that do not involve public speaking should not be forced to waste their time on irrelevant material, and even students who are interested in public speaking may be able to gain better experience outside of the classroom.

Many students (or their parents) are spending large amounts of money or accumulating large debts to attend college. If a student decides that she does not want to take a public speaking class, then she should not be forced to spend her money on it. Ultimately the college should be tailoring curricula towards the wants of students, since the students are the paying customers.

Perhaps more importantly, students should not be forced to take classes that fall outside of the scope of their future employment. Most students are in school to train for a profession (even if they desire to be a professional academic). Therefore, a student's course load should focus as much as possible on the skills and knowledge necessary for that profession. A pre-law student hoping to become a trial lawyer may need to take public speaking. However, a future statistician or surgeon may never need to speak in front of large groups. Why should these students be forced to waste their time and effort on a class that does not prepare them for their future life?

It should also be considered that even students who are interested in public speaking or are pursuing careers where public speaking is a necessary skill may be able to get better experience outside of the classroom. Many students while in high school became involved in the school debate team so that they can hone their public speaking skills. Others become involved in speaking at church to get over their fears of public speaking. Still others may have a natural talent for public speaking that requires no further instruction. Each of these groups of people might also feel that they were wasting their time if they were required to take a public speaking class.

Some critics of this point of view may contend that public speaking is part of a well-rounded education and that students should be forced to be well-rounded. This critique holds little water, however, because it is certainly not clear what 'well-rounded' means. Because of this, it is much better to offer a variety of electives, including public speaking, so that students might pursue their secondary and tertiary passions while in school. For example, the future statistician mentioned above may have a passion for performing in plays and would love to take acting and public speaking classes. Schools should offer these choices instead of dictating them.

In summary, it is important that schools not require students to take a public speaking class. While it is important to offer such a class for those that are interested, many students will find a required class to be a waste of their time, their money, or both. Still other students will find that they will be able to attain public speaking skills more effectively outside of the classroom.

Present your perspective on the issue below, using relevant reasons and/or examples to support your views.

"Progress should be the aim of any great society. People too often cling unnecessarily to obsolete ways of thinking and acting because of both a high comfort level and a fear of the unknown."

Keeping up with global progress is, doubtless, a desirable attribute of any society. However, to purport that the reasons certain societies may not progress at the same rate as "great" societies are its reluctance to break from its comfort zone and a fear of the unknown is to present an overly simplistic view. Such a view does not take into consideration the set of economic, political, and cultural constraints that affect every society's ability to progress on a global scale. Before exploring these constraints, it would be useful to examine the use of the word "great" in the above context. The concept of what makes a society great is highly subjective; some may equate greatness with military might or economic dominance, while others would emphasize cultural achievement or progress in care for less privileged citizens. Whatever one's definition of greatness, however, it is ludicrous to suggest that any society actively rejects the desire to be great. Many societies face the seemingly insurmountable struggle to maintain societal structure in the face of economic need and/or political upheaval; the desire for greatness can only come when a society's basic structure is intact.

Societies facing severe economic challenges are virtually unable to progress in areas like medicine, militia, and agriculture even if they want to do so. Countries like Bolivia use a majority of their limited resources to maintain an agricultural status quo. Bolivian farmers are not afraid of the unknown or passively content with their current situation, but are using all of their resources to maintain a functional economic climate and structure. Given this situation, the luxury of advancements in medicine, economics and military power is simply not possible.

Also, societies embroiled in political upheaval, such as Bangladesh, are unable to send its young and talented members to university where they can spearhead progress; the most viable sector of the population are required to serve in the military and/or to care for their families through difficult economic and political times. Maintaining a societal structure amid chaotic conditions engenders a lack of globally accepted progress, but as we have seen throughout time, episodes of great drama in any given society can yield important works of art, one such example being Albert Camus' *The Stranger*, written during the French Resistance.

Another point to consider is that in some cases, preservation of an entire society's cultural history, including its artistic contributions, is preserved only through its living members' rich oral tradition and active rejecting of progress in the worlds of technology, medicine, and science. This is evident when considering such so-called "primitive" societies as the African Masai or certain Native American tribes. The introduction of technology into the world of the Masai would inarguably lead to the demise of the entire society.

In conclusion, to devalue a society that isn't among the most progressive in the world is to discount the contributions a so-called "unprogressive" society can provide, such as artistic and cultural phenomena unique to a given society. Progress is a valuable tool for the advancement of a society, but blindly reaching for greatness can lead to a society's downfall just as much as ignoring it altogether can. The balance between accepting a society's constraints and highlighting its strengths is what will ultimately lead to a society's greatness.

Present your perspective on the issue below, using relevant reasons and/or examples to support your views.

"To achieve success, a person should set goals at an early age and continually measure him or herself against those goals."

It is not true that a person needs to set goals at an early age and constantly measure him or herself against those goals in order to achieve success. While many people find it helpful to set goals and measure performance against them, this is not necessary for success. Many people find success by chance or through the actions of others, without ever setting goals. Others find that the goals of their youth do not match up with what they would consider success as adults. Still others find success with merely a periodic look at their goals and progress.

Many people capture the traditional measures of success, such as health, wealth, and happiness, by chance. A close friend won a large lottery while in Las Vegas and is now quite content to spend his time playing golf around the world. He is certainly healthy, wealthy and happy, but he made no such plans as a youth. Others may find that they are able to achieve success because a successful parent or other loved one has paved the way for them. For example, the son-in-law of a wealthy landowner may find a successful career in real estate development because of a chance marriage, not because of meticulous goal setting and performance measurement.

Other people may find that the goals they planned as a youth are no longer relevant when they reach adulthood. Personally, I wanted to be a private detective or a garbage collector when I was in grammar school. Those are careers that I now know would not make me happy or fulfilled. As perceptions of success change across a lifetime, so to do goals need to change. If I had stuck to my original goals and constantly measured myself against them, I would not be a success in my own eyes today.

Many people do not feel the need to review or measure their progress against goals constantly in order to achieve success. A person my have the goal to retire at age 50. That person may be very successful if she sets out her goals, such as a budget, savings plan and investment plan, and then only periodically monitors her progress. In fact, many investment professionals advocate this approach so that people are not tempted to tinker too much with their plans. Another example may be in the dieter that weighs himself everyday. If someone sets a goal to be more healthy and lose 15 pounds, but becomes discouraged when he does not lose weight the first four days, that person may not be as successful as someone else who measures his progress periodically.

Some would point to the world of business to show that successful companies set goals early and measure often to achieve financial success. While this may be true, it is not necessarily applicable to personal success. There are undoubtedly a few people out there who knew what they wanted to be when they grew up, set goals, and achieved great success. However, this is more the exception than the rule. Many people who are successful did nothing of the sort. In fact many of these same people would not have been successful if they had clung to their early goals. Clearly, success can be achieved without early goal setting and constant measurement.

KAPLAN
Test Prep and Admissions

ANALYZE AN ARGUMENT ESSAYS

Discuss how well reasoned you find the following argument.

Recent studies have shown that the senior citizen population of Desert City is growing faster that that of any other major city in the country. It has also been show by medical researchers that 70% of seniors suffer from at least mild arthritis pain and that living in a warm, dry environment, like that of Desert City, can help to alleviate the pain of arthritis. In fact, more seniors suffer from arthritis than from any other single affliction. Therefore, seniors must be moving to Desert City in large numbers in order to enjoy relief from arthritis pain.

With the information provided, the assumptions leading to the conclusion drawn in this argument remain unfounded. The author uses the evidence that there has been a greater increase in the senior population of Desert City than in any other major city in the U.S., that 70% of all seniors suffer from at least mild arthritis pain, and that arthritis pain can be alleviated by a warm, dry climate, such as Desert City's to conclude that seniors are moving to Desert City in such large numbers in order to alleviate their arthritis pain. However, the author makes a number of unproved assumptions that hamper a reader's ability to believe the author's conclusion. If the author were to provide more evidence to support these assumptions, the argument would be much more effective.

The primary assumption underlying the author's conclusion is that Desert City has no attraction other than climate to draw seniors. It may be that there are outstanding geriatric physicians or state-of-the-art hospitals in Desert City that attract seniors, or that there is great entertainment that is geared towards the elderly in the city. Without evidence that these other attractions do not exist, it is difficult to conclude that seniors are moving in such large numbers solely for health effects related to the climate and arthritis.

Moreover, the author assumes that the large numbers of seniors moving to Desert City must be suffering arthritis pain severe enough to warrant relocation without any other motivation. The author cites a study that shows 70% of seniors have arthritis pain, but the reader does not know from this fact if there are sufficient numbers of seniors with severe enough pain that the increase in Desert City's senior population can be explained. For example, if a senior citizen suffers from arthritis that is easily treated with over the counter pain medication, that person is unlikely to relocate for that reason.

The author further assumes that there has not been a general increase in people of all ages relocating to Desert City of which seniors are just a part. If Desert City is simply the fastest growing city in the country, it would not necessarily follow that seniors are moving there for arthritis relief. The seniors could be moving as part of a whole family moving to Desert City. A related possibility is that Desert City has the largest number of people in late middle age, and is developing its growth in seniors simply through aging.

To strengthen this argument, the author could show that Desert City has no attraction that would draw seniors in particular other than the climate. More specific evidence of the status of arthritis pain in Desert City seniors would also improve the argument. If the author could show that the influx of new inhabitants from other age groups has remained the same, the anomalous nature of the senior relocation would be heightened. Until the author provides real evidence connecting the individual choice to move to Desert City with desire to alleviate arthritis pain, the argument remains unconvincing.

Discuss how well reasoned you find the following argument.

The following appeared in a letter to the editor of the Sun City Post newspaper:

"The tourism tax revenues of Sun City will continue to fall unless the city government takes action to bring our health resort industry up to the standard of other tourist destinations in our region. Our main competitor for tourists, Warm Springs City, completed two state-of-the-art spa complexes last year, and their level of tourism increased by over 20%; Sun City's tourist level actually declined for the fifth year in a row. If the city government does not sponsor the construction of a spa in Sun City, there is no chance that these trends will reverse."

The author of this letter to the editor would have readers believe that the only way to reverse Sun City's five-year trend of falling tourism is to have the city sponsor the construction of a new spa in the city. The author bases this conclusion mostly on evidence from the recent experience of Warm Springs—a city that rivals Sun City for tourism—and the new spas constructed there. The author's argument remains unconvincing because of significant unsupported assumptions and because of poorly defined vocabulary. If the author were to provide more support for his unfounded assumptions and better define some of his terms, the argument would be more compelling.

The author makes a number of unsupported assumptions. First, he assumes that there is no other explanation for the increase in Warm Springs' tourism other than the two new spas. To better validate this assumption, the author might have provided evidence showing that Sun City does not have other reasons for declining tourism, such as increasing crime levels, rampant disrepair, or construction projects that hamper a tourists' ability to reach Sun City.

Furthermore, he assumes that the only cause of Sun City's decline in tourism for the last five years is the lack of a new spa. This assumption is particularly difficult to accept since the only evidence provided is from Warm Springs in the very last year. The author provides no evidence that might explain the previous four years. In order to have a reader accept this assumption, the author might provide evidence such as a survey showing that tourists to Sun City have been disappointed by the lack of spas.

In addition, the author assumes that constructing one spa in Sun City will have the desired effect even though Warm Springs built two spas in the year that it enjoyed its increase in tourism. In order to convince his readers that one spa will be enough, the author might provide expert testimony showing that other, similar town have seen increases in tourism after building just one spa.

Finally, our author assumes that the city itself needs to sponsor the construction of a spa. To believe this assumption, the reader needs evidence that a spa will not be built using only private sources of capital. Finally, our author states that there "is no chance" that the trend will reverse without a new spa; implicitly this assumes that there is not another project that might draw more tourists. To believe this assumption, readers need evidence that tourists only want a spa in Sun City as opposed to a new amusement park or other tourist destination.

The author's argument also suffers from two poorly defined terms, which cause some confusion. First, the author uses the term "state-of-the-art" when discussing Warm Springs' two new spas. The author does not let the reader know what state-of-the-art means. If the spas in Warm Springs are so advanced that Sun City cannot replicate them, then the author's conclusion is in jeopardy. Second, the author interchangeably uses the terms "tourism levels" and "tourism tax revenues." Because the author does not distinctly draw a connection between the two, the reader is left wondering if there is a firm correlation between increasing tourism levels and increasing revenues.

The author of the letter to the editor does not give his readers a well-supported argument. The argument contains a large number of assumptions that are not properly validated. In addition, the author does not take the time to properly define some terms that would increase the understanding of his argument. Because of this, the argument remains unconvincing.

Discuss how well reasoned you find the following argument.

The following appeared in a memo from the Beach City office of the National Environment Protection Agency to the Director of the Agency:

"The amount of pollution in Beach City Harbor is staggering. This year alone 500 used car tires, 40,000 aluminum cans, 60,000 cigarette butts, and 75,000 glass bottles have been picked up from the city's beaches by our sanitation patrols. Additionally, the number of tourists visiting Beach City has grown by over 10% for each of the last 7 years, giving us reason to believe that levels of pollution will only grow in the future. If we cannot find a way to discourage the growth in tourism here, there is no chance of survival for the marine life in our harbor."

The Beach City office of the National Environmental Protection Agency would have the Director of the Agency believe that the survival of marine life in the Beach City Harbor depends on finding a way to discourage growth in tourism in Beach City. As evidence for this point, the city office cites the large amount of car tires, aluminum cans, cigarette butts, and glass bottles collected and the 10% annual growth in tourism to the city for the last 7 years. The argument remains unconvincing because of a number of unproved assumptions made by the Beach City office and because of a few pieces of vocabulary that require further definition for increased clarity in the argument.

The first unproved assumption made by the Beach City office is there actually has been growth in the amount of pollution. The office cites the amount of trash only in this year. This is not proof of growth since there is no evidence given about the amount of trash collected in the past. It could be that this level of pollution is actually down from previous years. Also, the memo does not tell us anything about collection methods. If the sanitation patrols were more diligent in picking up trash this year over previous years, it would skew any statistical trend. In order for the National Director to believe the story of growth in pollution, she would need additional information on previous years' pollution levels and on collection methods over the years.

The author's statement that there is a connection between increasing tourism and levels of pollution is yet another unproved assumption. The Beach City office offers no evidence that tourists are the ones polluting the harbor. It could be that most pollution comes from locals, in which case there would be little effect on marine life if tourism were curtailed. To convince the National Director that there is a link, the Beach City office should have offered evidence that shows tourists are primarily responsible for the pollution.

An additional unproved assumption is that past growth in tourism is indicative of future growth. The Beach City office states that the past growth in tourism gives the office "reason to believe that levels of pollution will only grow in the future." The National Director needs evidence to show that there will continue to be growth in tourism. For example, it could be that Beach City has not increased the number of hotel rooms in the city and was completely full during last year's peak tourist season. If the hospitality industry in Beach City has continued to grow its capacity, the National Director should know this.

Finally, yet another unproved assumption is that the growth in pollution insures the termination of all life in the harbor. The Beach City office offers no evidence that pollution is having an effect on the marine life in the harbor. If the National Director had evidence showing that marine life is slowly dying out with the increase in pollution or that similar harbors have had a complete loss of marine life with high levels of pollution, she would better be able to evaluate the argument.

The argument of the Beach City office of the National Environmental Protection Agency also suffers from ill-defined vocabulary. First, the office uses the term "staggering" to refer to the amount of pollution. The office only defines this term by giving examples of the numbers of certain pollutants collected in the last year. However, the term is largely out of context. It could be that 500 used tires or that 40,000 aluminum cans are actually small numbers to be collected from a harbor as large as Beach City's. The office also uses the phrase "discourage the growth" of tourism in Beach City as a requirement to allow for the possibility of future marine life in the harbor. The office does not give a clear sense for what is required. The National Director does not know if it is acceptable that the level stays at present heights, if it is necessary that the level actually drop, or if it is acceptable to have the level continue to grow at a lower rate.

The Beach City office of the National Environmental Protection Agency paints a dire picture in its memo to the National Director. However, its argument remains unproved until it provides additional evidence to fill in the holes left by its unproved assumptions. In addition the office should be more careful with the vocabulary that it uses in order to ensure that its message is clear.

Discuss how well reasoned you find the following argument.

The following is a recommendation from the manager of Family Friendly Restaurant:

"Family Friendly Restaurant needs to improve its facility to remain competitive in our city's restaurant market. Mega-Family Restaurant, recently opened in a suburb of our city, offers a video arcade, fine wood furniture, and 7 big-screen televisions. Due to a recession in our town, people report having less discretionary income for eating out. Therefore, if we are to hold our share of a shrinking restaurant market, we need to offer at least all the features of Mega-Family Restaurant."

The restaurant manager's argument is that Family Friendly Restaurant should upgrade its physical plant in order to remain competitive in a shrinking market for restaurants. However, the manager is not convincing because of the many unstated and unsupported assumptions that she makes and because of the ill-defined and confusing vocabulary that she uses. She presents only one real piece of evidence in support of her assertion that Family Friendly Restaurant must make improvements in order to remain competitive: people in town have less money for eating out because of a recession. Without further evidence, however, it is difficult to believe that Family Friendly Restaurant should engage in potentially costly renovations.

The argument is primarily plagued by a number of unsupported assumptions. First, the manager describes the different facilities Mega-Family restaurant provides as a starting level for improvements to Family Friendly Restaurant, indicating that the manager assumes Mega-Family restaurant is better equipped than Family Friendly Restaurant. However, no evidence is given to support this assumption. It could be that Family Friendly has other features that are valued by customers such as a salad bar or more booths so that waiting times are shorter. The manager also assumes that adding features such as big screen televisions will cause commercial success. The underlying assumption linking this evidence to the recommendation is that, all other factors being equal (quality of food, price of a meal), restaurant goers, having less money at their disposal, would base their dining decision on atmosphere—in this case, on a video arcade, fine wood furniture, and seven big screen televisions. However, we are given no reason to believe that this is true. If the manger were to offer evidence that the revenues and profits of restaurants with such amenities are higher, the reader would better be able to believe the conclusion.

Finally, the manager assumes that there are not other ways that Family Friendly restaurants can remain competitive. Perhaps Family Friendly could effectively compete with Mega-Family by having better food quality and lower prices. In all likelihood, people limiting their spending on eating out would generally place quality of food and price over purely atmospheric considerations. Further, even if food quality and prices were comparable, the additional expense that a video arcade might afford to consumers with children might make Mega-Family Restaurant less attractive during a recession. In this case,

Family Friendly Restaurant would do well not to waste money on expensive improvements that would deter rather than attract customers.

The manager's argument also suffers from ill-defined terms. Most notably, the manager describes Mega-Family's new location as in a "suburb" of the city. The reader is not told if this location is actually close enough to be considered a true competitive threat. If the two restaurants serve completely different markets, then there may be no reason to upgrade Family Friendly. Also, if the suburban location is considered superior—perhaps it is closer to people's homes—then upgrades to Family Friendly may not make any difference.

A second ill-defined term is the word "competitive". The manager seems to equate this to holding market share. However, the owners of Family Friendly may view competitiveness as retaining a decent return on investment. The manager gives us no information in the argument to determine if the potentially costly upgrades she suggests would offer a good return. It may be that lower levels of profit with the existing restaurant would be financially more attractive than keeping the same level of profits but spending a large amount of capital to do so.

In order to strengthen her argument, the manager would first have to prove that Mega-Family Restaurant, because of its greater success, is a relevant model for Family Friendly Restaurant. More than this, however, the manager must prove that Mega-Family Restaurant's success has resulted primarily from its video arcade, fine wood furniture, and big screen televisions and not from better food, lower prices, better location, or some other reason. The manager must also add evidence that consumers carefully watching their money will choose a restaurant based on external trappings rather than quality of food and lower prices. Finally, the manager should better define the terms she uses to give her readers a clearer understanding. Only under these circumstances would Family Friendly Restaurant benefit from remodeling itself on Mega-Family Restaurant.

Discuss how well reasoned you find the following argument.

The following appeared in a memo to the Mayor of Norchester from the School Board:

"The city of Norchester has a student-to-teacher ratio of 25:1 in its elementary schools, a ratio in line with the national average. Recent research by educational leaders, however, indicates that the highest acceptable ratio for optimal child learning is 22:1. While the city's ratio is slightly higher than the guideline, our town's population has been shrinking. Therefore, Norchester can respond to its current budget deficit by putting in place a teacher hiring freeze for the next 3 school years and still have a student-to-teacher ratio that is acceptable for child development."

The School Board of Norchester would have the city's mayor believe that a three year freeze on the hiring of teachers would not have a deleterious effect on child development in the city's elementary schools. On the surface, the school board's conclusion seems reasonable based on evidence that the town is shrinking in population. However, the argument itself is not convincing as it now stands because it fails to supports a number of its assumptions and also uses vocabulary that requires further definition.

The first unsupported assumption made by the School Board is that the nature of the population decline is such that the number of elementary school aged children is also declining. It could be that Norchester is losing population because older people or couples without children are moving or passing away. Thus, it could be that the number of children in the elementary school system could increase as the population decreases. Without evidence to the contrary, the school board's argument is weak. In a related manner, the school board assumes that there are not other factors that could contribute to an increase of children in the school system over the next three years. For example, the closing of a private school in the area might force more children into the public school system.

In addition, the assumption is that there will not be large changes in the other portion of the student to teacher ratio is unfounded. If the core of teachers in Norchester is reaching retirement age, there could be a large shift in the student to teacher ratio under a hiring freeze. Teachers might also leave for other reasons, for example a higher salary paid in a nearby town or the pressure and stress of increased class sizes. The school board gives no evidence to quantify the argument, thus making it difficult for the Mayor to evaluate the recommendation given.

The school board's argument could also be made more sound by including better definitions of some of the terms used. First, the school board states that the current ratio is "slightly higher" than the guideline because it is at 25:1 instead of 22:1. However the board does not tell us if this "slight" difference is material in the eyes of recent research. It could be true that the extra three students indeed has a small effect on student learning, but it could be that an extra three students have a disastrous effect on the learning for all of the students. Second, the school board states that after the three year freeze, the ratio will still be "acceptable for child development." The board does not defined exactly what "acceptable" is. It could be that they expect that the ratio will remain the same in which case the Mayor still does not know if 25:1 is okay. Or it could be that the board expects some other ratio at the end of three years. Without specific and effective definitions, it is difficult to evaluate their proposal.

The school board could improve their argument significantly if they included more evidence to support the argument. Specifically, the Mayor needs more information on what exactly what effects the hiring freeze will have on both parts of the student teacher ratio. Also, the board needs to better define a few key terms, so that the Mayor can make an informed decision on the board's recommendation.

Chapter Seven: **GMAT**
Essay Prompts

This chapter contains 25 sample prompts for the Issue task and 25 sample prompts for the Argument task. For your convenience, blank space is provided for you to plan your essays. Please use extra paper if necessary, or practice typing your essay on a computer. Prompts that are marked by an asterisk (*) are those for which sample essays are found in the following chapter.

ANALYSIS OF AN ISSUE PROMPTS

Discuss the extent to which you agree or disagree with the opinion stated below. Support your position with reasons and/or examples from your experience, observations, or reading.

> "Television and radio broadcasts should be closely policed to prevent inappropriate material from airing; this will strengthen the moral fiber of our country's citizens."

_____

_____

_____

_____

_____

_____

_____

_____

_____

_____

Discuss the extent to which you agree or disagree with the opinion stated below. Support your position with reasons and/or examples from your experience, observations, or reading.

"Individual awards should not be used in youth activities—they will only cause children to think that there can only be one person who deserves praise in any given pursuit."*

_____

_____

_____

_____

_____

_____

Discuss the extent to which you agree or disagree with the opinion stated below. Support your position with reasons and/or examples from your experience, observations, or reading.

"Schools should require that students participate in interscholastic sports to ensure that young adults receive a well-rounded education."

_____

_____

_____

_____

_____

_____

_____

Discuss the extent to which you agree or disagree with the opinion stated below. Support your position with reasons and/or examples from your experience, observations, or reading.

> "A person can expect to have a successful career if he or she learns how to work in a team environment."

_____

_____

_____

_____

_____

_____

_____

Discuss the extent to which you agree or disagree with the opinion stated below. Support your position with reasons and/or examples from your experience, observations, or reading.

> "In order to have success, one must learn to balance personal and professional achievement."

_____

_____

_____

_____

_____

_____

_____

_____

Discuss the extent to which you agree or disagree with the opinion stated below. Support your position with reasons and/or examples from your experience, observations, or reading.

"The quality of a business can best be judged by looking at the quality of its highest-level managers."

_____

_____

_____

_____

_____

_____

_____

Discuss the extent to which you agree or disagree with the opinion stated below. Support your position with reasons and/or examples from your experience, observations, or reading.

"Leaders of democratic countries need to rely on their own best judgment rather than following the will of the people."*

_____

_____

_____

_____

_____

_____

_____

_____

Discuss the extent to which you agree or disagree with the opinion stated below. Support your position with reasons and/or examples from your experience, observations, or reading.

"Compromising with one's employees is more effective than demanding results from them."

_____

_____

_____

_____

_____

_____

_____

Discuss the extent to which you agree or disagree with the opinion stated below. Support your position with reasons and/or examples from your experience, observations, or reading.

"Recent high-profile corporate scandals point to a desperate need for more ethics classes in business school."

_____

_____

_____

_____

_____

_____

_____

_____

Discuss the extent to which you agree or disagree with the opinion stated below. Support your position with reasons and/or examples from your experience, observations, or reading.

"The importance of winning should be deemphasized in children's sporting activities. Only the act of participation should matter."

_____

_____

_____

_____

_____

_____

_____

Discuss the extent to which you agree or disagree with the opinion stated below. Support your position with reasons and/or examples from your experience, observations, or reading.

"Any manager who wants improved performance from his or her staff should rely heavily on praising a job well done and should seldom, if ever, criticize a sub-par effort."

_____

_____

_____

_____

_____

_____

_____

Discuss the extent to which you agree or disagree with the opinion stated below. Support your position with reasons and/or examples from your experience, observations, or reading.

"Our educational system should be structured, from the earliest grades, to teach our students how to compete in an increasingly global marketplace."

_____

_____

_____

_____

_____

_____

_____

Discuss the extent to which you agree or disagree with the opinion stated below. Support your position with reasons and/or examples from your experience, observations, or reading.

"A manager will get more out of staff members if he or she gives them the responsibility to follow through with a project. A manager will never be successful by carving off individual pieces of work for each member of his or her team—this will only cause employees to feel that they do not have a vested interest in the success of a project."

_____

_____

_____

_____

_____

_____

_____

Discuss the extent to which you agree or disagree with the opinion stated below. Support your position with reasons and/or examples from your experience, observations, or reading.

"Government needs to regulate industry to ensure that the environment is protected. Without regulation, companies will always strive for profits at the expense of the natural world."*

_____

_____

_____

_____

_____

_____

_____

Discuss the extent to which you agree or disagree with the opinion stated below. Support your position with reasons and/or examples from your experience, observations, or reading.

"Parents should be held responsible for the actions of their minor children."

_____

_____

_____

_____

_____

_____

_____

Discuss the extent to which you agree or disagree with the opinion stated below. Support your position with reasons and/or examples from your experience, observations, or reading.

"When deciding on a future career, students should consider where their interests lie instead of attempting to maximize their earning ability."

_____

_____

_____

_____

_____

_____

_____

_____

Discuss the extent to which you agree or disagree with the opinion stated below. Support your position with reasons and/or examples from your experience, observations, or reading.

"The ultimate goal of a business career should be attaining financial security."

_____

_____

_____

_____

_____

_____

_____

_____

Discuss the extent to which you agree or disagree with the opinion stated below. Support your position with reasons and/or examples from your experience, observations, or reading.

"The only music worth listening to is classical music, since it is the only musical genre that has proven its popularity over the course of centuries."

_____

_____

_____

_____

_____

_____

_____

Discuss the extent to which you agree or disagree with the opinion stated below. Support your position with reasons and/or examples from your experience, observations, or reading.

"Employees respond best to monetary compensation. No incentive will engender better performance than a raise in salary or a big bonus for a job well done."*

_____

_____

_____

_____

_____

_____

_____

_____

_____

Discuss the extent to which you agree or disagree with the opinion stated below. Support your position with reasons and/or examples from your experience, observations, or reading.

"No person acting by himself or herself can be as creative or effective in achieving a goal as a team of highly qualified people would be."

_____

_____

_____

_____

_____

_____

_____

_____

Discuss the extent to which you agree or disagree with the opinion stated below. Support your position with reasons and/or examples from your experience, observations, or reading.

"People would do better to focus on long-term goals, rather than short-term satisfaction."

_____

_____

_____

_____

_____

_____

_____

_____

_____

Discuss the extent to which you agree or disagree with the opinion stated below. Support your position with reasons and/or examples from your experience, observations, or reading.

"The only history that we should teach our children is our own country's history. This will boost their patriotic feelings."*

Discuss the extent to which you agree or disagree with the opinion stated below. Support your position with reasons and/or examples from your experience, observations, or reading.

"Some economists believe that the role government plays in the business world should be very limited in order to improve the efficiency of the business world. Other economists believe that heavy government involvement is necessary to ensure that businesses do not unfairly treat consumers or competitors."

Discuss the extent to which you agree or disagree with the opinion stated below. Support your position with reasons and/or examples from your experience, observations, or reading.

> "People in business focus too much on the goal of reaching the top of their profession. Few realize that the key to success is to focus on the steps leading to a destination, not on the destination itself."

_____

_____

_____

_____

_____

_____

_____

_____

Discuss the extent to which you agree or disagree with the opinion stated below. Support your position with reasons and/or examples from your experience, observations, or reading.

> "Some parents believe that their children should receive as broad an education as possible; but children would be better served by studies that prepare them for a specific career."

_____

_____

_____

_____

_____

_____

_____

_____

ANALYSIS OF AN ARGUMENT PROMPTS

Discuss how well reasoned you find the following arguments. In your discussion be sure to analyze the line of reasoning and the use of evidence in the argument. For example, you may need to consider what questionable assumptions underlie the thinking and what alternative explanations or counterexamples might weaken the conclusion. You can also discuss what sort of evidence would strengthen or refute the argument, what changes in the argument would make it more logically sound, and what, if anything, would help you better evaluate its conclusion.

The following appeared in a report from the business department of Plane Corporation:

"When Plane Corporation had its headquarters in Sepia City, near its major production plants, its profit levels were much lower than they are today now that Plane Corporation is headquartered in Chiltress City, which is over 1,000 miles away. Clearly, Plane Corporation has benefited from the change of headquarters because it allows upper management to focus more on the strategic vision of the company and allows the manufacturing bosses to focus on production without the distraction of being micromanaged by upper management."

Discuss how well reasoned you find the following arguments. In your discussion be sure to analyze the line of reasoning and the use of evidence in the argument. For example, you may need to consider what questionable assumptions underlie the thinking and what alternative explanations or counterexamples might weaken the conclusion. You can also discuss what sort of evidence would strengthen or refute the argument, what changes in the argument would make it more logically sound, and what, if anything, would help you better evaluate its conclusion.

The following appeared in a report submitted for discussion at the board meeting of the Los Altos Rockets, a professional baseball team:

"Our attendance levels have been falling to the point where we have 5,000 fewer fans per game than we did five seasons ago. As everyone here knows, 5 years ago the owner of the Renegades moved his baseball team to Los Altos and began charging less for tickets than we charge. This is clearly the cause of our problems. The only course of action to stem our decline in ticket sales is to drop our price below the price for a Renegades game. This will increase our attendance and, thus, allow us to attract more businesses as sponsors. In the end, we will be more profitable after this move."

Discuss how well reasoned you find the following arguments. In your discussion be sure to analyze the line of reasoning and the use of evidence in the argument. For example, you may need to consider what questionable assumptions underlie the thinking and what alternative explanations or counterexamples might weaken the conclusion. You can also discuss what sort of evidence would strengthen or refute the argument, what changes in the argument would make it more logically sound, and what, if anything, would help you better evaluate its conclusion.

The following appeared in the business section of the local newspaper in Thousand Acres City:

"Recent studies have shown that senior citizens (those over age 65) devote 60% of their discretionary income to playing golf or purchasing golf products. With the huge 'baby-boom' generation approaching this age, Thousand Acres should take note and prepare for a golf-related boom. The city council should approve a new golf course, and local businesses should begin to offer more golf-related products for sale, or the city will miss out."

_____

_____

_____

_____

_____

_____

_____

_____

_____

_____

_____

_____

_____

_____

Discuss how well reasoned you find the following arguments. In your discussion be sure to analyze the line of reasoning and the use of evidence in the argument. For example, you may need to consider what questionable assumptions underlie the thinking and what alternative explanations or counterexamples might weaken the conclusion. You can also discuss what sort of evidence would strengthen or refute the argument, what changes in the argument would make it more logically sound, and what, if anything, would help you better evaluate its conclusion.

The following appeared in a memo to the president of Baby-And-Me Bread Company:

"Late last year we switched the supplier we use for bread bags in our Windy City bakery plant to AAA Plastics. This year we have seen over 5,000 defects in bags and each defective bag causes a need to throw out the loaf of bread. In our Bentonville bakery plant, where we use ZZZ Plastics, there have only been 1,000 defects in our bread bags. Even though AAA plastics charge considerably less for their bread bags, we should switch our Windy City plant to ZZZ Plastics in order to save money."*

Discuss how well reasoned you find the following arguments. In your discussion be sure to analyze the line of reasoning and the use of evidence in the argument. For example, you may need to consider what questionable assumptions underlie the thinking and what alternative explanations or counterexamples might weaken the conclusion. You can also discuss what sort of evidence would strengthen or refute the argument, what changes in the argument would make it more logically sound, and what, if anything, would help you better evaluate its conclusion.

The following appeared in the editorial section of a statewide newspaper:

"Last week, two firefighters from every major city in the state traveled to the State Capitol to protest a bill being considered by the State Legislature that would cut funding for city firefighting forces by 10%. Since the average staff of a city firefighting department is 34, many more firefighters stayed behind. Evidently, the other firefighters are less concerned with the budget cuts. The State Legislature should not listen to the protests of a vocal minority and should go ahead with the proposed cuts."

Discuss how well reasoned you find the following arguments. In your discussion be sure to analyze the line of reasoning and the use of evidence in the argument. For example, you may need to consider what questionable assumptions underlie the thinking and what alternative explanations or counterexamples might weaken the conclusion. You can also discuss what sort of evidence would strengthen or refute the argument, what changes in the argument would make it more logically sound, and what, if anything, would help you better evaluate its conclusion.

The following appeared in an advertisement from ABC Drinking Glasses:

"Both ABC Drinking Glasses and our main competitor XYZ Drinking Glasses intend to unveil a new line of ceramic coffee mugs in January. Over the last 5 years, we have sold 5 million more plastic drinking glasses than XYZ. Therefore if you wish to have a more trusted, higher quality ceramic coffee mug, you should buy ABC brand coffee mugs."

Discuss how well reasoned you find the following arguments. In your discussion be sure to analyze the line of reasoning and the use of evidence in the argument. For example, you may need to consider what questionable assumptions underlie the thinking and what alternative explanations or counterexamples might weaken the conclusion. You can also discuss what sort of evidence would strengthen or refute the argument, what changes in the argument would make it more logically sound, and what, if anything, would help you better evaluate its conclusion.

The following appeared in an advertisement for the reelection of Mayor Carter:

"A vote to reelect Mayor Carter is a vote for increased prosperity in our city. Over the last four years since Mayor Carter was first elected, 1,000 new jobs have been created, the city's tax revenues are up 20%, and 50% of our citizens have had increases in their wages. Clearly, Mayor Carter has been good for the livelihood of our citizens."

Discuss how well reasoned you find the following arguments. In your discussion be sure to analyze the line of reasoning and the use of evidence in the argument. For example, you may need to consider what questionable assumptions underlie the thinking and what alternative explanations or counterexamples might weaken the conclusion. You can also discuss what sort of evidence would strengthen or refute the argument, what changes in the argument would make it more logically sound, and what, if anything, would help you better evaluate its conclusion.

> The following appeared in a memorandum to the President of Sparky Dog Food Company:
>
> "In order to increase production of Sparky Dog Food to meet future demand, we should begin construction on a new plant in Wayward City as soon as possible. Of all the cities that we have examined for a new plant, Wayward has the largest population and the most technical colleges; therefore, we should be able to staff our plant very quickly with qualified employees. In addition, Wayward has two meat companies, so we should be able to acquire the ingredients for our dog food at low cost."

Discuss how well reasoned you find the following arguments. In your discussion be sure to analyze the line of reasoning and the use of evidence in the argument. For example, you may need to consider what questionable assumptions underlie the thinking and what alternative explanations or counterexamples might weaken the conclusion. You can also discuss what sort of evidence would strengthen or refute the argument, what changes in the argument would make it more logically sound, and what, if anything, would help you better evaluate its conclusion.

> The following appeared in a memorandum to the Dean of the Culinary Institute of West Apria:

> "Over the last two years, our main competitor, the Culinary Institute of East Apria, has offered cooking classes over the Internet. Over that time period, they have attracted 5,000 students to attend on-line classes, and have also seen a decrease in their food costs, since on-line students practice with food they buy themselves. Over the same time period, our school has seen a 10% decline in our student body, and food costs have remained steady as a percentage of revenue. In order to avert financial disaster, we should begin to offer on-line classes as soon as possible."

Discuss how well reasoned you find the following arguments. In your discussion be sure to analyze the line of reasoning and the use of evidence in the argument. For example, you may need to consider what questionable assumptions underlie the thinking and what alternative explanations or counterexamples might weaken the conclusion. You can also discuss what sort of evidence would strengthen or refute the argument, what changes in the argument would make it more logically sound, and what, if anything, would help you better evaluate its conclusion.

The following appeared in a speech given by the new president of Lovelace's, a major department store:

"I believe that good customer service is at the heart of good business. My first actions as president will be to increase the number of sales clerks in our stores, to open our stores earlier and close our stores later, and to offer free lollipops to all children in our stores. This emphasis on customer service will distinguish us from our many competitors, drive more business our way, and increase our profits."*

Discuss how well reasoned you find the following arguments. In your discussion be sure to analyze the line of reasoning and the use of evidence in the argument. For example, you may need to consider what questionable assumptions underlie the thinking and what alternative explanations or counterexamples might weaken the conclusion. You can also discuss what sort of evidence would strengthen or refute the argument, what changes in the argument would make it more logically sound, and what, if anything, would help you better evaluate its conclusion.

The following appeared in a national newspaper:

"The National Society of Architects each year polls its members to see how much new business they have generated in the last year. The Society's poll is a great way to predict future spending on construction projects. If architects are gaining new business at a higher rate than the previous year, surely construction spending should also rise based on the plans that are generated by architects."

Discuss how well reasoned you find the following arguments. In your discussion be sure to analyze the line of reasoning and the use of evidence in the argument. For example, you may need to consider what questionable assumptions underlie the thinking and what alternative explanations or counterexamples might weaken the conclusion. You can also discuss what sort of evidence would strengthen or refute the argument, what changes in the argument would make it more logically sound, and what, if anything, would help you better evaluate its conclusion.

The following is excerpted from the business plan for a new coffee shop in Wyattsville:

"Of the five cities in Wyatt Valley, Wyattsville is the most attractive place to open a new coffee shop. Wyattsville has the largest population in the region and over 85% of its citizens drink coffee, a number 5% higher than the national average. In addition, there is an abundance of cheap rental property available in the city center because of an overbuilding of strip malls five years ago, so a store can be opened at lower expense than in other cities."

Discuss how well reasoned you find the following arguments. In your discussion be sure to analyze the line of reasoning and the use of evidence in the argument. For example, you may need to consider what questionable assumptions underlie the thinking and what alternative explanations or counterexamples might weaken the conclusion. You can also discuss what sort of evidence would strengthen or refute the argument, what changes in the argument would make it more logically sound, and what, if anything, would help you better evaluate its conclusion.

The following appeared as part of a promotional campaign to sell advertising on channels provided by the local cable television company:

"Advertising with Cable Communications Corporation is a great way to increase your profits. Recently the Adams Car Dealership began advertising with Cable Communications and over the last 30 days, sales are up 15% over the previous month. Let us increase your profits, just as we did for Adams Cars!"✱

Discuss how well reasoned you find the following arguments. In your discussion be sure to analyze the line of reasoning and the use of evidence in the argument. For example, you may need to consider what questionable assumptions underlie the thinking and what alternative explanations or counterexamples might weaken the conclusion. You can also discuss what sort of evidence would strengthen or refute the argument, what changes in the argument would make it more logically sound, and what, if anything, would help you better evaluate its conclusion.

The following appeared in a memo to the Superintendent of Schools in Jerseytown:

"The school district in nearby Yorktown has seen a dramatic increase in school attendance associated with adding more computer classes to the elective curriculum of their high school. Jerseytown School District should immediately buy more computers so that our town can also enjoy higher attendance rates."

Discuss how well reasoned you find the following arguments. In your discussion be sure to analyze the line of reasoning and the use of evidence in the argument. For example, you may need to consider what questionable assumptions underlie the thinking and what alternative explanations or counterexamples might weaken the conclusion. You can also discuss what sort of evidence would strengthen or refute the argument, what changes in the argument would make it more logically sound, and what, if anything, would help you better evaluate its conclusion.

The following is excerpted from the business plan for a new nursing home in West Bridgetown:

"The population of our nation is aging. In the region in which West Bridgetown sits, there are over 10,000 residents aged 65 years or older. Because there is not a state-of-the-art nursing home facility in West Bridgetown, there must be pent-up demand for nursing home services. Therefore, opening a nursing home in West Bridgetown will be very profitable."

Discuss how well reasoned you find the following arguments. In your discussion be sure to analyze the line of reasoning and the use of evidence in the argument. For example, you may need to consider what questionable assumptions underlie the thinking and what alternative explanations or counterexamples might weaken the conclusion. You can also discuss what sort of evidence would strengthen or refute the argument, what changes in the argument would make it more logically sound, and what, if anything, would help you better evaluate its conclusion.

The following appeared in a memorandum to the president of Top Shape Fitness Centers:

"We currently operate no fitness centers in the western half of our nation. However, recent medical surveys have shown that 30% of the citizens in the West meet the definition of "obese." Our services are clearly needed in the West. Therefore, if Top Shape Fitness Centers were to expand into the western half of the nation, we would more than double our profits."

Discuss how well reasoned you find the following arguments. In your discussion be sure to analyze the line of reasoning and the use of evidence in the argument. For example, you may need to consider what questionable assumptions underlie the thinking and what alternative explanations or counterexamples might weaken the conclusion. You can also discuss what sort of evidence would strengthen or refute the argument, what changes in the argument would make it more logically sound, and what, if anything, would help you better evaluate its conclusion.

The following appeared in an open letter to the Governor that was published in a major newspaper:

"Our state needs to reduce the property tax levied on businesses in order to encourage more investment within the state. The current tax rate is 1.0% of assessed value, which is 33% higher than the national average. If our state were to drop the property tax rate to 0.5%, below the national average, it would attract more businesses to the state and help solve our unemployment problems."

Discuss how well reasoned you find the following arguments. In your discussion be sure to analyze the line of reasoning and the use of evidence in the argument. For example, you may need to consider what questionable assumptions underlie the thinking and what alternative explanations or counterexamples might weaken the conclusion. You can also discuss what sort of evidence would strengthen or refute the argument, what changes in the argument would make it more logically sound, and what, if anything, would help you better evaluate its conclusion.

The following appeared in a regional fitness journal:

"A recent survey of this journal's readers found that over 80% are or plan to be on a low-carbohydrate diet. This should serve as a warning to restaurants in our region. If they do not add low-carbohydrate meals to their menus, they could stand to lose 80% of their business."*

Discuss how well reasoned you find the following arguments. In your discussion be sure to analyze the line of reasoning and the use of evidence in the argument. For example, you may need to consider what questionable assumptions underlie the thinking and what alternative explanations or counterexamples might weaken the conclusion. You can also discuss what sort of evidence would strengthen or refute the argument, what changes in the argument would make it more logically sound, and what, if anything, would help you better evaluate its conclusion.

The following appeared in the editorial section of a local newspaper:

"The children in our town suffer from obesity at a rate double the national average. The Superintendent of our school system believes that the problem lies in having too little funding to provide a balanced diet in our school cafeterias. If our city does not provide adequate funding for better meals, our town will soon have an even greater obesity problem."

Discuss how well reasoned you find the following arguments. In your discussion be sure to analyze the line of reasoning and the use of evidence in the argument. For example, you may need to consider what questionable assumptions underlie the thinking and what alternative explanations or counterexamples might weaken the conclusion. You can also discuss what sort of evidence would strengthen or refute the argument, what changes in the argument would make it more logically sound, and what, if anything, would help you better evaluate its conclusion.

The following appeared in a medical journal:

"Recent research by psychiatrists has shown that people convicted of hate crimes have elevated neural activity in the prefrontal cortex of their brain when shown images of the groups of people that they claim to hate. If doctors can devise a way to control neural activity in the prefrontal cortex, then the perpetrators of hate crimes can be cured of their violent tendencies."

Discuss how well reasoned you find the following arguments. In your discussion be sure to analyze the line of reasoning and the use of evidence in the argument. For example, you may need to consider what questionable assumptions underlie the thinking and what alternative explanations or counterexamples might weaken the conclusion. You can also discuss what sort of evidence would strengthen or refute the argument, what changes in the argument would make it more logically sound, and what, if anything, would help you better evaluate its conclusion.

The following appeared in a national newspaper:

"Recent research by a team of economists has shown that wages for unskilled laborers tend to be higher for those that work in traditionally dangerous jobs, such as mining. The researchers have used this evidence to recommend that all companies make their workplaces safer. They believe that this will reduce the wages required by workers and thus make businesses more profitable."

Discuss how well reasoned you find the following arguments. In your discussion be sure to analyze the line of reasoning and the use of evidence in the argument. For example, you may need to consider what questionable assumptions underlie the thinking and what alternative explanations or counterexamples might weaken the conclusion. You can also discuss what sort of evidence would strengthen or refute the argument, what changes in the argument would make it more logically sound, and what, if anything, would help you better evaluate its conclusion.

The following investment advice was listed in a financial journal:

"The percentage of the population over the age of 65 who enjoy playing bocce ball is 24%, more than double the percentage for people under 65. In addition, the number of people aged over 65 years is expected to more than double within the next 7 years. Knowing these facts makes it obvious that we should all buy the stock of Bocce Corporation, the largest maker of bocce ball equipment."

Discuss how well reasoned you find the following arguments. In your discussion be sure to analyze the line of reasoning and the use of evidence in the argument. For example, you may need to consider what questionable assumptions underlie the thinking and what alternative explanations or counterexamples might weaken the conclusion. You can also discuss what sort of evidence would strengthen or refute the argument, what changes in the argument would make it more logically sound, and what, if anything, would help you better evaluate its conclusion.

The following appeared on the editorial page of a national newspaper:

"The ready availability of low interest rate loans in this nation has allowed more people to own homes than ever before. However, many of these new homeowners have lower credit ratings than those who owned homes before the availability of low interest rate loans. Therefore, we should expect to see a dramatic increase in the rate of foreclosures in this country over the next 5 to 10 years."

_____

_____

_____

_____

_____

_____

_____

_____

_____

_____

_____

_____

_____

_____

_____

Discuss how well reasoned you find the following arguments. In your discussion be sure to analyze the line of reasoning and the use of evidence in the argument. For example, you may need to consider what questionable assumptions underlie the thinking and what alternative explanations or counterexamples might weaken the conclusion. You can also discuss what sort of evidence would strengthen or refute the argument, what changes in the argument would make it more logically sound, and what, if anything, would help you better evaluate its conclusion.

The following appeared in a health and medicine journal:

"Oxycodone is a prescription drug popular with doctors for treating severe pain. However, Oxycodone is also an opium-based drug that can be highly addictive if abused. Since the patent for Oxycodone is expiring in the next year, and cheaper generic versions will then be available for prescription, we should expect to see a rise in Oxycodone addictions."

Discuss how well reasoned you find the following arguments. In your discussion be sure to analyze the line of reasoning and the use of evidence in the argument. For example, you may need to consider what questionable assumptions underlie the thinking and what alternative explanations or counterexamples might weaken the conclusion. You can also discuss what sort of evidence would strengthen or refute the argument, what changes in the argument would make it more logically sound, and what, if anything, would help you better evaluate its conclusion.

The following appeared in a memorandum to the Chief Executive Officer of Tasty-Ice, a company that manufactures and distributes ice cream:

"It is time to reintroduce our goat-milk ice cream product that we took off the market three years ago. The only reason we stopped producing this product is that prices for goat milk three years ago were at 30-year highs. Now prices for the milk have fallen to more reasonable levels. Moreover, our major competitors have also stopped producing goat-milk ice cream. This will allow us to position our goat-milk ice cream as a premium product and to charge a premium price. Therefore, introducing a goat-milk product now will greatly improve our profits."*

_____

_____

_____

_____

_____

_____

_____

_____

_____

_____

_____

_____

_____

_____

Chapter Eight: **GMAT Sample Essays**

Here are sample top scoring essays for five of the sample Issue prompts and five of the sample Argument prompts found in the previous chapter. Remember that an essay does not have to be perfect to receive a top score. Review these essays and note which qualities earned them a score of 6.

ANALYSIS OF AN ISSUE ESSAYS

Discuss the extent to which you agree or disagree with the opinion stated below. Support your position with reasons and/or examples from your experience, observations, or reading.

> "Individual awards should not be used in youth activities—they will only cause children to think that there can only be one person who deserves praise in any given pursuit."

The author of the statement above would have her readers believe that individual awards in children's activities are counter-productive because they teach our youths to be overly competitive. While it should not be the aim of youth activities to promote hyper-competition between children, it does not follow that individual awards should not be used. In fact, individual awards have the benefit of teaching valuable lessons to children. Through the bestowal of individual honors, children will learn that notable efforts deserve praise, they will see role models in their peers in terms of how to perform, and they will also gain knowledge of how our competitive world works.

The first major benefit of individual awards in youth activities is that it teaches children that there are rewards for stellar efforts. Pavlov showed decades ago the power of positive reinforcement and everything from dog training to child psychology has adopted its tenets. If there is a positive prize, such as an individual award, children will learn to strive for better results, whether the activity is youth soccer or other activity. My eleven year-old niece has developed into a fine young poet primarily because of the praise and awards she received as a grammar school student in poetry exercises.

Another positive factor associated with individual awards in youth sports is that children will gain necessary role models in their peer group. If a child has dreams of being a star basketball player, he or she can always look to the professional leagues and model themselves after Vince Carter or Tim Duncan. However, young children cannot possible mimic the behavior of these international stars on the court. A child would be much better off trying to compete with the acknowledged star of the youth league in order to improve on his skills. When I was a young swimmer, I did not ever try to train to compete with the Olympic athletes. I simply tried to become the best on my team, then the best in my league, and so on. I benefited from watching the work ethic and strokes of the awarded athletes around me, not the stars that I could not possibly compare myself to.

The final benefit of individual awards is that it teaches children that we live in a competitive world. There is no reason that teachers, parents, and coaches should teach their children to cheat to get ahead. However, children must learn that there is a competitive world waiting on the other side of childhood where better performers are more successful.

Skeptics of this viewpoint might disparage these arguments by stating that children do learn to be cutthroat from individual awards or that individual awards kill a sense of team play. Even individual awards can be structured in such a way that these concerns will be moot. First of all, awards can be given in a variety of activities so that the individual talent of every participant is recognized. Young Jim may be the best basketball player, but Timmy can win for best acting skills. Second, multiple awards can be given for the same activity. Again, this will emphasize that everyone is good at something. Tina might win for best soccer defense while Alexis wins for best shooting. Finally, awards can be given for best spirit or best team player. Recognizing the ability to sacrifice for the common good and be a team player will only encourage this activity in the future lives of youths.

While individual awards may develop competition between children, they can be structured in a way to prevent children from becoming overly focused on competition. In addition, individual awards have a number of important benefits. Among these benefits are the behavioral effects of positive reinforcement, the granting of young role models, and the lessons provided in the way that the "real" world works.

Discuss the extent to which you agree or disagree with the opinion stated below. Support your position with reasons and/or examples from your experience, observations, or reading.

"Leaders of democratic countries need to rely on their own best judgment rather than following the will of the people."

In representative democracies, voters select leaders to make decisions. This is in contrast to direct democracy, where voters make decisions directly. Although there are isolated examples of direct democracy, in local Swiss government, in referendums, and in petitions for change, direct democracy is difficult to practice, and elected representatives make most decisions in most democratic nations. In representative democracy, leaders must rely on their best judgment and not always follow the "will of the people." Not only are leaders selected for this very role, but also they typically have more information upon which to make decisions, and more time to weigh the issues than do voters. Also, judging the "will of the people" is difficult.

Two advantages that elected leaders have over voting citizens are greater quantities of information and time. For example, the office of the President of the United States receives information from many parts of the executive branch, and has hundreds of researchers collecting and distilling information. Few voters would have the time or the expertise to distill and make use of such information. In addition, the President has a job where he or she is afforded the time to make important decisions, and where he or she must make decisions constantly. It would be impractical to expect American voters to similarly devote large portions of their time to ponder questions of foreign trade or domestic policy, and to make quick, important decisions when such decisions must be made.

A final reason that leaders should act on their own judgment is the difficulty in precisely determining public opinion. Much of the work in determining public opinion is currently done through polling small "representative" samples of the public. Polls, however, can be skewed by many factors including how a question is asked, and what time of day the poll administrator calls. Also, many respondents are unsure of their answers, and seek merely to please the administrators. When groups of individuals are placed in groups to discuss policies, or when respondents are presented with certain facts, the results can vary dramatically from poll results. Opinion poll results are also known to contradict each other, to move wildly in a short period of time, and, sometimes, to be inaccurate. On many issues, it would be very difficult to assess public opinion with a high degree of accuracy.

An elected leader has an obligation to act according to her best interest because he or she has more information, more time, and a defined role tailored for making decisions for the people. In addition, a leader has little chance of knowing the "true" will of the people at every moment because of the logistical difficulties inherent in measuring the opinions of people.

Discuss the extent to which you agree or disagree with the opinion stated below. Support your position with reasons and/or examples from your experience, observations, or reading.

"Government needs to regulate industry to ensure that the environment is protected. Without regulation, companies will always strive for profits at the expense of the natural world."

It may not be true that companies will "always" strive for profits at the expense of the environment; however, government authorities should take an active role in policing the actions of corporate entities to ensure that commitment to the profit motive does not have deleterious effects on our environment. Some companies do show a serious concern for the natural world, but even a few transgressors can cause significant harm to the ecosystem. Regulators must lay down the primary line of defense in protecting the environment, making sure that a series of small offenses do not combine to have a major impact.

The primary concern of companies is to increase their profits and therefore the value of the enterprise. Because of this, companies are given a strong incentive to slash costs wherever possible. Examples may include putting runoff from a factory directly into a stream, river, or ocean without treating it first or allowing smoke from a coal burning power plant to flow unhindered into the atmosphere. Building treatment facilities or installing smoke stack scrubbers are almost never in the best interests of individual companies. Since companies do not face the costs of polluting streams or the atmosphere, they will increase profits by polluting.

In fact, some of the worst pollution industries have never voluntarily taken pollution control measures. Before recent legislation and enforcement that requires the use of smoke stack scrubbers in coal burning power plants, all the coal plants in the United States were letting SOx and NOx gasses flow directly into the atmosphere. Similarly, the mining industry never treated mine runoff before environmental regulations required them to do so. The oil refining industry is another that has had to make considerable changes against its will to improve its environmental track record.

Some may argue that the past thirty years or so have seen more and more companies displaying a "green," or ecologically informed, sensibility in their decision-making and that therefore government regulation is no longer needed. This development, however, should not lull government leaders into a reduced degree of vigilance. Even if the majority of business concerns were environmentally responsible, it would only take one company's negligence to bring about an ecological disaster. Most of the environmental tragedies of the last few decades—for example, Love Canal, the Exxon Valdez, and the real-life events depicted in "Erin Brockovich"—have been attributable to individual corporations. Even businesses that one might characterize as "environmentally aware" may choose to skirt environmental regulations by incremental degrees in the pursuit of greater profitability. If every company, however, were to sanction such small infractions, the collective effect could be considerable.

While it is not true that companies will always sacrifice the environment for increased profits, it is definitely true that government needs to regulate industry to protect the natural world. Without regulation, too many companies would be tempted by profits to slash the costs required for environmental cleanup or would never see a reason to improve their current polluting operations. Government watchfulness in matters of environmental protection will provide the requisite insurance against all manifestations of ecological disregard, from the single catastrophic event to the stealthy accumulation of cut corners.

Discuss the extent to which you agree or disagree with the opinion stated below. Support your position with reasons and/or examples from your experience, observations, or reading.

"Employees respond best to monetary compensation. No incentive will engender better performance than a raise in salary or a big bonus for a job well done."

While compensation plays an important role in encouraging optimal employee performance, money is not the most effective incentive. Money works more at the foundational level of motivation, convincing an employee to accept a job. Other, less tangible methods must be employed to engender peak performance once the employee is at work. These methods may range from public praise for a job well done to greater degrees of responsibility in the decision-making process.

Less straightforward methods of reward can be very effective in fostering exemplary performance. Some of these methods may also retain a compensatory element. Many firms, for example, reward high-performing executives with the option to buy shares of the company's stock at prices lower than the normal trading range of the stock. While money is still involved, the long-term aspect of this reward encourages a similarly long-term commitment to the employer, and a focus on years to come rather than on next week's paycheck.

Many other types of incentives have no financial element. Simple words of praise, if delivered consistently and, when warranted, before the employee's peer group, can do much to win a subordinate's commitment to a higher level of performance. When I began my first job after college at a consulting firm, my manager got the most out of me by praising a job well done. I was always highly motivated to again earn her praise.

Promotions can also have positive effects, as long as the promotion is truly one of responsibility and not in title alone. Many motivated people dream of having the responsibility to make decisions for themselves at work and often wish to have their "boss's job." When a person gets a true promotion, they often feel that added responsibility deserves added efforts and put even more of themselves into their work.

Finally, employees can also be motivated is through inspirational leadership. Those that pour their hearts out for a political campaign are rarely doing so because of the financial rewards that they might reap. In fact, many volunteer their time and tireless efforts with no expectation of financial reward. They work so hard because they believe in the positive effect that their candidate or policy might have, if elected or enacted. This same motivation can also work in a company. Employees will often respond well to a hard-working, fair, and dedicated manager.

None of this is to say that money does not play a role in motivation. However, monetary compensation serves as what the eminent twentieth century motivational expert Frederick Herzberg termed a "dissatisfier." According to Herzberg, if an employee perceived himself or herself to be underpaid, that perception worked to increase dissatisfaction and strongly reduce the motivation to perform beyond, or even at, expectations. Conversely, if the employee perceived himself or herself to be compensated fairly, or overpaid, this might have engendered some sense of personal satisfaction or comfort, but it wouldn't have necessarily translated into outstanding job performance. The perception of insufficient compensation can dissatisfy an employee, but the perception of sufficient compensation is not a great driver to higher performance. On some level, the employee may feel naturally entitled to the higher rate of pay.

While it is true that remuneration is a necessary ingredient in the motivation of employees, it is not sufficient unto itself. Most people enjoy the sense of belonging to a winning team and of contributing to a worthy endeavor. They also may respond well to praise or increases in responsibility. Still other incentives involve longer-term financial compensation without a raise in salary or a big bonus.

Discuss the extent to which you agree or disagree with the opinion stated below. Support your position with reasons and/or examples from your experience, observations, or reading.

"The only history that we should teach our children is our own country's history. This will boost their patriotic feelings."*

The author of the opinion above would have his or her readers believe that schools in this country should only teach American history to students because this will increase their patriotism. There are, however, many negative effects of teaching only a unilateral view of history, including the inability to learn from the mistakes and successes of others, the lack of understanding of other cultures, and the feeling of over-importance that children may derive. It also remains unclear if teaching only American history would actually have the salubrious effect of increasing patriotism. Therefore, I do not agree with the opinion expressed above.

The first negative effect of teaching only American history is that it does not let our children, who are the future leaders of this country, learn from the mistakes of others. The study of history allows young people to see how difficult situations were handled in the past. Students might learn to avoid the mistakes of Neville Chamberlain in backing down to Hitler or the success of negotiated peace from Anwar Sadat and Menachem Begin by studying foreign histories. If students studied only American history, they would miss out on many of these valuable lessons.

The second ill effect is that studying only American history does not allow students to gain an appreciation and understanding of foreign cultures. In this increasingly global marketplace in which we live, it is critical that our political and business leaders of tomorrow understand their counterparties in other nations. Without studying global history, our future leaders would not understand the critical and delicate situations in North Korea or the Middle East. If our leaders do not understand the background to these situations, there could be disastrous effects. It would also be very important for business leaders to understand the culture and history of the markets into which they hope to sell American goods.

The final negative factor is that our children might become overly intrepid if they believe that the only history worth noting is American history. Not only would our future political leaders not have an understanding of their counterparties as discussed above, but also they may develop into overbearing and unilateral negotiators. The situation of North Korea outlined above could be greatly compounded if our future leaders did not understand the situation, and as a result attempted to bully the North Koreans into acting a certain way. Similarly, our future business leaders would not be as effective if they tried to control partners in other nations.

Some might argue that the patriotic benefits derived from teaching only American history would outweigh the negatives as outlined. While I do not believe this would be the case even if the patriotic benefits were significant, I further believe that the benefits would not materialize under most circumstances. If our schools taught only American history, but taught it in a balanced and fair manner, there would be much for our young people to regret about the actions of our predecessors. This might actually hamper patriotism. For example, Americans are responsible for hundreds of years of slavery, for the massacre of indigenous peoples, for fighting a bloody civil war, for racial discrimination, for treating Vietnam War veterans as outcasts, and for supporting totalitarian administrations in other nations. While the history of the United States is full of laudable accomplishments, if it is taught in a balance manner, our students would not necessarily be more patriotic.

It does not make sense to teach our children only the history of this nation. There could be several negative effects, including the loss of important examples, of cultural understanding, and of proper decorum. In addition, the opinion that the main benefit of teaching only American history is increased patriotism is unsubstantiated. It does not follow that a fair and balanced portrayal of American history would augment patriotism.

ANALYSIS OF AN ARGUMENT ESSAYS

Discuss how well reasoned you find the following arguments. In your discussion be sure to analyze the line of reasoning and the use of evidence in the argument. For example, you may need to consider what questionable assumptions underlie the thinking and what alternative explanations or counterexamples might weaken the conclusion. You can also discuss what sort of evidence would strengthen or refute the argument, what changes in the argument would make it more logically sound, and what, if anything, would help you better evaluate its conclusion.

The following appeared in a memo to the president of Baby-And-Me Bread Company:

"Late last year we switched the supplier we use for bread bags in our Windy City bakery plant to AAA Plastics. This year we have seen over 5,000 defects in bags and each defective bag causes a need to throw out the loaf of bread. In our Bentonville bakery plant, where we use ZZZ Plastics, there have only been 1,000 defects in our bread bags. Even though AAA plastics charge considerably less for their bread bags, we should switch our Windy City plant to ZZZ Plastics in order to save money."

The author of the memorandum to the President of Baby-And-Me Bread Company concludes that the company would save money if it switched its plastic bag supplier to its Windy City plant from AAA Plastics to ZZZ Plastics. To support this conclusion, the author cites the 5,000 defects in bags since the Windy City plant switched to AAA Plastics and the 4,000 fewer defects that are seen at the Bentonville plant, which uses ZZZ Plastics. The author makes several assumptions in this argument that are not supported by evidence, making his argument less effective. In addition, the author fails to properly define some vocabulary. These two facts make the argument weak.

The argument assumes that there is not a production volume difference between the Windy City and Bentonville plants which might explain the difference in bag defects. It may be that the Windy City plant uses one million bags per year and is experiencing only a 0.5% defect rate. If the Bentonville plant only uses one hundred thousand bags per year, then its defect rate would be double at 1.0% per year. Without information on the production volumes of the two plants, it is difficult to see if the defect rate at AAA Plastics is actually worse than the defect rate at ZZZ Plastics. The author also assumes that ZZZ Plastics would actually be able to effectively serve the Windy City bakery plant. The President of Baby-And-Me is not given any information on freight charges and the distance between ZZZ Plastics and the Windy City plant versus the distance between AAA and the Windy City Plant. It could be that the additional freight charges associated with shipping from ZZZ Plastics to Windy City would negate any savings from lower numbers of defective bags. In addition, the President is given no information on the volume that ZZZ can support. If Baby-And-Me is already purchasing all the production of ZZZ Plastics' bags, ZZZ may not be able to supply the Windy City plant. Yet another assumption is that there is not a third plastics supplier that would be better than both AAA and ZZZ. Without information on pricing and defect rates from all potential suppliers, the President will not be able to decide the best way to save money.

To further weaken the argument, the author uses some confusing vocabulary. First, the author states that AAA Plastics charges "considerably less" for bags than does ZZZ Plastics. Without information on the actual prices charged by the two suppliers and how much is lost when a loaf must be thrown out, it is difficult to say if the switch should actually occur. If AAA bags cost so much less than ZZZ that it exceeds the cost of the lost bread product, then it certainly is not worth the switch. The second piece of confusing vocabulary is the phrase "bakery plant." The author uses the phrase to describe both plants, but gives no information about similarities or differences between the two plants. It could be that Windy City produces more of a particular product that is susceptible to bag tears. If this is the case, switching bag suppliers would not necessarily help ameliorate the bag defect situation.

By failing to give evidence support assumptions made in his argument, the author of the memorandum to the President of Baby-And-Me fails to write a convincing case for switching bag suppliers at the Windy City bakery plant. The author also fails to clear up certain pieces of vocabulary, which make it even more difficult to believe the conclusion given. The author could write a stronger argument if he were to include more information about production volumes at the Windy City and Bentonville bakery plants, shipping costs, supplier ability to serve, supplier costs and defect rates, and similarities or differences between the products produced at the two plants.

Discuss how well reasoned you find the following arguments. In your discussion be sure to analyze the line of reasoning and the use of evidence in the argument. For example, you may need to consider what questionable assumptions underlie the thinking and what alternative explanations or counterexamples might weaken the conclusion. You can also discuss what sort of evidence would strengthen or refute the argument, what changes in the argument would make it more logically sound, and what, if anything, would help you better evaluate its conclusion.

The following appeared in a speech given by the new president of Lovelace's, a major department store:

"I believe that good customer service is at the heart of good business. My first actions as president will be to increase the number of sales clerks in our stores, to open our stores earlier and close our stores later, and to offer free lollipops to all children in our stores. This emphasis on customer service will distinguish us from our many competitors, drive more business our way, and increase our profits."

The new president of Lovelace's Department Store concludes that certain improvements in aspects of customer service will increase the store's profits by distinguishing the store from its competitors and capturing more business. However, the conclusion is decidedly difficult to evaluate given that there is little real evidence to back up the conclusion. The president only mentions the specific steps he will take, such as increasing staffing levels and store hours. The argument ultimately rests on a large number of unsupported assumptions. Without further evidence, the argument will remain unconvincing.

The first major assumption is that the specific actions to improve customer service will actually distinguish Lovelace's from its "many competitors." Since we are not given any specifics regarding Lovelace's current hours and staffing levels or those of its main competitors, it is impossible to tell if improvements will actually distinguish the department store. For example, if Lovelace's is open fewer hours than its competitors right now, an increase in store hours may only bring Lovelace's in line with the industry. Similarly, it may be that Lovelace's staffing levels have been lacking and that most competitors already offer free lollipops to children. In order to show that his actions will actually distinguish Lovelace's, the new president must show that the improvements will be unique in the industry.

Whether the actions taken by the new president will actually drive more business to Lovelace's is another example of an unsupported assumption. We are given no evidence that customers actually desire any of the customer service related improvements offered by the new president. It could be that customers are already happy with the current hours and staffing levels and will not be impressed by improvements in those areas. It also seems plausible that, while most children would disagree, many parents would not want their children consuming a sugar filled lollipop every time they go to the store. If the president were to offer evidence, such as customer surveys, that show a demand for these customer service improvements, his argument would be much more persuasive.

The final assumption is that the customer service improvements will increase profits. The new president offers no financial details, making this theory difficult to accept. Even if it is true that additional business—i.e., revenue—will follow the customer service improvements, it would not necessarily follow that profits would rise. It could be that the costs associated with the improvements, such as extra pay for staffing, extra utilities for staying open more, and the cost of lollipops, would actually negate the extra gross margin captured by selling more. Without a detailed cost/benefit analysis of the steps, the conclusion made by the new president is impossible to evaluate.

The new president of Lovelace's focus on customer service may very well be the path to better performance for Lovelace's Department Store. However, the argument made by the president is unconvincing as it now stands. The argument needs large amounts of additional evidence to be more credible. Specifically, the president should have included additional details about Lovelace's current customer service levels relative to its competitors, data regarding the demand for additional customer service by customers, and financial details on the costs and benefits associated with the proposed changes.

Discuss how well reasoned you find the following arguments. In your discussion be sure to analyze the line of reasoning and the use of evidence in the argument. For example, you may need to consider what questionable assumptions underlie the thinking and what alternative explanations or counterexamples might weaken the conclusion. You can also discuss what sort of evidence would strengthen or refute the argument, what changes in the argument would make it more logically sound, and what, if anything, would help you better evaluate its conclusion.

The following appeared as part of a promotional campaign to sell advertising on channels provided by the local cable television company:

"Advertising with Cable Communications Corp. is a great way to increase your profits. Recently the Adams Car Dealership began advertising with Cable Communications and over the last 30 days, sales are up 15% over the previous month. Let us increase your profits, just as we did for Adams Cars!"

The promotional campaign by Cable Communications Corporation argues that all businesses would benefit from advertising with the cable television company in the form of increased profitability. As evidence to back up this assertion, the promotional campaign notes the experience of the Adams Car Dealership, a recent advertiser with Cable Communications Corporation. Over the last 30 days, Adams Cars has seen a 15% increase in sales over the previous month. The argument as it now stands is unconvincing because it is missing evidence that would make the argument more well reasoned and also suffers from poorly defined vocabulary, which makes the argument less easy to understand.

The argument presupposes that the example of the Adams Car Dealership is relevant for other businesses. It could be that there is a particular advantage from advertising for car dealerships because car buyers are willing to travel around to buy a car. The same may not be said, for example, of a dry cleaner. In general, people will take their dry cleaning business to the closest dry cleaner because it is a commodity service and a relatively small expenditure. Thus, advertising would be much more effective for a car dealership than a dry cleaner.

In order to convince business owners that they should advertise with Cable Communications, the promotional campaign should show additional evidence from a wide variety of business that have benefited by advertising with the company. The argument presupposes that the 15% increase in sales at Adams Car Dealership is a direct result of the recent advertising campaign with Cable Communications Corporation. It could be that the dealership had announced a sale for this month or that the previous month's sales were seasonably low—for example sales in March might always be better than sales in February due to some exogenous factor. In order to better believe that Adams benefited from the advertising campaign with Cable Communications, business owners need evidence that there was not some other factor causing the 15% increase. Perhaps evidence could be shown comparing the last 30 days sales with the same period in the previous year, or the last time the dealership was running the same promotions.

The final area of presupposition is that business owners do not have a better option for advertising. A company may get a higher increase in profits by advertising in print media or the yellow pages. In order for business owners to make an informed decision regarding their advertising expenditures, they need to see a comparison between Cable Communication's offering and the offerings of other advertising outlets.

The argument also suffers from poorly defined vocabulary. The first piece of such vocabulary is the word "recently." From just this word, it is impossible to tell when the advertising began. If Adam's advertising began three months ago, it would not be very impressive that sales increased 15% between month two and month three of the advertising campaign. Why would there not have been a boost before the most recent month? If the promotional campaign told business owners exactly when Adams began advertising, the owners would have a better ability to evaluate the argument's conclusion.

The author should also clarify the phrase "increase your profits." The promotional campaign's argument gives no details on the fees associated with advertising with Cable Communications. If Adams Cars had to develop an ad and pay large sums to Cable Communications to run the ad, the total cost of advertising with the cable company very well may have exceeded the additional profits derived from increased sales. Without additional information in this regard, business owners cannot possibly evaluate the argument's conclusion.

In order to craft a well-reasoned argument, the promotional campaign by Cable Communications needs to better define its vocabulary and offer more evidence. To better convince business owners of the benefits of advertising with Cable Communications, the company should provide additional details regarding the relevance of cable advertising to multiple business types, the exact nature of Adams' increase in sales, the ability of cable advertising to outperform other forms of advertising, and the true costs of advertising with Cable Communications. With this additional information, the promotional campaign would be much more convincing when it concludes that advertising with Cable Communications is a great way to increase a business's profits.

Discuss how well reasoned you find the following arguments. In your discussion be sure to analyze the line of reasoning and the use of evidence in the argument. For example, you may need to consider what questionable assumptions underlie the thinking and what alternative explanations or counterexamples might weaken the conclusion. You can also discuss what sort of evidence would strengthen or refute the argument, what changes in the argument would make it more logically sound, and what, if anything, would help you better evaluate its conclusion.

The following appeared in a regional fitness journal:

"A recent survey of this journal's readers found that over 80% are or plan to be on a low-carbohydrate diet. This should serve as a warning to restaurants in our region. If they do not add low-carbohydrate meals to their menus, they could stand to lose 80% of their business."

It appears that the low-carb revolution is affecting nearly every aspect of the food industry in our country. The author of this particular argument suggests that restaurants need to add low-carbohydrate meals to their menus or they could lose 80% of their business. As evidence to back up this conclusion, the author notes that a recent survey of the journal's readers found that 80% are or plan to be on a low-carbohydrate diet. The conclusion is not valid, however, because the argument contains a serious flaw in logic—namely that the readers of a fitness journal are representative of all people in the region. In addition, the argument has a number of flaws in logic that need to be redressed with additional evidence.

The logical flaw in the argument revolves around the evidence used by the author. He or she cites a survey of the readers of a fitness journal in order to draw a conclusion about all restaurant patrons in the region. This is a problematic logical leap. There is no reason for restaurant owners to believe that fitness journal subscribers behave as the general population does. Just because 80% of the readers of the fitness journal are already on or are considering a low-carbohydrate diet does not mean that the same is true of the general population. Therefore, there is no reason to believe that 80% of restaurant patrons will be looking for low-carbohydrate meals. In order to correct this flaw, the author needs to show evidence that the readers of the journal do behave as the rest of the population does, or include other evidence showing that 80% of all restaurant patrons are looking for low-carbohydrate options. If the author cannot offer either of these pieces of information, he or she needs to qualify her conclusion.

The argument is also plagued by gaps in logic. Without further evidence to shore up the argument, it becomes difficult to evaluate the author's conclusion. The first such gap is the implicit belief that the low-carbohydrate diet craze has not already affected the restaurant industry. Some portion of the 80% cited by the author is already on low-carbohydrate diets and presumably has been for some time. Restaurants may already have lost business due to this phenomenon and, therefore, do not stand to lose an additional 80% of business. In order to better evaluate the conclusion, the author should provide additional details on the breakdown of the 80%, and how long people have been on the diet.

A second gap in logic is the notion that restaurants do not already have a sufficient amount of low-carbohydrate options. It could be that subscribers to the low-carbohydrate diet are proficient at finding low-carbohydrate meals on just about any menu. Alternatively, the dieters could also be happy eating only the low-carbohydrate components of any standard entrée. To support her conclusion, the author should show evidence that the dieters are not satisfied with the low-carbohydrate options now offered and that this may prevent them from eating out.

Finally, the author needs to support the implication that low-carbohydrate dieters actually stick to their diets when they eat out. It could be that the dieters use restaurant experiences as a time to cheat on the diet. If this were true, then restaurants need not worry about losing business. The author needs to offer evidence that the dieters stick to their diets while eating out.

In summary, it is difficult to accept the conclusion that restaurants in the region risk losing 80% of their business if they do not add low-carbohydrate options to their menus given the current state of the author's argument. In order to craft a better argument, the author should first eliminate her logical flaw by not drawing a conclusion regarding all restaurant patrons from evidence about only one sub-group of the population. The author also needs to provide additional evidence about the low-carbohydrate dieters and their needs in order to not leave large lapses in logic.

Discuss how well reasoned you find the following arguments. In your discussion be sure to analyze the line of reasoning and the use of evidence in the argument. For example, you may need to consider what questionable assumptions underlie the thinking and what alternative explanations or counterexamples might weaken the conclusion. You can also discuss what sort of evidence would strengthen or refute the argument, what changes in the argument would make it more logically sound, and what, if anything, would help you better evaluate its conclusion.

The following appeared in a memorandum to the Chief Executive Officer of Tasty-Ice, a company that manufactures and distributes ice cream:

"It is time to reintroduce our goat milk ice cream product that we took off the market 3 years ago. The only reason we stopped producing this product is that prices for goat milk three years ago were at 30-year highs. Now prices for the milk have fallen to more reasonable levels. Moreover, our major competitors have also stopped producing goat milk ice cream. This will allow us to position our goat milk ice cream as a premium product and to charge a premium price. Therefore, introducing a goat milk product now will greatly improve our profits."

While goat milk ice cream may not be exciting to the average consumer, it is certainly possible that the author of this memorandum to the CEO of Tasty-Ice is correct that the reintroduction of goat milk ice cream will "greatly improve" the profits of Tasty-Ice Company. However, the argument is not well reasoned as written. The author supports his assertion by citing the lack of competition in the market place, which will allow Tasty-Ice to produce a premium product, and the reduction in goat milk prices over the last three years. In order to craft a better argument, the author needs to avoid questionable assumptions and offer better definitions for the vocabulary that he uses.

The first questionable assumption made by the author is that demand for goat milk ice cream has not changed over the last three years. The author states that the "only reason" that the company stopped making goat milk ice cream is that the input prices for goat milk had soared to levels that were unprecedented in recent history. From this fact we can gather that three years ago, the company was actually able to sell goat milk ice cream. However, there are no assurances that people still will want to buy the product. A counterexample could be that in the interim years, medical researchers had found negative health effects from consuming goat milk, or perhaps the palate of the consumer has changed in that time period. The author should have shown evidence that demand remains intact, such as a survey of consumers.

Assuming that the lack of competition will actually allow Tasty-Ice to position the goat milk ice cream as a premium product is questionable at best. A counterexample could be that goat milk ice cream has always been viewed as an inferior good, and consumers will not buy premium goat milk ice cream. Another possibility is that the Tasty-Ice brand is viewed as a down-market brand and consumers will not accept a premium product from Tasty-Ice, even if it is made in a premium way. In order for the CEO of Tasty-Ice to believe that the company can produce a premium goat milk product and charge a premium price, he or she needs evidence that shows that goat milk ice cream can be a premium product and that Tasty-Ice can be seen as a premium brand.

The final questionable assumption is that the margins associated with the goat milk product will be sufficient to "greatly improve" profits at Tasty-Ice. The argument does not include any financial data on how much it will cost to produce goat milk ice cream, what price the market will bear for the product, and how many units can be sold. Without this information, it is impossible to tell if the introduction of a goat milk ice cream line will vastly improve profits.

The assumptions are not the only reason the information in the memorandum does no present a strong argument. The author of the memorandum states that goat milk prices have fallen to "more reasonable" levels over the last three years. The CEO can properly deduce from this statement that prices are no longer at 30-year highs, but he or she does not know how far they have fallen. It could be that the company only had a highly profitable goat milk ice cream line when goat milk was at $2 per gallon, then the milk went to a thirty year high of $4 per gallon, and now is at $3 per gallon. If this were true, the phrase "more reasonable" would be deceiving. By actually telling the CEO the facts behind goat milk pricing, the author would have a more compelling argument.

The author also states that Tasty-Ice will be able to charge a "premium price" for the new goat milk line. Based on this phrasing, the CEO does not know specifically how much the company will be able to charge for a gallon of ice cream. Related to this point, if a premium price will not deliver a profit because of the costs of inputs, then the company certainly should not bring back the product line. Again, more information on this topic would make the argument better reasoned.

The author the argument sent to the CEO of Tasty-Ice Company is not well reasoned because of its questionable assumptions and unspecified terms. The CEO will not be able to properly evaluate the conclusion that the reintroduction of a Tasty-Ice goat milk ice cream will greatly improve the profits of the company. If the author were to include more evidence on market demand, the premium nature of a new product, and financial information on pricing, inputs and margins, the CEO would better be able to evaluate the conclusion.

GRE & GMAT Resources

Vocabulary Builder

A

Abandon (*n*): total lack of inhibition

Abase: to humble, disgrace

Abash: to embarrass

Abatement: decrease, reduction

Abdicate: to give up a position, right, or power

Aberrant: atypical, not normal

Aberration: something different from the usual or normal

Abet: to aid, act as accomplice

Abeyance: temporary suppression or suspension

Abhor: to loathe, detest

Abiding: enduring, continuing

Abject: miserable, pitiful

Abjure: to reject, abandon formally

Ablution: act of cleansing

Abnegate: to deny, renounce

Abolitionist: one who opposes the practice of slavery

Abominate: to hate

Abortive: interrupted while incomplete

Abridge: to condense, shorten

Abrogate: to abolish or invalidate by authority

Abscond: to depart secretly

Absolve: to forgive, free from blame

Abstain: to refrain deliberately from something

Abstemious: moderate in appetite

Abstruse: difficult to comprehend

Abut: to touch, to be in contact with

Abyss: an extremely great depth

Accede: to express approval; agree to

Accessory: attachment, ornament; accomplice, partner

Accolade: praise, distinction

Accommodating: helpful

Accord: to reconcile, come to an agreement

Accost: to approach and speak to someone

Accretion: growth in size or increase in amount

Accrue: to accumulate, grow by additions

Acerbic: bitter, sharp in taste or temper

Acidulous: sour in taste or manner

Acme: highest point, summit

Acquiesce: to agree, comply quietly

Acquittal: release from blame

Acrid: harsh, bitter

Acrimony: bitterness, animosity

Acuity: sharpness

Acumen: sharpness of insight

Adage: old saying or proverb

Adamant: uncompromising, unyielding

Adjacent: next to

Adjunct: something added, attached, or joined

Admonish: to caution or reprimand

Adroit: skillful, accomplished, highly competent

Adulation: high praise

Adulterate: to corrupt or make impure

Adumbrate: to sketch, outline in a shadowy way

Adventitious: accidental

Adversarial: antagonistic, competitive

Adverse: unfavorable, unlucky, harmful

Aerial: having to do with the air

Aerie: nook or nest built high in the air

Aesthetic: pertaining to beauty or art

Affable: friendly, easy to approach

Affected (*adj*): pretentious, phony

Affinity: fondness, liking; similarity

Affront (*n*): personal offense, insult

Agenda: plan, schedule

Aggrandize: to make larger or greater in power

Aggregate (*n*): collective mass or sum; total

Aggrieve: to afflict, distress

Agile: well coordinated, nimble

Agitation: commotion, excitement; uneasiness

Agnostic: one doubting that people can know God

Agrarian: relating to farming or rural matters

Alacrity: cheerful willingness, eagerness; speed

Alchemy: medieval chemical philosophy based on quest to change metal into gold

Algorithm: mechanical problem-solving procedure

Alias: assumed name

Alienated: distanced, estranged

Aligned: precisely adjusted; committed to one side or party

Allay: to lessen, ease, or soothe

Allegory: symbolic representation

Alliteration: repetition of the beginning sounds of words

Allocation: allowance, portion, share

Allure (*v*): to entice by charm; attract

Allusion: indirect reference

Allusiveness: quality of making many indirect references

Altercation: noisy dispute

Altruism: unselfish concern for others' welfare

Amalgam: mixture, combination, alloy

Ambidextrous: able to use both hands equally well

Ambiguous: uncertain; subject to multiple interpretations

Ambivalence: attitude of uncertainty; conflicting emotions

Ambulatory: itinerant; related to walking around

Ameliorate: to make better, improve

Amenable: agreeable, cooperative

Amend: to improve or correct flaws in

Amenity: pleasantness; something increasing comfort

Amiable: friendly, pleasant, likable

Amicable: friendly, agreeable

Amity: friendship

Amoral: unprincipled, unethical

Amorous: strongly attracted to love; showing love

Amorphous: having no definite form

Amortize: to diminish by installment payments

Amphitheater: arena theater with rising tiers around a central open space

Ample: abundant, plentiful

Amplify: to increase, intensify

Amulet: ornament worn as a charm against evil spirits

Anachronism: something chronologically inappropriate

Anachronistic: outdated

Analgesia: a lessening of pain

Analogous: comparable, parallel

Anarchy: absence of government or law; chaos

Anathema: ban, curse; something shunned or disliked

Ancillary: accessory, subordinate, helping

Anecdote: short, usually funny account of an event

Angular: characterized by sharp angles; lean and gaunt

Animation: enthusiasm, excitement

Animosity: hatred, hostility

Annul: to cancel, nullify, declare void, or make legally invalid

Anodyne: something that calms or soothes pain

Anoint: to apply oil to, esp. as a sacred rite

Anomaly: irregularity or deviation from the norm

Anonymity: condition of having no name or an unknown name

Antagonist: foe, opponent, adversary

Antecedent (*adj*): coming before in place or time

Antedate: dated prior to the actual occurrence

Antediluvian: prehistoric, ancient beyond measure

Antepenultimate: third from last

Anterior: preceding, previous, before, prior (to)

Anthology: collection of literary works

Anthropomorphic: attributing human qualities to nonhumans

Antipathy: dislike, hostility; extreme opposition or aversion

Antiquated: outdated, obsolete

Antiquity: ancient times; the quality of being old or ancient

Antithesis: exact opposite or direct contrast

Apace: done quickly

Apathetic: indifferent, unconcerned

Apathy: lack of feeling or emotion

Aperture: an opening or hole

Aphasia: inability to speak or use words

Aphelion: point in a planet's orbit that is farthest from the sun

Aphorism: old saying or short pithy statement

Aplomb: poise, confidence

Apocryphal: not genuine; fictional

Apostate (*n*): one who renounces a religious faith

Apostrophe: speech to the reader or someone not present; a superscript sign (')

Apothegm: a short, instructive saying

Apotheosis: glorification; glorified ideal

Appease: to satisfy, placate, calm, pacify

Append: to attach

Appraise: to evaluate the value of something

Apprehension: the act of comprehending; fear, foreboding

Apprise: to give notice of; inform

Approbation: praise; official approval

Appropriate (*v*): to take possession of

Arable: suitable for cultivation

Arbitrary: depending solely on individual will; inconsistent

Arbitrator: mediator, negotiator

Arboreal: relating to trees; living in trees

Arboretum: place where trees are displayed and studied

Arcane: secret, obscure, known only to a few

Archaic: antiquated, from an earlier time; outdated

Archipelago: large group of islands

Ardent: passionate, enthusiastic, fervent

Ardor: great emotion or passion

Arduous: extremely difficult, laborious

Arraign: to call to court to answer a charge

Arrogate: to demand, claim arrogantly

Arsenal: ammunition storehouse

Articulate (*adj*): well-spoken, expressing oneself clearly

Artifact: historical relic, item made by human craft

Artisan: craftsperson; expert

Artless: open and honest

Ascend: to rise or climb

Ascendancy: state of rising, ascending; power or control

Ascertain: to determine, discover, make certain of

Ascetic (*adj*): self-denying, abstinent, austere

Ascribe: to attribute to, assign

Ashen: resembling ashes; deathly pale

Asinine: lacking intelligence or sound judgment

Askance: scornfully

Askew: crooked, tilted

Asocial: unable or unwilling to interact socially

Asperity: harshness, roughness

Aspersion: false rumor, damaging report, slander

Aspire: to have great hopes; to aim at a goal

Assail: to attack, assault

Assay: to analyze or estimate

Assent (*v*): to express agreement

Assiduous: diligent, persistent, hardworking

Assignation: appointment for lovers' meeting; assignment

Assimilation: act of blending in, becoming similar

Assonance: resemblance in sound, especially in vowel sounds; partial rhyme

Assuage: to make less severe, ease, relieve

Astral: exalted, elevated in position; relating to the stars

Astringent: harsh, severe, stern

Astute: having good judgment

Asunder (*adv*): into different parts

Asymmetrical: not corresponding in size, shape, position, etcetera

Atone: to make amends for a wrong

Atrocious: monstrous, shockingly bad, wicked

Atrophy (*v*): to waste away, wither from disuse

Attenuate: to make thin or slender; weaken

Attest: to testify, stand as proof of, bear witness

Audacious: bold, daring, fearless

Audible: capable of being heard

Audit (*n*): formal examination of financial records

Auditory: having to do with hearing

Augment: to expand, extend

Augury (*adj*): prophecy, prediction of events

August: dignified, awe-inspiring, venerable

Auspicious: having favorable prospects, promising

Austere: stern, strict, unadorned

Authoritarian: extremely strict, bossy

Autocrat: dictator

Autonomous: separate, independent

Auxiliary: supplementary, reserve

Avarice: greed

Avenge: to retaliate, take revenge for an injury or crime

Aver: to declare to be true, affirm

Averse: being disinclined toward something

Aversion: intense dislike

Avert: to turn (something) away; prevent

Aviary: large enclosure housing birds

Avow: to state openly or declare

Awry: crooked, askew, amiss

Axiom: premise, postulate, self-evident truth

B

Bacchanalian: drunkenly festive

Baleful: harmful, with evil intentions

Balk (*v*): to refuse, shirk; prevent

Ballad: folk song, narrative poem

Balm: soothing, healing influence

Ban (*v*): to forbid, outlaw

Banal: trite and overly common

Bane: something causing ruin, death, or destruction

Banter: playful conversation

Base: being of low value or position

Bastion: fortification, stronghold

Bay (*v*): to bark, especially in a deep, prolonged way

Beatific: appearing to be saintly, angelic

Becalm: to make calm or still; keep motionless by lack of wind

Becloud: to confuse; darken with clouds

Beguile: to deceive, mislead; charm

Behemoth: huge creature

Belabor: to insist repeatedly or harp on

Beleaguer: to harass, plague

Belfry: bell tower, room in which a bell is hung

Belie: to misrepresent; expose as false

Belittle: to represent as unimportant, make light of

Bellicose: warlike, aggressive

Belligerent: hostile, tending to fight

Bellow: to roar, shout

Bemuse: to confuse, stupefy; plunge deep into thought

Benchmark: standard of measure

Benefactor: someone giving aid or money

Beneficent: kindly, charitable; doing good deeds; producing good effects

Benighted: unenlightened

Benign: kindly, gentle or harmless

Benison: blessing

Bent: a natural inclination toward something

Bequeath: to give or leave through a will; to hand down

Bereaved: suffering the death of a loved one

Beseech: to beg, plead, implore

Besmear: to smear

Bespatter: to spatter

Bestial: beastly, animal-like

Bestow: to give as a gift

Betoken: to indicate, signify, give evidence of

Bevy: group

Bias: prejudice, slant

Bibliophile: book lover

Bicker: to have a petty argument

Bifurcate: divide into two parts

Bilateral: two-sided

Bilious: bad-natured

Bilk: to cheat, defraud

Billet: board and lodging for troops

Biped: two-footed animal

Bisect: to cut into two (usually equal) parts

Blanch: to pale; take the color out of

Blandish: to coax with flattery

Blasphemous: cursing, profane, irreverent

Blatant: glaring, obvious, showy

Blight (*v*): to afflict, destroy

Blithe: joyful, cheerful, or without appropriate thought

Bludgeon: to hit as with a short heavy club

Bluster: to boast or make threats loudly

Boisterous: rowdy, loud, unrestrained

Bolster: to support; reinforce

Bombastic: using high-sounding but meaningless language

Bonanza: extremely large amount; something profitable

Bonhomie: good-natured geniality; atmosphere of good cheer

Boon: blessing, something to be thankful for

Boor: crude person, one lacking manners or taste

Botanist: scientist who studies plants

Bountiful: plentiful

Bouquet: a bunch of cut flowers

Bourgeois: middle-class

Bovine: relating to cows

Brazen: bold, shameless, impudent; of or like brass

Breach: act of breaking, violation

Brevity: the quality of being brief in time

Brigand: bandit, outlaw

Broach: to mention or suggest for the first time

Bromide: a dull, commonplace person or idea

Brusque: rough and abrupt in manner

Buffet (*v*): to strike, hit

Buffoon: clown or fool

Bulwark: defense wall; anything serving as defense

Burgeon: to sprout or flourish

Burly: brawny, husky

Burnish: to polish, make smooth and bright

Bursar: treasurer

Bustle: commotion, energetic activity

Butt: person or thing that is object of ridicule

Buttress (*v*): to reinforce or support

Byway: back road

C

Cabal: a secret group seeking to overturn something

Cacophonous: jarring, unpleasantly noisy

Cadaver: dead body

Cadence: rhythmic flow of poetry; marching beat

Cajole: to flatter, coax, persuade

Calamitous: disastrous, catastrophic

Callous: thick-skinned, insensitive

Callow: immature, lacking sophistication

Calumny: false and malicious accusation, misrepresentation, slander

Canard: a lie

Candid: frank or fair

Candor: honesty of expression

Canny: smart; founded on common sense

Canonize: to declare a person a saint; raise to highest honors

Canvass: to examine thoroughly; conduct a poll

Capacious: large, roomy; extensive

Capitulate: to submit completely, surrender

Capricious: impulsive, whimsical, without much thought

Careen: to lean to one side

Carnal: of the flesh

Carom: to strike and rebound

Carp (*v*): to find fault, complain constantly

Cartography: science or art of making maps

Cast (*n*): copy, replica

Cast (*v*): to fling, to throw

Castigate: to punish, chastise, criticize severely

Cataclysmic: disastrous

Categorical: absolute, without exception

Catharsis: purification, cleansing

Catholic: universal; broad and comprehensive

Caucus: smaller group within an organization; a meeting of such a group

Caulk: to make watertight

Causality: cause-and-effect relationship

Caustic: biting, sarcastic; able to burn

Cavalcade: a procession

Cavalier(*adj*): carefree, happy; with lordly disdain

Cavil: to raise trivial objections

Cavort: to frolic, frisk

Cede: to surrender possession of something

Celerity: rapidity of motion or action

Censorious: severely critical

Censure: to criticize or find fault with

Centripetal: directed or moving toward the center

Certitude: assurance, certainty

Cessation: temporary or complete halt

Cession: act of surrendering something

Chagrin: shame, embarrassment, humiliation

Chalice: goblet, cup

Champ (*v*): chew noisily

Champion (*v*): to defend or support

Chaotic: extremely disorderly

Charlatan: quack, fake

Chary: watchful, cautious, extremely shy

Chastise: to punish, discipline, scold

Chattel: piece of personal property

Chauvinist: someone prejudiced in the belief of their kind's superiority

Cheeky: lacking prudence or discretion

Cherubic: sweet, innocent, resembling a cherub angel

Chicanery: trickery, fraud, deception

Chide: to scold, express disapproval

Chimerical: fanciful, imaginary, visionary; impossible

Choice (*adj*): specially selected, preferred

Choleric: easily angered, short-tempered

Chortle: to chuckle

Chromatic: relating to color

Chronicler: one who keeps records of historical events

Churlish: rude

Circuitous: roundabout

Circumlocution: roundabout, lengthy way of saying something

Circumnavigate: to sail completely around

Circumscribe: to encircle; set limits on, confine

Circumspect: cautious, wary

Circumvent: to go around; avoid

Cistern: tank for rainwater

Citadel: fortress or stronghold

Civil: polite; relating to citizens

Civility: courtesy, politeness

Clairvoyant (*adj*): having ESP, psychic

Clamor (*n*): noisy outcry

Clamor (*v*): to make a noisy outcry

Clandestine: secretive, concealed for a darker purpose

Clarity: clearness; clear understanding

Cleave: to split or separate; to stick, cling, adhere

Clemency: merciful leniency

Clement: mild

Cloister (*v*): to confine, seclude

Cloying: indulging to excess

Coagulate: to clot or change from a liquid to a solid

Coalesce: to grow together or cause to unite as one

Coddle: to baby, treat indulgently

Coerce: to compel by force or intimidation

Coffer: strongbox, large chest for money

Cogent: logically forceful, compelling, convincing

Cognate: related, similar, akin

Cognition: mental process by which knowledge is acquired

Cognomen: family name; any name, especially a nickname

Cohabit: to live together

Coherent: intelligible, lucid, understandable

Collate: to arrange in an order

Collateral: accompanying

Collected: acting calm and composed

Colloquial: characteristic of informal speech

Colloquy: dialogue or conversation, conference

Collusion: collaboration, complicity, conspiracy

Comeliness: physical grace and beauty

Commend: to compliment, praise

Commensurate: proportional

Commission: fee payable to an agent; authorization

Commodious: roomy, spacious

Communicable: transmittable

Commute: to change a penalty to a less severe one

Compatriot: fellow countryman

Compendious: summarizing completely and briefly

Compensate: to repay or reimburse

Complacent: self-satisfied, smug, affable

Complaisant: agreeable, friendly

Complement: to complete, perfect

Compliant: submissive and yielding

Complicity: knowing partnership in wrongdoing

Composed: acting calm

Composure: a calm manner or appearance

Compound (*adj*): complex; composed of several parts

Compound (*v*): to combine, add to

Compress (*v*): to reduce, squeeze

Compulsive: obsessive, fanatic

Compunctious: feeling guilty or having misgivings

Compunction: feeling of uneasiness caused by guilt or regret

Concatenate: linked together

Concave: curving inward

Concede: to yield, admit

Conceptualize: to envision, imagine

Concerto: musical composition for orchestra and soloist(s)

Conciliatory: overcoming distrust or hostility

Concomitant: accompanying something

Concord: agreement

Concur: to agree

Condone: to pardon or forgive; overlook, justify, or excuse a fault

Conduit: tube, pipe, or similar passage

Confection: something sweet to eat

Confiscate: to appropriate, seize

Conflagration: big, destructive fire

Confluence: meeting place; meeting of two streams

Confound: to baffle, perplex

Congeal: to become thick or solid, as a liquid freezing

Congenial: similar in tastes and habits

Congenital: existing since birth

Conglomerate: collected group of varied things

Congress: formal meeting or assembly

Congruity: correspondence, harmony, agreement

Conjecture: speculation, prediction

Conjugal: pertaining to marriage

Conjure: to evoke a spirit, cast a spell

Connive: to conspire, scheme

Connoisseur: a person with refined taste

Consanguineous: of the same origin; related by blood

Conscientious: governed by conscience; careful and thorough

Consecrate: to declare sacred; dedicate to a goal

Consensus: unanimity, agreement of opinion or attitude

Consequential: important

Consign: to commit, entrust

Consistent: containing no contradictions, being harmonious

Consolation: something providing comfort or solace for a loss or hardship

Consolidate: to combine, incorporate

Consonant (*adj*): consistent with, in agreement with

Constituent: component, part; citizen, voter

Constrained: forced, compelled; confined, restrained

Constraint: something that forces or compels; something that restrains or confines

Constrict: to inhibit

Construe: to explain or interpret

Consummate (*adj*): accomplished, complete, perfect

Consummate (*v*): to complete, fulfill

Contend: to battle, clash; compete

Contentious: quarrelsome, disagreeable, belligerent

Continence: self-control, self-restraint

Contravene: to contradict, deny, act contrary to

Contrite: deeply sorrowful and repentant for a wrong

Contumacious: rebellious

Contusion: bruise

Conundrum: riddle, puzzle or problem with no solution

Convalescence: gradual recovery after an illness

Convene: to meet, come together, assemble

Conventional: typical, customary, commonplace

Convex: curved outward

Convivial: sociable; fond of eating, drinking, and people

Convoke: to call together, summon

Convoluted: twisted, complicated, involved

Copious: abundant, plentiful

Coquette: woman who flirts

Cornucopia: abundance

Corporeal: having to do with the body; tangible, material

Corpulence: obesity, fatness, bulkiness

Correlation: association, mutual relation of two or more things

Corroborate: to confirm, verify

Corrode: to weaken or destroy

Corrugate: to mold in a shape with parallel grooves and ridges

Cosmetic (*adj*): relating to beauty; affecting the surface of something

Cosmography: science that deals with the nature of the universe

Cosmopolitan: sophisticated, free from local prejudices

Cosset: to pamper, treat with great care

Coterie: group of people with a common interest or purpose

Countenance (*n*): facial expression; look of approval or support

Countenance (*v*): to favor, support

Countermand: to annul, cancel, make a contrary order

Countervail: to counteract, to exert force against

Coven: group of witches

Covert: hidden; secret

Covet: to strongly desire something possessed by another

Cower: to cringe in fear

Crass: crude, unrefined

Craven: cowardly

Credence: acceptance of something as true or real

Credible: plausible, believable

Credulous: gullible, trusting

Creed: statement of belief or principle

Crescendo: gradual increase in volume of sound

Criterion: standard for judging, rule for testing

Cryptic: puzzling

Cuisine: characteristic style of cooking

Culmination: climax, final stage

Culpable: guilty, responsible for wrong

Culprit: guilty person

Cumulative: resulting from gradual increase

Cupidity: greed

Curator: caretaker and overseer of an exhibition, esp. in a museum

Curmudgeon: cranky person

Cursory: hastily done, superficial

Curt: abrupt, blunt

Curtail: to shorten

Cutlery: cutting instruments; tableware

Cygnet: young swan

Cynic: person who distrusts the motives of others

D

Dally: to act playfully or waste time

Daunt: to discourage, intimidate

Dearth: lack, scarcity, insufficiency

Debase: to degrade or lower in quality or stature

Debauch: to corrupt, seduce from virtue or duty; indulge

Debilitate: to weaken, enfeeble

Debunk: to discredit, disprove

Debutante: young woman making debut in high society

Decadence: decline or decay, deterioration

Decamp: to leave suddenly

Decapitate: to behead

Decathlon: athletic contest with ten events

Deciduous: losing leaves in the fall; short-lived, temporary

Declivity: downward slope

Decorous: proper, tasteful, socially correct

Decorum: proper behavior, etiquette

Decry: to belittle, openly condemn

Defamatory: slanderous, injurious to the reputation

Defame: to disgrace or slander

Defer: to submit or yield

Deference: respect, honor

Deferential: respectful and polite in a submissive way

Deficient: defective, not meeting a normal standard

Defile: to make unclean or dishonor

Definitive: clear-cut, explicit or decisive

Deflation: decrease, depreciation

Deform: to disfigure, distort

Deft: skillful, dexterous

Defunct: no longer existing, dead, extinct

Delectable: appetizing, delicious

Delegate (*v*): to give powers to another

Deleterious: harmful, destructive, detrimental

Delineation: depiction, representation

Delta: tidal deposit at the mouth of a river

Deluge (*n*): flood

Deluge (*v*): to submerge, overwhelm

Demagogue: leader or rabble-rouser who usually uses appeals to emotion or prejudice

Demarcation: borderline; act of defining or marking a boundary or distinction

Demean: to degrade, humiliate, humble

Demise: death

Demote: to reduce to a lower grade or rank

Demotion: lowering in rank or grade

Demur: to express doubts or objections

Denigrate: to slur or blacken someone's reputation

Denounce: to accuse, blame

Denunciation: public condemnation

Deplete: to use up, exhaust

Deplore: to express or feel disapproval of; regret strongly

Deploy: to spread out strategically over an area

Depose: to remove from a high position, as from a throne

Depravity: sinfulness, moral corruption

Deprecate: to belittle, disparage

Depreciate: to lose value gradually

Deride: to mock, ridicule, make fun of

Derisive: expressing ridicule or scorn

Derivative: copied or adapted; not original

Derive: to originate; take from a certain source

Derogate: to belittle, disparage

Descry: to discover or reveal

Desecrate: to abuse something sacred

Desiccate: to dry completely, dehydrate

Desist: to stop doing something

Despondent: feeling discouraged and dejected

Despot: tyrannical ruler

Destitute: very poor, poverty-stricken

Desultory: at random, rambling, unmethodical

Detached: separate, unconnected

Determinate: having defined limits; conclusive

Detestation: extreme hatred

Detractor: one who takes something away

Detrimental: causing harm or injury

Deviate: to stray, wander

Deviation: departure, exception, anomaly

Devoid: totally lacking

Devout: deeply religious

Dexterous: skilled physically or mentally

Diabolical: fiendish; wicked

Dialect: regional style of speaking

Diaphanous: allowing light to show through; delicate

Diatribe: bitter verbal attack

Dichotomy: division into two parts

Dictum: authoritative statement; popular saying

Didactic: excessively instructive

Differentiate: to distinguish between two items

Diffidence: shyness, lack of confidence

Diffract: to cause to separate into parts, esp. light

Diffuse: widely spread out

Dilapidated: in disrepair, run-down, neglected

Dilate: to enlarge, swell, extend

Dilatory: slow, tending to delay

Dilettante: an amateur

Diluvial: relating to a flood

Diminutive: small

Diplomacy: discretion, tact

Dirge: funeral hymn

Disabuse: to free from a misconception

Disaffected: discontented and disloyal

Disarray: clutter, disorder

Disband: to break up

Disbar: to expel from legal profession

Disburse: to pay out

Discern: to perceive something obscure

Disclaim: to deny, disavow

Disclose: to confess, divulge

Discomfit: to cause perplexity and embarrassment

Discompose: to disturb the composure or serenity

Disconcerting: bewildering, perplexing, slightly disturbing

Disconsolate: unable to be consoled; extremely sad

Discordant: harsh-sounding, badly out of tune

Discredit: to dishonor or disgrace

Discredited: disbelieved, discounted; disgraced, dishonored

Discrepancy: difference between

Discrete: distinct, separate

Discretionary: subject to one's own judgment

Discursive: wandering from topic to topic

Disdain: to regard with scorn and contempt

Disengaged: disconnected, disassociated

Disgorge: to vomit, discharge violently

Disheveled: untidy, disarranged, unkempt

Disinclined: averse, unwilling, lacking desire

Disingenuous: sly and crafty

Disinterest: lack of interest or a disadvantage

Disjointed: lacking coherence or order, being separated

Disparage: to belittle, speak disrespectfully about

Disparate: dissimilar, different in kind

Disparity: contrast, dissimilarity

Dispassionate: free from emotion; impartial, unbiased

Dispel: to drive out or scatter

Dispense: to distribute, administer

Dispense with: to suspend the operation of, do without

Disperse: to break up, scatter

Dispirit: to dishearten, make dejected

Dispute: to debate, to quarrel

Disquieted: feeling anxiety, being disturbed, lacking peace

Disregard: to neglect, pay no attention to

Disrepute: disgrace, dishonor

Dissemble: to pretend, disguise one's motives

Disseminate: to spread far and wide

Dissension: difference of opinion

Dissimulate: to disguise or put on a false appearance

Dissipate: to scatter; to pursue pleasure to excess

Dissociate: to separate; remove from an association

Dissonant: harsh and unpleasant sounding

Dissuade: to persuade someone to alter original intentions

Distaff: the female branch of a family

Distend: to swell, inflate, bloat

Distraught: very worried and distressed

Distrust (*n*): disbelief and suspicion

Dither (*v*): to move or act confusedly or without clear purpose

Diurnal: daily

Diverge: to move in different directions, to deviate from a source

Divest: to get rid of

Divine (*v*): to foretell or know by inspiration

Divisive: creating disunity or conflict

Docile: tame, willing to be taught

Doctrinaire: rigidly devoted to theories

Dogged (*adj*): persistent, stubborn

Dogmatic: rigidly fixed in opinion, opinionated

Doldrums: a period of despondency

Doleful: sad, mournful

Dolor: sadness

Dolt: idiot, dimwit, foolish person

Domineer: to rule over something in a tyrannical way

Dormant: at rest, inactive, in suspended animation

Dotage: senile condition, mental decline

Dotard: senile old person

Doting: excessively fond, loving to excess

Doughty: courageous

Dour: sullen and gloomy; stern and severe

Dowry: money or property given by a bride to her husband

Draft (*v*): to plan, outline; to recruit, conscript

Draw: to attract, to pull toward

Drivel: stupid talk; slobber

Droll: amusing in a wry, subtle way

Dross: waste produced during metal smelting; garbage

Dudgeon: angry indignation

Dulcet: pleasant sounding, soothing to the ear

Dumb: unable to speak

Dupe (*n*): fool, pawn

Dupe (*v*): to deceive, trick

Duplicity: deception, dishonesty, double-dealing

Durability: strength, sturdiness

Duress: threat of force or intimidation; imprisonment

Dwindle: to shrink or decrease

Dyspeptic: suffering from indigestion; gloomy and irritable

E

Earthy: crude

Ebb (*v*): to fade away, recede

Ebullient: exhilarated, full of enthusiasm and high spirits

Eclectic: selecting from various sources

Ecstatic: joyful

Eddy: air or wind current

Edict: law, command, official public order

Edifice: building

Edify: to instruct morally and spiritually

Editorialize: to express an opinion on an issue

Efface: to erase or make illegible

Effervescent: bubbly, lively

Efficacious: effective, efficient

Effigy: stuffed doll; likeness of a person

Effluvia: outpouring of gases or vapors

Effrontery: impudent boldness; audacity

Effulgent: brilliantly shining

Effusive: expressing emotion without restraint

Egregious: conspicuously bad

Egress: exit

Elation: exhilaration, joy

Elegy: mournful poem, usually about the dead

Elevated: high in status, exalted

Elicit: to draw out, provoke

Eloquence: fluent and effective speech

Elucidate: to explain, clarify

Emaciated: skinny, scrawny, gaunt, esp. from hunger

Emancipate: to set free, liberate

Embellish: to ornament, make attractive with decoration or details; add details to a
            statement

Embezzle: to steal money in violation of a trust

Embroil: to involve in; cause to fall into disorder

Emend: to correct a text

Eminent: celebrated, distinguished; outstanding, towering

Emollient: having soothing qualities, esp. for skin

Emotive: appealing to or expressing emotion

Empathy: identification with another's feelings

Emulate: to copy, imitate

Enchant: to charm or attract

Encipher: to translate a message into code

Encomium: warm praise

Encumber: to hinder, burden, restrict motion

Endemic: belonging to a particular area, inherent

Endogamous: marrying within a specific group due to law or custom

Enervate: to weaken, sap strength from

Engender: to produce, cause, bring about

Enigmatic: puzzling, inexplicable

Enjoin: to urge, order, command; forbid or prohibit, as by judicial order

Enmity: hostility, antagonism, ill-will

Ennui: boredom, lack of interest and energy

Enormity: state of being gigantic or terrible

Ensconce: to settle comfortably into a place

Enshroud: to cover, enclose with a dark cover

Entail: to involve as a necessary result, necessitate

Enthrall: to captivate, enchant, enslave

Entice: to lure or tempt

Entity: something with its own existence or form

Entomologist: scientist who studies insects

Entreat: to plead, beg

Entrenched: established solidly

Enumerate: to count, list, itemize

Enunciate: to pronounce clearly

Eon: indefinitely long period of time

Ephemeral: momentary, transient, fleeting

Epicure: person with refined taste in food and wine

Epigram: short, witty saying or poem

Epigraph: quotation at the beginning of a literary work

Epilogue: concluding section of a literary work

Epithet: an abusive word or phrase

Epitome: representative of an entire group; summary

Epochal: very significant or influential; defining an epoch or time period

Equanimity: calmness, composure

Equestrian (*n*): one who rides on horseback

Equine: relating to horses

Equitable: fair

Equity: justice, fairness

Equivocal: ambiguous, open to two interpretations

Equivocate: to use vague or ambiguous language intentionally

Eradicate: to erase or wipe out

Errant: straying, mistaken, roving

Erratic: wandering and unpredictable

Erroneous: in error; mistaken

Ersatz: fake

Erudite: learned, scholarly

Eschew: to abstain from, avoid

Esoteric: understood only by a learned few

Espouse: to support or advocate; to marry

Estimable: admirable

Esurient: hungry, greedy

Ethereal: not earthly, spiritual, delicate

Ethos: beliefs or character of a group

Etymology: origin and history of a word; study of words

Eulogy: high praise, often in a public speech

Euphemism: use of an inoffensive word or phrase in place of a more distasteful one

Euphony: pleasant, harmonious sound

Euphoria: feeling of well-being or happiness

Eurythmics: art of harmonious bodily movement

Euthanasia: mercy killing; intentional, easy and painless death

Evade: to avoid, dodge

Evanescent: momentary, transitory, short-lived

Evince: to show clearly, display, signify

Evoke: to inspire memories; to produce a reaction

Exacerbate: to aggravate, intensify the bad qualities of

Exalt: to glorify, to elevate

Excommunicate: to bar from membership in the church

Excoriate: to denounce

Exculpate: to clear of blame or fault

Execrable: utterly detestable

Exemplary: serving as an example, commendable

Exhort: to urge or incite by strong appeals

Exhume: to remove from a grave; uncover a secret

Exigent: urgent; excessively demanding

Exonerate: to clear of blame

Exorbitant: extravagant, greater than reasonable

Exorcise: to expel evil spirits

Expansive: sweeping, comprehensive; tending to expand

Expatiate: to wander; to discuss or describe at length

Expatriate (*n*): one who lives outside one's native land

Expatriate (*v*): to drive someone from his/her native land

Expedient (*adj*): convenient, efficient, practical

Expiate: to atone for, make amends for

Explicable: capable of being explained

Explicit: clearly defined, specific; forthright in expression

Exponent: one who champions or advocates

Expound: to elaborate; to expand or increase

Expunge: to erase, eliminate completely

Expurgate: to censor

Extemporaneous: unrehearsed, on the spur of the moment

Extenuate: to lessen the seriousness, strength, or effect of

Extol: to praise

Extort: to obtain something by threats

Extraneous: irrelevant, unrelated, unnecessary

Extrapolate: to estimate

Extremity: outermost or farthest point

Extricate: to free from, disentangle, free

Extrinsic: not inherent or essential, coming from without

Extrovert: an outgoing person

Exuberant: lively, happy, and full of good spirits

Exude: to give off, ooze

Exult: to rejoice

F

Fabricate: to make or devise; construct

Fabricated: constructed, invented; faked, falsified

Facade: face, front; mask, superficial appearance

Facetious: witty in an inappropriate way

Facile: very easy

Facilitate: to aid, assist

Facility: aptitude, ease in doing something

Facsimile: an exact copy

Fallacious: wrong, unsound, illogical

Fallible: capable of failing

Fallow: uncultivated, unused

Fanaticism: extreme devotion to a cause

Farcical: absurd, ludicrous

Fastidious: careful with details

Fathom (*v*): to measure the depth of, gauge; to understand

Fatuous: stupid; foolishly self-satisfied

Fault: break in a rock formation; mistake or error

Fawn (*v*): to flatter excessively, seek the favor of

Faze: to bother, upset, or disconcert

Fealty: intense loyalty

Feasible: possible, capable of being done

Feckless: ineffective, careless, irresponsible

Fecund: fertile, fruitful, productive

Federation: union of organizations; union of several states, each of which retains local power

Feign: to pretend, give a false impression; to invent falsely

Feisty: excitable, easily drawn into quarrels

Felicitous: suitable, appropriate; well-spoken

Felicity: feeling great happiness

Fell (*v*): to chop, cut down

Fell: cruel

Fervid: passionate, intense zealous

Fetid: foul-smelling, putrid

Fetter: to bind, chain, confine

Fey: otherworldly; doomed

Fickle: unreliable

Fictive: fictional, imaginary

Fidelity: loyalty

Fiendish: excessively bad or cruel

Filch: to steal

Filial: appropriate for a child

Filibuster: use of obstructive tactics in a legislative assembly to prevent adoption of a measure

Finesse: refinement or skill at a task or in a situation

Finicky: fussy, difficult to please

Fission: process of splitting into two parts

Fissure: a crack or break

Fitful: intermittent, irregular

Fixity: being fixed or stable

Flaccid: limp, flabby, weak

Flag: to loose energy and strength

Flagrant: outrageous, shameless

Flamboyant: flashy, garish; exciting, dazzling

Flammable: combustible, being easily burned

Fledgling: young bird just learning to fly; beginner, novice

Flippant: disrespectful, casual

Flora: plants

Florid: gaudy, extremely ornate; ruddy, flushed

Flounder: to falter, waver; to muddle, struggle

Flout: to treat contemptuously, scorn

Fluctuate: to alternate, waver

Flurried: to become agitated and confused

Fluster: to agitate or confuse

Fodder: raw material; feed for animals

Foible: minor weakness or character flaw

Foil (v): to defeat, frustrate

Foist: to pass off as genuine

Foliate: to grow, sprout leaves

Foment: to arouse or incite

Forage: to wander in search of food

Forbearance: patience, restraint, leniency

Ford (v): to cross a body of water at a shallow place

Foreboding: dark sense of evil to come

Foreclose: to rule out; to seize debtor's property for lack of payments

Forensic: relating to legal proceedings; relating to debates

Forensics: study of argumentation and debate

Forestall: to prevent, delay; anticipate

Forethought: anticipation, foresight

Forfend: to prevent

Forgo: to go without, refrain from

Formulate: to conceive, devise; to draft, plan; to express, state

Forsake: to abandon, withdraw from

Forswear: to repudiate, renounce, disclaim, reject

Forte (n): strong point, something a person does well

Fortnight: two weeks

Fortuitous: happening by luck, fortunate

Foster (v): to nourish, cultivate, promote

Foundation: groundwork, support; institution established by donation to aid a certain cause

Founder (v) to fall helplessly; sink

Fracas: noisy dispute

Fractious: unruly, rebellious

Fragmentation: division, separation into parts, disorganization

Fratricide: the killing of a brother or sister

Fraudulent: deceitful, dishonest, unethical

Fraught: full of, accompanied by

Frenetic: wildly frantic, frenzied, hectic

Frenzied: feverishly fast, hectic, and confused

Frivolous: petty, trivial; flippant, silly

Frugal: thrifty; cheap

Fulminate: to explode with anger

Fulsome: excessive, overdone, sickeningly abundant

Funereal: mournful, appropriate to a funeral

Furor: rage, fury

Furtive: secret, stealthy

Fusion: process of merging things into one

G

Gainsay: to deny

Gall (*n*): bitterness; careless nerve

Gall (*v*): to exasperate and irritate

Gallant: a very fashionable young man

Gambol: to dance or skip around playfully

Game (*adj*): courageous

Gargantuan: giant, tremendous

Garner: to gather and store

Garrulous: very talkative

Gauche: crude, socially awkward

Gaucherie: a tactless or awkward act

Gaunt: thin and bony

Gavel: mallet used for commanding attention

Genre: type, class, category

Genteel: stylish, elegant in manner or appearance

Geriatric: relating to old age or the process of aging

Germinate: to begin to grow (as in a seed or idea)

Gestation: growth process from conception to birth

Gibe (*v*): to make heckling, taunting remarks

Girth: distance around something

Glib: fluent in an insincere manner; offhand, casual

Glower: to glare, stare angrily and intensely

Gluttony: eating and drinking to excess

Gnostic: having to do with knowledge

Goad: to prod or urge

Gossamer: something light, delicate, or tenuous

Gouge: scoop out; extort

Gradation: process occurring by regular degrees or stages; variation in color

Grandiloquence: pompous talk, fancy but meaningless language

Grandiose: magnificent and imposing; exaggerated and pretentious

Granular: having a grainy texture

Grasp (*v*): to perceive and understand; to hold securely

Gratis: free, costing nothing

Gratuitous: free, voluntary; unnecessary and unjustified

Gratuity: something given voluntarily, tip

Gregarious: outgoing, sociable

Grievous: causing grief or sorrow; serious and distressing

Grimace: facial expression showing pain or disgust

Grimy: dirty, filthy

Gross (*adj*): obscene; blatant, flagrant

Gross (*n*): total before deductions

Grovel: to humble oneself in a demeaning way

Grubby: dirty, sloppy

Guile: trickery, deception

Gullible: easily deceived

Gustatory: relating to sense of taste

Gyrate: to move in a circular motion

H

Habitat: dwelling place

Hackneyed: worn out by over-use

Hail: to greet with praise

Hallow: to make holy; treat as sacred

Hamlet: small village

Hapless: unfortunate, having bad luck

Harangue: a pompous speech

Harbinger: precursor, sign of something to come

Hardy: robust, vigorous

Harmony: accord, tranquility, agreement

Harrowing: extremely distressing, terrifying

Hasten: to hurry, to speed up

Haughty: arrogant and condescending

Headlong: recklessly

Heathen: pagan; uncivilized and irreligious

Hectic: hasty, hurried, confused

Hector: a bully, braggart

Hedonism: pursuit of pleasure as a goal

Hegemony: leadership, domination, usually by a country

Heinous: shocking, wicked, terrible

Hemicycle: semicircular form or structure

Heretical: opposed to an established religious orthodoxy

Hermetic: tightly sealed

Heterodox: unorthodox, not widely accepted

Heterogeneous: composed of unlike parts, different, diverse

Hew: to cut with an ax

Hiatus: a gap or a break

Hidebound: excessively rigid; dry and stiff

Hinder: to hamper

Hindsight: perception of events after they happen

Hinterland: wilderness

Hoary: very old; whitish or gray from age

Holistic: emphasizing importance of the whole and interdependence of its parts

Holocaust: widespread destruction, usually by fire

Homage: public honor and respect

Homogenous: composed of identical parts

Homonym: word identical in pronunciation but different in meaning

Hone: to sharpen

Honor (*v*): to praise, glorify, pay tribute to

Humane: merciful, kindly

Husband (*v*): to farm; manage carefully and thriftily

Hutch: pen or coop for animals; shack, shanty

Hydrate: to add water to

Hyperbole: purposeful exaggeration for effect

Hyperventilate: to breathe abnormally fast

Hypochondria: unfounded belief that one is often ill

Hypocrite: person claiming beliefs or virtues he or she doesn't really possess

Hypothermia: abnormally low body temperature

Hypothesis: assumption subject to proof

Hypothetical: theoretical, speculative

I

Iconoclast: one who attacks traditional beliefs

Idealism: pursuit of noble goals

Idiosyncrasy: peculiarity of temperament, eccentricity

Ignoble: dishonorable, not noble in character

Ignominious: disgraceful and dishonorable

Ignoramus: an ignorant person

Ilk: type or kind

Illicit: illegal, improper

Illimitable: limitless

Illusory: unreal, deceptive

Illustrious: famous, renowned

Imbue: to infuse; dye, wet, moisten

Immaculate: spotless; free from error

Immaterial: extraneous, inconsequential, nonessential; not consisting of matter

Immense: enormous, huge

Immerse: to bathe, dip; to engross, preoccupy

Immobile: not moveable; still

Immunological: relating to immune system

Immure: to imprison

Immutable: unchangeable, invariable

Impair: to damage, injure

Impasse: blocked path, dilemma with no solution

Impassioned: with passion

Impassive: showing no emotion

Impeach: to charge with misdeeds in public office; accuse

Impeccable: flawless, without fault

Impecunious: poor, having no money

Impediment: barrier, obstacle; speech disorder

Imperative: essential; mandatory

Imperious: arrogantly self-assured, domineering, overbearing

Impertinent: rude

Imperturbable: not capable of being disturbed

Impervious: impossible to penetrate; incapable of being affected

Impetuous: quick to act without thinking

Impious: not devout in religion

Implacable: inflexible, incapable of being pleased

Implant: to set securely or deeply; to instill

Implausible: improbable, inconceivable

Implicate: to involve in a crime, incriminate

Implicit: implied, not directly expressed

Impolitic: unwise

Importune: to ask repeatedly, beg

Impose: to inflict, force upon

Imposing: dignified, grand

Impotent: powerless, ineffective, lacking strength

Impound: to seize and confine

Impoverish: to make poor or bankrupt

Imprecation: curse

Impregnable: totally safe from attack, able to resist defeat

Impressionable: easily influenced or affected

Impromptu: spontaneous, without rehearsal

Improvident: without planning or foresight, negligent

Imprudent: unwise

Impudent: arrogant and rude

Impugn: to call into question, attack verbally

Inane: foolish, silly, lacking significance

Incandescent: shining brightly

Incarnadine: blood-red in color

Incarnate: having bodily form

Incendiary: combustible, flammable, burning easily

Incense (*v*): to infuriate, enrage

Inception: beginning

Incessant: continuous, never ceasing

Inchoate: just begun; disorganized

Incipient: beginning to exist or appear; in an initial stage

Incisive: perceptive, penetrating

Incognito: in disguise, concealing one's identity

Incommunicado: lacking a means to communicate

Incongruous: incompatible, not harmonious

Incontrovertible: unquestionable, beyond dispute

Incorrigible: incapable of being corrected

Incredulous: skeptical, doubtful

Inculcate: to teach, impress in the mind

Inculpate: to blame, charge with a crime

Incumbent (*adj*): holding a specified office, often political; required, obligatory

Incursion: sudden invasion

Indefatigable: never tired

Indefensible: inexcusable, unforgivable

Indelible: permanent, not erasable

Indenture: bound to another by contract

Indicative: showing or pointing out, suggestive of

Indict: to accuse formally, charge with a crime

Indigenous: native, occurring naturally in an area

Indigent: very poor

Indignant: angry, incensed, offended

Indisputable: not disputed, unquestioned

Indolent: habitually lazy, idle

Indomitable: fearless, unconquerable

Indubitable: unquestionable

Induce: to persuade; bring about

Induct: to place ceremoniously in office

Inebriated: drunk, intoxicated

Inept: clumsy, awkward

Inert: unable to move, tending to inactivity

Inestimable: too great to be estimated

Inevitable: certain, unavoidable

Inexorable: inflexible, unyielding

Inextricable: incapable of being disentangled

Infallible: incapable of making a mistake

Infamy: reputation for bad deeds

Infatuated: strongly or foolishly attached to, inspired with foolish passion, overly in love

Infer: to conclude, deduce

Infernal: hellish, diabolical

Infiltrate: to pass secretly into enemy territory

Infinitesimal: extremely tiny

Infirmity: disease, ailment

Infringe: to encroach, trespass; to transgress, violate

Infuriate: to anger, provoke, outrage

Infuriating: provoking anger or outrage

Ingenious: original, clever, inventive

Ingenuous: straightforward, open; naive and unsophisticated

Inglorious: lacking fame or honor, shameful

Ingrained: an innate quality, deep-seated

Ingrate: ungrateful person

Ingratiate: to bring oneself purposely into another's good graces

Ingress: entrance

Inhibit: to hold back, prevent, restrain

Inimical: hostile, unfriendly

Iniquity: sin, evil act

Initiate: to begin, introduce; to enlist, induct

Inject: to force into; to introduce into conversation

Injunction: command, order

Injurious: causing injury

Inkling: hint; vague idea

Innate: natural, inborn

Innateness: state of being natural or inborn

Innocuous: harmless; inoffensive

Innovate: to invent, modernize, revolutionize

Innuendo: indirect and subtle criticism, insinuation

Innumerable: too many to be counted

Inquest: investigation; court or legal proceeding

Insatiable: never satisfied

Inscrutable: impossible to understand fully

Insentient: unfeeling, unconscious

Insidious: sly, treacherous, devious

Insinuate: to suggest, say indirectly, imply

Insipid: bland, lacking flavor; lacking excitement

Insolent: insulting and arrogant

Insoluble: not able to be solved or explained

Insolvent: bankrupt, unable to pay one's debts

Instigate: to incite, urge, agitate

Insubstantial: modest, insignificant

Insufficiency: lacking in something

Insular: isolated, detached

Insuperable: insurmountable, unconquerable

Insurgent (*adj*): rebellious, insubordinate

Insurrection: rebellion

Integral: central, indispensable

Integrity: decency, honest; wholeness

Intemperate: not moderate

Inter: to bury

Interdict: to forbid, prohibit

Interject: to interpose, insert

Interlocutor: someone taking part in a dialogue

Interloper: trespasser; meddler in others' affairs

Interminable: endless

Internecine: deadly to both sides

Interpolate: to insert; change by adding new words or material

Interpose: to insert; to intervene

Interregnum: interval between reigns

Intersect: to divide by passing through or across

Intersperse: to distribute among, mix with

Interstice: a space between things

Intimation: clue, suggestion

Intractable: not easily managed

Intramural: within an institution like a school

Intransigent: uncompromising, refusing to be reconciled

Intrepid: fearless

Intrigued: interested, curious

Intrinsic: inherent, internal

Introspective: contemplating one's own thoughts and feelings

Introvert: someone given to self-analysis

Intuitive: instinctive, untaught

Inundate: to cover with water; overwhelm

Inure: to harden; accustom; become used to

Invective: verbal abuse

Inveigh: protest strongly

Investiture: ceremony conferring authority

Inveterate: confirmed, long-standing, deeply rooted

Invidious: likely to provoke ill will, offensive

Inviolable: safe from violation or assault

Invoke: to call upon, request help

Irascible: easily angered

Iridescent: showing many colors

Irreverent: disrespectful

Irrevocable: conclusive, irreversible

Itinerant: wandering from place to place, unsettled

J

Jaded: tired by excess or overuse; slightly cynical

Jangling: clashing, jarring; harshly unpleasant (in sound)

Jargon: nonsensical talk; specialized language

Jaundice: yellowish discoloration of skin

Jaundiced: affected by jaundice; prejudiced or embittered

Jettison: to cast off, throw cargo overboard

Jibe: to shift suddenly from one side to the other

Jingoism: belligerent support of one's country

Jocular: jovial, playful, humorous

Jubilee: special anniversary

Judicious: sensible, showing good judgment

Juggernaut: huge force destroying everything in its path

Juncture: point where two things are joined

Jurisprudence: philosophy of law

Juxtaposition: side-by-side placement

K

Keen: having a sharp edge; intellectually sharp, perceptive

Kernel: innermost, essential part; seed grain, often in a shell

Keynote: note or tone on which a musical key is founded; main idea of a speech, program, etcetera

Kindle: to set fire to or ignite; excite or inspire

Kinetic: relating to motion; characterized by movement

Kismet: fate

Knell: sound of a funeral bell; omen of death or failure

Kudos: fame, glory, honor

L

Laceration: cut or wound

Lachrymose: tearful

Lackadaisical: idle, lazy; apathetic, indifferent

Lackluster: dull

Laconic: using few words

Laggard: dawdler, loafer, lazy person

Lambaste: disapprove angrily

Lament (v): to deplore, grieve

Lampoon (v): to attack with satire, mock harshly

Languid: lacking energy, indifferent, slow

Languor: listlessness

Lap (v): to drink using the tongue; to wash against

Lapidary: relating to precious stones

Larceny: theft of property

Larder: place where food is stored

Largess: generosity; gift

Larynx: organ containing vocal cords

Lascivious: lewd, lustful

Lassitude: lethargy, sluggishness

Latent: present but hidden; potential

Latitude: freedom of action or choice

Laudable: deserving of praise

Lavish: to give plentiful amounts of

Laxity: carelessness

Legerdemain: trickery

Legible: readable

Legislate: to decree, mandate, make laws

Lenient: easygoing, permissive

Lethargy: indifferent inactivity

Levitate: to rise in the air or cause to rise

Levity: humor, frivolity, gaiety

Lexicon: dictionary, list of words

Liberal (*adj*): tolerant, broad-minded; generous, lavish

Liberation: freedom, emancipation

Libertarian: one who believes in unrestricted freedom

Libertine: one without moral restraint

Libidinous: lustful

License: freedom to act

Licentious: immoral; unrestrained by society

Lien: right to possess and sell the property of a debtor

Limpid: clear and simple; serene; transparent

Lineage: ancestry

Liniment: medicinal liquid used externally to ease pain

Lionize: to treat as a celebrity

Lissome: easily flexed, limber, agile

Listless: lacking energy and enthusiasm

Literal: word for word; upholding the exact meaning of word

Literate: able to read and write; well-read and educated

Lithe: moving and bending with ease; graceful

Litigation: lawsuit

Livid: discolored from a bruise; reddened with anger

Loathe: to abhor, despise, hate

Locomotion: movement from place to place

Lodged: fixed in one position

Lofty: noble, elevated in position

Logo: corporate symbol

Loiter: to stand around idly

Loquacious: talkative

Low (*v*): to make a sound like a cow, moo

Lucid: clear and easily understood

Ludicrous: laughable, ridiculous

Lugubrious: sorrowful, mournful

Lull: to soothe

Lumber (*v*): to move slowly and awkwardly

Luminary: bright object; celebrity; source of inspiration

Luminous: bright, brilliant, glowing

Lunar: relating to the moon

Lurid: harshly shocking, sensational; glowing

Luxuriance: elegance, lavishness

Lyrical: suitable for poetry and song; expressing feeling

M

Macabre: gruesome, producing horror

Machination: plot or scheme

Macrobiotics: art of prolonging life by special diet of organic, nonmeat substances

Macrocosm: system regarded as an entity with subsystems

Maelstrom: whirlpool; turmoil; agitated state of mind

Magnanimous: generous, noble in spirit

Magnate: powerful or influential person

Magnitude: extent, greatness of size

Mainstay: chief support

Maladroit: clumsy, tactless

Malady: illness

Malapropism: humorous misuse of a word

Malcontent: discontented person, one who holds a grudge

Malediction: curse

Malefactor: evil-doer; culprit

Malevolent: ill-willed; causing evil or harm to others

Malfunction (*n*): breakdown, failure

Malfunction (*v*): to fail to work

Malice: animosity, spite, hatred

Malinger: to evade responsibility by pretending to be ill

Malleable: capable of being shaped

Malodorous: foul-smelling

Manifest (*adj*): obvious

Manifold: diverse, varied, comprised of many parts

Mannered: artificial or stilted in character

Manual (*adj*): hand-operated; physical

Manumission: release from slavery

Mar: to damage, deface; spoil

Marginal: barely sufficient

Maritime: relating to the sea or sailing

Martial: warlike, pertaining to the military

Martinet: strict disciplinarian, one who rigidly follows rules

Martyr: person dying for his/her beliefs

Masochist: one who enjoys pain or humiliation

Materialism: preoccupation with material things

Matriculate: to enroll as a member of a college or university

Matrilineal: tracing ancestry through mother's line rather than father's

Maudlin: overly sentimental

Maverick: a person who resists adherence to a group

Mawkish: sickeningly sentimental

Meager: scanty, sparse

Meander: to wander aimlessly without direction

Meaningful: significant

Meddler: person interfering in others' affairs

Medieval: relating to the Middle Ages

Megalith: huge stone used in prehistoric structures

Megalomania: mental state with delusions of wealth and power

Melancholy: sadness, depression

Melodious: having a pleasing melody

Menagerie: various animals kept together for exhibition

Mendacious: dishonest

Mendacity: a lie, falsehood

Mendicant: beggar

Mercenary (*adj*): motivated only by greed

Mercenary (*n*): soldier for hire in foreign countries

Mercurial: quick, shrewd, and unpredictable

Meretricious: gaudy, falsely attractive

Meridian: circle passing through the two poles of the earth

Meritorious: deserving reward or praise

Metamorphosis: change, transformation

Metaphor: figure of speech comparing two different things

Meticulous: extremely careful, fastidious, painstaking

Metronome: time-keeping device used in music

Mettle: courageousness; endurance

Microbe: microorganism

Microcosm: tiny system used as analogy for larger system

Migratory: wandering from place to place with the seasons

Militate: to operate against, work against

Minatory: menacing, threatening

Minimal: smallest in amount, least possible

Miniscule: very small

Mirth: frivolity, gaiety, laughter

Misanthrope: person who hates human beings

Misapprehend: to misunderstand, fail to know

Misconstrue: to misunderstand, fail to discover

Miscreant: one who behaves criminally

Miserliness: extreme stinginess

Misgiving: apprehension, doubt, sense of foreboding

Mishap: accident; misfortune

Misnomer: an incorrect name or designation

Missive: note or letter

Mitigate: to soften, or make milder

Mnemonic: relating to memory; designed to assist memory

Mobility: ease of movement

Mock (*v*): to deride, ridicule

Moderate (*adj*): reasonable, not extreme

Moderate (*v*): to make less excessive, restrain; regulate

Modicum: a small amount

Mollify: to calm or make less severe

Mollusk: sea animal with a soft body

Molt (*v*): to shed hair, skin, or an outer layer periodically

Momentous: important

Monastic: extremely plain or secluded, as in a monastery

Monochromatic: having one color

Monogamy: custom of marriage to one person at a time

Monolith: large block of stone

Monologue: dramatic speech performed by one actor

Monotony: lack of variation; wearisome sameness

Montage: composite picture

Moot: debatable; previously decided

Morbid: gruesome; relating to disease; abnormally gloomy

Mordacious: caustic, biting

Mordant: sarcastic

Mores: customs or manners

Moribund: dying, decaying

Morose: gloomy, sullen, or surly

Mote: small particle, speck

Motley: many-colored; composed of diverse parts

Mottle: to mark with spots

Multifaceted: having many parts, many-sided

Multifarious: diverse

Mundane: worldly; commonplace

Munificent: generous

Munitions: ammunition

Mutability: changeability

Myopic: near-sighted

Myriad: immense number, multitude

N

Nadir: lowest point

Naiveté: a lack of worldly wisdom

Narrative: account, story

Nascent: starting to develop, coming into existence

Nebulous: vague, cloudy

Necromancy: black magic

Nefarious: vicious, evil

Negligent: careless, inattentive

Negligible: not worth considering

Nemesis: a formidable, often victorious opponent

Neologism: new word or expression

Neonate: newborn child

Neophyte: novice, beginner

Nether: located under or below

Nettle (*v*): to irritate

Neutrality: disinterest, impartiality

Neutralize: to balance, offset

Nicety: elegant or delicate feature; minute distinction

Niche: recess in a wall; best position for something

Niggardly: stingy

Niggling: trifle, petty

Nihilism: belief that existence and all traditional values are meaningless

Noisome: stinking, putrid

Nomenclature: terms used in a particular science or discipline

Nominal: existing in name only; negligible

Non sequitur: conclusion not following from apparent evidence

Nonentity: an insignificant person

Novitiate: period of being a beginner or novice

Noxious: harmful, unwholesome

Nullify: to make legally invalid; to counteract the effect of

Numismatics: coin collecting

Nutritive: relating to nutrition or health

O

Obdurate: stubborn

Obeisance: a show of respect or submission

Obfuscate: to confuse, obscure

Objurgate: scold

Obliging: accommodating, agreeable

Oblique: indirect, evasive; misleading, devious

Obliterate: demolish completely, wipe out

Obloquy: abusive language; ill repute

Obscure (*adj*): dim, unclear; not well known

Obscurity: place or thing that's hard to perceive

Obsequious: overly submissive, brownnosing

Obsequy: funeral ceremony

Obsolete: no longer in use

Obstinate: stubborn

Obstreperous: troublesome, boisterous, unruly

Obtrusive: pushy, too conspicuous

Obtuse: insensitive, stupid, dull

Obviate: to make unnecessary; to anticipate and prevent

Occlude: to shut, block

Odious: hateful, contemptible

Officious: too helpful, meddlesome

Offshoot: branch

Ominous: menacing, threatening, indicating misfortune

Omnipotent: having unlimited power

Omniscient: having infinite knowledge

Omnivorous: eating everything; absorbing everything

Onerous: burdensome

Ontology: theory about the nature of existence

Opalescent: iridescent, displaying colors

Opaque: impervious to light; difficult to understand

Opine: to express an opinion

Opportune: appropriate, fitting

Opportunist: one who takes advantage of circumstances

Opprobrious: disgraceful, contemptuous

Optimum: the most favorable degree

Opulence: wealth

Oracle: person who foresees the future and gives advice

Oration: lecture, formal speech

Orator: lecturer, speaker

Orchestrate: to arrange music for performance; to coordinate, organize

Ordain: to make someone a priest or minister; to order

Orifice: an opening

Ornithologist: scientist who studies birds

Orotund: pompous

Oscillate: to move back and forth

Ossify: to turn to bone; to become rigid

Ostensible: apparent

Ostentatious: showy

Ostracism: exclusion, temporary banishment

Ouster: expulsion, ejection

Overabundance: excess, surfeit

Overstate: to embellish, exaggerate

Overt: in the open, obvious

Overture: musical introduction; proposal, offer

Overweening: arrogant

Overwrought: agitated, overdone

P

Pacific: calm, peaceful

Pacifist: one opposed to war

Pacify: to restore calm, bring peace

Paean: a song of praise or thanksgiving

Palatial: like a palace, magnificent

Palaver: idle talk

Paleontology: study of past geological eras through fossil remains

Palette: board for mixing paints; range of colors

Palisade: fence made up of stakes

Pall (*n*): covering that darkens or obscures; coffin

Pall (*v*): to lose strength or interest

Palliate: to make less serious, ease

Pallid: lacking color or liveliness

Palpable: obvious, real, tangible

Palpitation: trembling, shaking, irregular beating

Paltry: pitifully small or worthless

Panacea: cure-all

Panache: flamboyance, verve

Pandemic: spread over a whole area or country

Panegyric: elaborate praise; formal hymn of praise

Panoply: impressive array

Panorama: broad view; comprehensive picture

Paradigm: ideal example, model

Paradox: contradiction, incongruity; dilemma, puzzle

Paradoxical: self-contradictory but true

Paragon: model of excellence or perfection

Paramount: supreme, dominant, primary

Paraphrase: to reword, usually in simpler terms

Parch: to dry or shrivel

Pare: to trim

Pariah: outcast

Parity: equality

Parley: discussion, usually between enemies

Parochial: of limited scope or outlook, provincial

Parody: humorous imitation

Parry: to ward off or deflect

Parsimony: stinginess

Partisan (*adj*): biased in favor of

Partisan (*n*): strong supporter

Pastiche: piece of literature or music imitating other works

Patent (*adj*): obvious, unconcealed

Patent (*n*): official document giving exclusive right to sell an invention

Pathogenic: causing disease

Pathos: pity, compassion

Patrician: aristocrat

Patricide: murder of one's father

Patrimony: inheritance or heritage derived from one's father

Patronize: to condescend to, disparage; to buy from

Paucity: scarcity, lack

Pauper: very poor person

Pavilion: tent or light building used for shelter or exhibitions

Peccadillo: minor sin or offense

Peculation: theft of money or goods

Pedagogue: teacher

Pedant: one who pays undue attention to book learning and rules; one that displays learning ostentatiously

Pedestrian (*adj*): commonplace

Pediment: triangular gable on a roof or facade

Peerless: unequaled

Pejorative: having bad connotations; disparaging

Pellucid: transparent; translucent; easily understood

Penance: voluntary suffering to repent for a wrong

Penchant: inclination

Pending (*prep*): during, while awaiting

Penitent: expressing sorrow for sins or offenses, repentant

Pensive: thoughtful

Penultimate: next to last

Penumbra: partial shadow

Penury: extreme poverty

Perambulate: walk about

Percipient: discerning, able to perceive

Perdition: complete and utter loss; damnation

Peregrinate: to wander from place to place

Peremptory: imperative; dictatorial

Perennial: present throughout the years; persistent

Perfidious: faithless, disloyal, untrustworthy

Perfunctory: done in a routine way; indifferent

Perihelion: point in orbit nearest to the sun

Peripatetic: moving from place to place

Periphrastic: containing too many words

Perjure: to tell a lie under oath

Permeable: penetrable

Pernicious: very harmful

Perpetuity: continuing forever

Perplexing: puzzling, bewildering

Personification: act of attributing human qualities to objects or abstract qualities

Perspicacious: shrewd, astute, keen-witted

Pert: lively and bold

Pertinacious: persistent, stubborn

Pertinent: applicable, appropriate

Perturbation: disturbance

Perusal: close examination

Pervasive: present throughout

Pervert (v): to cause to change in immoral way; to misuse

Pestilence: epidemic, plague

Pettish: fretful

Petulance: rudeness, peevishness

Phalanx: massed group of soldiers, people, or things

Philanderer: pursuer of casual love affairs

Philanthropy: love of humanity; generosity to worthy causes

Philistine: narrow-minded person, someone lacking appreciation for art or culture

Philology: study of words

Phlegm: coldness or indifference

Phlegmatic: calm in temperament; sluggish

Phoenix: mythical, immortal bird that lives for 500 years, burns itself to death, and rises from its ashes

Phonetics: study of speech sounds

Phonic: relating to sound

Picayune: petty, of little value

Piddling: trivial

Piety: devoutness

Pilfer: to steal

Pillage: to loot, especially during a war

Pillory: ridicule and abuse

Pinnacle: peak, highest point of development

Pious: dedicated, devout, extremely religious

Pique: fleeting feeling of hurt pride

Pithy: profound, substantial; concise, succinct, to the point

Pittance: meager amount or wage

Placate: to soothe or pacify

Placid: calm

Plaintiff: injured person in a lawsuit

Plaintive: expressing sorrow

Plait: to braid

Plangent: loud sound; wailing sound

Plastic: flexible; pliable

Platitude: stale, overused expression

Plaudit: applause

Plebeian: crude, vulgar; low-class

Plenitude: abundance, plenty

Plethora: excess, overabundance

Pliant: pliable, yielding

Pluck: to pull strings on musical instrument

Plucky: courageous, spunky

Plummet: to fall, plunge

Pluralistic: including a variety of groups

Ply (*v*): to use diligently; to engage; to join together

Pneumatic: relating to air; worked by compressed air

Poach: to steal game or fish; cook in boiling liquid

Podium: platform or lectern for orchestra conductors or speakers

Poignant: emotionally moving

Polar: relating to a geographic pole; exhibiting contrast

Polarize: to tend towards opposite extremes

Polemic: controversy, argument; verbal attack

Politic: shrewd and practical; diplomatic

Polyglot: speaker of many languages

Pompous: self-important

Ponderous: weighty, heavy, large

Pontificate: to speak in a pretentious manner

Pore (*v*): to study closely or meditatively

Porous: full of holes, permeable to liquids

Portent: omen

Portly: stout, dignified

Posit: to put in position; to suggest an idea

Posterior: bottom, rear

Posterity: future generations; all of a person's descendants

Potable: drinkable

Potentate: monarch or ruler with great power

Poverty: lacking money or possessions

Pragmatic: practical; moved by facts rather than abstract ideals

Prattle: meaningless, foolish talk

Precarious: uncertain

Precept: principle; law

Precipice: edge, steep overhang

Precipitate (*adj*): sudden and unexpected

Precipitate (*v*): to throw down from a height; to cause to happen

Precipitous: hasty, quickly, with too little caution

Précis: short summary of facts

Preclude: to rule out

Precocious: unusually advanced at an early age

Precursor: forerunner, predecessor

Predestine: to decide in advance

Predicament: difficult situation

Predicate (*v*): to found or base on

Predictive: relating to prediction, indicative of the future

Predilection: preference, liking

Predisposition: tendency, inclination

Preeminent: celebrated, distinguished

Premeditate: to consider, plan beforehand

Premonition: forewarning; presentiment

Preponderance: majority in number; dominance

Prepossessing: attractive, engaging, appealing

Preposterous: absurd, illogical

Presage: to foretell, indicate in advance

Prescient: having foresight

Presentiment: premonition, sense of foreboding

Prestidigitation: sleight of hand

Presumptuous: rude, improperly bold

Pretext: excuse, pretended reason

Prevalent: widespread

Prevaricate: to lie, evade the truth

Primeval: ancient, primitive

Primordial: original, existing from the beginning

Pristine: untouched, uncorrupted

Privation: lack of usual necessities or comforts

Probity: honesty, high-mindedness

Proclivity: tendency, inclination

Procure: to obtain

Prodigal: wasteful, extravagant, lavish

Prodigious: vast, enormous, extraordinary

Proficient: expert, skilled in a certain subject

Profligate: corrupt, degenerate

Profundity: great depth

Profuse: lavish, extravagant

Progenitor: originator, forefather, ancestor in a direct line

Progeny: offspring, children

Prognosticate: to predict

Progressive: favoring progress or change; moving forward

Proliferation: propagation, reproduction; enlargement, expansion

Prolific: productive, fertile

Prolix: tedious; wordy

Prologue: introductory section of a literary work or play

Promontory: piece of land or rock higher than its surroundings

Promulgate: to make known publicly

Propagate: to breed

Propensity: inclination, tendency

Propinquity: nearness

Propitiate: to win over, appease

Propitious: favorable, advantageous

Proponent: advocate, defender, supporter

Propriety: appropriateness

Prosaic: relating to prose; dull, commonplace

Proscribe: to condemn; to forbid, outlaw

Prose: ordinary language used in everyday speech

Prosecutor: person who initiates a legal action or suit

Proselytize: to convert to a particular belief or religion

Prostrate: lying face downward, lying flat on the ground

Protagonist: main character in a play or story, hero

Protean: readily assuming different forms or characters

Protestation: declaration

Protocol: ceremony and manners observed by diplomats

Protract: to prolong, draw out, extend

Protrusion: something that sticks out

Provident: prudent, frugal

Providential: prudent, lucky

Provincial: rustic, unsophisticated, limited in scope

Provocation: cause, incitement to act or respond

Prowess: bravery, skill

Proximity: nearness

Proxy: power to act as substitute for another

Prudent: careful, cautious

Prurient: lustful, exhibiting lewd desires

Pseudonym: pen name; fictitious or borrowed name

Puerile: childish, immature, silly

Pugilism: boxing

Pugnacious: quarrelsome, eager and ready to fight

Pulchritude: beauty

Pulverize: to pound, crush, or grind into powder; destroy

Pummel: to pound, beat

Punctilious: careful in observing rules of behavior or ceremony

Pundit: an authority or critic

Pungent: strong or sharp in smell or taste

Punitive: having to do with punishment

Purgation: process of cleansing, purification

Purge (*v*): to cleanse or free from impurities

Puritanical: adhering to a rigid moral code

Purport: to profess, suppose, claim

Pusillanimous: cowardly

Putrid: rotten

Q

Quack (*n*): faker; one who falsely claims to have medical skill

Quadrilateral: four-sided polygon

Quadruped: animal having four feet

Quaff: to drink heartily

Quagmire: marsh; difficult situation

Quandary: dilemma, difficulty

Quarantine: isolation period, originally 40 days, to prevent spread of disease

Quaternary: consisting of or relating to four units or members

Quell: to crush or subdue

Querulous: inclined to complain, irritable

Query (*n*): question

Quibble: to argue about insignificant and irrelevant details

Quicken: to hasten, arouse, excite

Quiescence: inactivity, stillness

Quiescent: inactive, at rest

Quintessence: most typical example; concentrated essence

Quiver (*v*): to shake slightly, tremble, vibrate

Quixotic: overly idealistic, impractical

Quotidian: occurring daily; commonplace

R

Raconteur: witty, skillful storyteller

Radical (*adj*): fundamental; drastic

Raging: violent, wild

Rail (*v*): to scold with bitter or abusive language

Raillery: lighthearted jesting

Rally (*v*): to assemble; recover, recuperate

Ramble (*v*): to roam, wander; to babble, digress

Ramification: implication, outgrowth, or consequence

Rampant: unrestrained

Rancor: bitter hatred

Rapacious: greedy; predatory

Rapport: relationship of trust and respect

Rapprochement: having a cordial relationship

Rapt: deeply absorbed

Rarefy: to make thinner, purer, or more refined

Ratify: to approve formally, confirm

Ratiocination: methodical, logical reasoning

Ration (*n*): portion, share

Ration (*v*): to supply; to restrict consumption of

Rationale: line of reasoning

Raucous: harsh-sounding; boisterous

Ravenous: extremely hungry

Ravine: deep, narrow gorge

Raze: to tear down, demolish

Reactionary (*adj*): marked by extreme conservatism, esp. in politics

Rebarbative: irritating; repellent

Rebuff (*n*): blunt rejection

Rebuke (*v*): to reprimand, scold

Rebut: to refute by evidence or argument

Recalcitrant: resisting authority or control

Recant: to retract a statement, opinion, etcetera

Recapitulate: to review with a brief summary

Receptive: open to others' ideas; congenial

Recidivism: tendency to repeat previous behavior

Reciprocate: to show or feel in return

Reclusive: shut off from the world

Recondite: relating to obscure learning; known to only a few

Recount (*v*): to describe facts or events

Recreant: disloyal; cowardly

Recruit (*v*): to draft, enlist; to seek to enroll

Rectify: to correct

Rectitude: moral uprightness

Recurrence: repetition

Redress (*n*): relief from wrong or injury

Redundancy: unnecessary repetition

Refectory: room where meals are served

Reform (*v*): to change, correct

Refract: to deflect sound or light

Refractory: obstinately resistant

Refuge: escape, shelter

Refurbish: to renovate

Refute: to contradict, discredit

Regal: magnificent, splendid, fit for royalty

Regard: high esteem

Regimen: government rule; systematic plan

Regress: to move backward; revert to an earlier form or state

Rehabilitate: to restore to good health or condition; reestablish a person's good reputation

Reiterate: to say again, repeat

Rejoinder: response

Rejuvenate: to make young again; renew

Relegate: to assign to a class, especially to an inferior one

Relent: to become gentler in attitude

Relinquish: to renounce or surrender something

Relish (*v*): to enjoy greatly

Remediable: capable of being corrected

Reminiscence: remembrance of past events

Remission: lessening, relaxation

Remit: to send (usually money) as payment

Remonstrate: to protest or object

Remote: distant, isolated

Remuneration: pay or reward for work, trouble, etcetera

Renascent: reborn, coming into being again

Renegade: traitor, person abandoning a cause

Renege: to go back on one's word

Renitent: resisting pressure, obstinate

Renounce: to give up or reject a right, title, person, etcetera

Renown: fame, widespread acclaim

Rent (*adj*): torn apart

Repast: meal or mealtime

Repeal: to revoke or formally withdraw (often a law)

Repent: to regret a past action

Repentant: apologetic, guilty, remorseful

Replete: abundantly supplied

Replicate: to duplicate, repeat

Repose: relaxation, leisure

Reprehend: to criticize

Reprehensible: blameworthy, disreputable

Repress: to restrain or hold in

Repression: act of restraining or holding in

Reprise: repetition, esp. of a piece of music

Reproach (*v*): to find fault with; blame

Reprobate: morally unprincipled person

Reprove: to criticize or correct

Repudiate: to reject as having no authority

Requiem: hymns or religious service for the dead

Requite: to return or repay

Rescind: to repeal, cancel

Residue: remainder, leftover, remnant

Resilient: able to recover quickly after illness or bad luck; able to bounce back into shape

Resolute: determined; with a clear purpose

Resolve (*n*): determination, firmness of purpose

Resolve (*v*): to conclude, determine

Resonate: to echo

Respire: to breathe

Respite: interval of relief

Resplendent: splendid, brilliant

Restitution: act of compensating for loss or damage

Restive: impatient, uneasy, restless

Restorative: having the power to renew or revitalize

Restrained: controlled, repressed, restricted

Resuscitate: to revive, bring back to life

Retard (*v*): to slow, hold back

Reticent: not speaking freely; reserved

Retinue: group of attendants with an important person

Retiring: shy, modest, reserved

Retort: cutting response

Retract: to draw in or take back

Retrench: to regroup, reorganize

Retroactive: applying to an earlier time

Retrograde: having a backward motion or direction

Retrospective: looking back to the past

Revelry: boisterous festivity

Revere: to worship, regard with awe

Revert: to backslide, regress

Revile: to criticize with harsh language, verbally abuse

Revitalize: to renew; give new energy to

Revoke: to annul, cancel, call back

Revulsion: strong feeling of repugnance or dislike

Rhapsody: emotional literary or musical work

Rhetoric: persuasive use of language

Ribald: humorous in a vulgar way

Riddle (*v*): to make many holes in; permeate

Rife: widespread, prevalent; abundant

Rift: an open space; to divide

Righteous: morally right

Riposte: a retort

Risqué: bordering on being inappropriate or indecent

Robust: strong and healthy; hardy

Rococo: very highly ornamented

Roil: to disturb or cause disorder

Root (*v*): to dig with a snout (like a pig)

Rooted: to have an origin or base

Rostrum: stage for public speaking

Rotund: round in shape; fat

Rue: to regret

Ruffled: irritated

Ruminate: to contemplate, reflect upon

Rustic: rural

S

Saccharine: excessively sweet or sentimental

Sacrosanct: extremely sacred; beyond criticism

Sagacious: shrewd, wise

Salacious: lustful

Salient: prominent or conspicuous

Sallow: sickly yellow in color

Salubrious: healthful

Salutation: greeting

Sanction: permission, support; law; penalty

Sanctuary: haven, retreat

Sanguine: ruddy; cheerfully optimistic

Sap (*v*): to weaken gradually

Sapient: wise

Sardonic: cynical, scornfully mocking

Satiate: to satisfy

Saunter: to amble; walk in a leisurely manner

Savant: learned person

Scabbard: sheath for sword or dagger

Scabrous: dealing with indecent things; blemished

Scale (*v*): to climb to the top of

Scantiness: barely enough, meager

Scarcity: not enough, insufficient

Scenario: plot outline; possible situation

Schism: a division or separation; disharmony

Scintilla: very small amount

Scintillate: to sparkle, flash

Scion: descendent, child

Score (*n*): notation for a musical composition

Score (*v*): to make a notch or scratch

Scrivener: professional copyist

Scrupulous: restrained; careful and precise

Scurrilous: vulgar, low, indecent

Secant: straight line intersecting a curve at two points

Secede: to withdraw formally from an organization

Sectarian: narrow-minded; relating to a group or sect

Secular: not specifically pertaining to religion

Sedentary: inactive, stationary; sluggish

Sedition: behavior promoting rebellion

Seismology: science of earthquakes

Seminal: relating to the beginning or seeds of something

Senescent: aging, growing old

Sententious: having a moralizing tone

Sentient: aware, conscious, able to perceive

Sepulchral: typical of a place of burial

Sequester: to remove or set apart; put into seclusion

Seraphic: angelic, pure, sublime

Serendipity: habit of making fortunate discoveries by chance

Serrated: saw-toothed, notched

Servile: submissive, obedient

Shard: piece of broken glass or pottery

Shirk: to avoid a task due to laziness or fear

Sidle: to cause to turn sideways; to move along one side

Simian: apelike; relating to apes

Simper: to smirk, smile foolishly

Simulated: fake, made to look real

Sinecure: well-paying job or office that requires little or no work

Singe: to burn slightly, scorch

Sinuous: winding; intricate, complex

Skulk: to move in a stealthy or cautious manner; sneak

Slake: to calm down or moderate

Slight: to treat as unimportant; insult

Slipshod: careless, hasty

Slough: to discard or shed

Sluggard: lazy, inactive person

Smelt (*v*): to melt metal in order to refine it

Smutty: obscene, indecent

Snippet: tiny part, tidbit

Sobriety: seriousness

Sobriquet: nickname

Sodden: thoroughly soaked; saturated

Sojourn: visit, stay

Solace: comfort in distress; consolation

Solarium: room or glassed-in area exposed to the sun

Solecism: grammatical mistake

Solicitous: concerned, attentive; eager

Solidarity: unity based on common aims or interests

Soliloquy: literary or dramatic speech by one character, not addressed to others

Solipsism: belief that the self is the only reality

Solstice: shortest or longest day of the year

Soluble: capable of being solved or dissolved

Somber: dark and gloomy; melancholy, dismal

Somnambulist: sleepwalker

Somnolent: drowsy, sleepy; inducing sleep

Sonic: relating to sound

Sonorous: producing a full, rich sound

Sophist: person good at arguing deviously

Sophistry: deceptive reasoning or argumentation

Sophomoric: immature and overconfident

Soporific: sleepy or tending to cause sleep

Sordid: filthy; contemptible and corrupt

Sovereign: having supreme power

Spartan: austere, severe, grave; simple, bare

Specious: deceptively attractive

Speculation: contemplation; act of taking business risks for financial gain

Speculative: involving assumption; uncertain; theoretical

Sporadic: infrequent, irregular

Sportive: frolicsome, playful

Sprightly: lively, animated, energetic

Spur (*v*): to prod

Spurious: lacking authenticity; counterfeit, false

Spurn: to reject or refuse contemptuously; scorn

Squabble: quarrel

Squalid: filthy; morally repulsive

Squander: to waste

Staccato: marked by abrupt, clear-cut sounds

Stagnant: immobile, stale

Staid: self-restrained to the point of dullness

Stalwart: strong, unwavering

Stand (*n*): group of trees

Stasis: motionless state; standstill

Stately: grand, unapproachable

Steadfast: immovable

Stentorian: extremely loud

Stigma: mark of disgrace or inferiority

Stilted: stiff, unnatural

Stint (*n*): period of time spent doing something

Stint (*v*): to be sparing or frugal

Stipend: allowance; fixed amount of money paid regularly

Stockade: enclosed area forming defensive wall

Stoic: indifferent to or unaffected by emotions

Stolid: having or showing little emotion

Stratagem: trick designed to deceive an enemy

Stratify: to arrange into layers

Striate: striped, grooved

Stricture: something that restrains; negative criticism

Strident: loud, harsh, unpleasantly noisy

Stringent: imposing severe, rigorous standards

Stripling: an adolescent boy

Stultify: to impair or reduce to uselessness

Stupefy: to dull the senses of; stun, astonish

Stymie: to block or thwart

Subdued: suppressed, stifled

Subjection: dependence, obedience, submission

Subjugate: to conquer, subdue; enslave

Sublimate: to repress impulses

Sublime: awe-inspiring; of high spiritual or moral value

Subliminal: subconscious; imperceptible

Submissive: tending to be meek and submit

Subpoena: notice ordering someone to appear in court

Subterfuge: trick or tactic used to avoid something

KAPLAN
Test Prep and Admissions

Subterranean: hidden, secret; underground

Subvert: to undermine or corrupt

Succinct: terse, brief, concise

Succulent: juicy; full of vitality or freshness

Sufferable: bearable

Suffragist: one who advocates extended voting rights

Sully: to soil, stain, tarnish; taint

Sumptuous: lavish, splendid

Superabundance: excessive

Superannuated: too old, obsolete, outdated

Supercilious: arrogant, haughty, overbearing, condescending

Supererogatory: nonessential

Superfluous: extra, more than necessary

Supersede: to take the place of; replace

Supervise: to direct or oversee the work of others

Supplant: to replace, substitute

Supple: flexible, pliant

Supplicant: one who asks humbly and earnestly

Supposition: assumption

Surfeit: excessive amount

Surly: rude and bad-tempered

Surmise: to make an educated guess

Surmount: to conquer, overcome

Surreptitious: characterized by secrecy

Susceptible: vulnerable, unprotected

Sustenance: supplying the necessities of life

Sybarite: person devoted to pleasure and luxury

Sycophant: self-serving flatterer, yes-man

Symbiosis: cooperation, mutual helpfulness

Symposium: meeting with short presentations on related topics

Synchronous: happening at the same time

Syncopation: temporary irregularity in musical rhythm

Synthesis: blend, combination

Synthetic: artificial, imitation

T

Tableau: vivid description, striking incident or scene

Tacit: silently understood or implied

Taciturn: uncommunicative, not inclined to speak much

Tactful: skillful in dealing with others

Tactile: relating to the sense of touch

Talisman: something producing a magical effect

Tandem: acting as a group or in partnership

Tangential: digressing, diverting

Tangible: able to be sensed; perceptible, measurable

Tantamount: equivalent in value or significance; amounting to

Tarnished: corroded, discolored; discredited, disgraced

Tawdry: gaudy, cheap, showy

Taxonomy: science of classification

Technocrat: strong believer in technology; technical expert

Teeter: to waver or move unsteadily

Temerity: recklessness

Temperance: restraint, self-control, moderation

Tempered: moderated, restrained

Tempestuous: stormy, raging, furious

Temporal: relating to time; chronological

Tenable: defensible, reasonable

Tenacious: stubborn, holding firm

Tendentious: biased

Tenet: belief, doctrine

Tensile: capable of withstanding physical stress

Tenuous: weak, insubstantial

Tepid: lukewarm; showing little enthusiasm

Terminal (*adj*): concluding, final; fatal

Terminal (*n*): depot, station

Terrestrial: earthly; down-to-earth, commonplace

Terse: concise, brief, free of extra words

Testament: statement of belief; will

Testimonial: statement testifying to a truth; something given in tribute to a person's achievement

Tether (*v*): to bind, tie

Theocracy: government by priests representing a god

Theology: study of God and religion

Theoretical: abstract

Thrall: a person in servitude, enslaved

Threnody: a sad poem or song

Thwart: to block or prevent from happening; frustrate

Tidings: news

Timorous: timid, shy, full of apprehension

Tinge: to color slightly

Tirade: long violent speech; verbal assault

Titan: person of colossal stature or achievement

Toady: flatterer, hanger-on, yes-man

Tome: book, usually large and academic

Tonal: relating to pitch or sound

Topography: art of making maps or charts

Torpid: lethargic; unable to move; dormant

Torrid: burning hot; passionate

Torsion: act of twisting and turning

Tortuous: having many twists and turns; highly complex

Tottering: barely standing

Tractable: obedient, yielding

Trammel: to impede or hamper

Transcend: to rise above, go beyond

Transcendent: rising above, going beyond

Transcription: copy, reproduction; record

Transfiguration: a change; an exalting change

Transgress: to trespass, violate a law

Transient (*adj*): temporary, short-lived, fleeting

Transitory: short-lived, existing only briefly

Translucent: partially transparent

Transmute: to change in appearance or shape

Transpire: to happen, occur; become known

Travesty: parody, exaggerated imitation, caricature

Tremulous: trembling, quivering; fearful, timid

Trenchant: acute, sharp, incisive; forceful, effective

Trepidation: fear and anxiety

Trifling: of slight worth, trivial, insignificant

Trite: shallow, superficial

Trounce: to beat severely, defeat

Troupe: group of actors

Truculent: savage and cruel; fierce; ready to fight

Truism: something that is obviously true

Truncate: to cut off, shorten by cutting

Trying: difficult to deal with

Tryst: agreement between lovers to meet; rendezvous

Tumult: state of confusion; agitation

Tundra: treeless plain found in Arctic or subarctic regions

Turbid: muddled; unclear

Turbulence: commotion, disorder

Turgid: swollen, bloated

Turpitude: inherent vileness, foulness, depravity

Tyrannical: oppressive; dictatorial

Tyro: beginner, novice

U

Ubiquitous: being everywhere simultaneously

Umbrage: offense, resentment

Unadulterated: absolutely pure

Unanimity: state of total agreement or unity

Unavailing: hopeless, useless

Unbending: inflexible, unyielding

Unbridled: unrestrained

Unconscionable: unscrupulous; shockingly unfair or unjust

Unctuous: greasy, oily; smug and falsely earnest

Undaunted: resolute even in adversity

Undermine: to sabotage, thwart

Undocumented: not certified, unsubstantiated

Undulating: moving in waves

Unequivocal: absolute, certain

Unfailing: not likely to fail, constant, infallible

Unfettered: free, unrestrained

Unfrock: to strip of priestly duties

Ungracious: rude, disagreeable

Unheralded: unannounced, unexpected

Unidimensional: having one size or dimension

Uniform (*adj*): consistent and unchanging; identical

Unimpeachable: beyond question

Uninitiated: not familiar with an area of study

Unobtrusive: modest, unassuming

Unpolished: lacking sophistication

Unruffled: poised, calm

Unscrupulous: dishonest

Unsoiled: clean, pure

Unsolicited: unrequested

Unstinting: generous

Unsullied: clean

Unswayable: unable to change

Untoward: not favorable; unruly

Untrammeled: unhampered

Unwarranted: groundless, unjustified

Unwitting: unconscious; unintentional

Unyielding: firm, resolute

Upbraid: to scold sharply

Uproarious: loud and forceful

Upsurge: sudden rise

Urbane: courteous, refined, suave

Usurp: to seize by force

Usury: practice of lending money at exorbitant rates

Utilitarian: efficient, functional, useful

Utopia: perfect place

V

Vacillate: to waver, show indecision

Vacuous: empty, void; lacking intelligence, purposeless

Valiant: brave, courageous

Validate: to authorize, certify, confirm

Valorous: brave, valiant

Vanquish: to conquer, defeat

Vapid: tasteless, dull

Variable: changeable, inconstant

Variegated: varied; marked with different colors

Vaunted: boasted about, bragged about

Vehemently: strongly, urgently

Venal: willing to do wrong for money

Vendetta: prolonged feud marked by bitter hostility

Venerable: respected because of age

Veneration: adoration, honor, respect

Vent (*v*): to express, say out loud

Veracious: truthful, accurate

Veracity: accuracy, truth

Verbatim: word for word

Verbose: wordy

Verdant: green with vegetation; inexperienced

Verdure: fresh, rich vegetation

Verified: proven true

Verisimilitude: quality of appearing true or real

Verity: truthfulness; belief viewed as true and enduring

Vermin: small creatures offensive to humans

Vernacular: everyday language used by ordinary people; specialized language of a
profession

Vernal: related to spring

Versatile: adaptable, all-purpose

Verve: energy, vitality

Vestige: trace, remnant

Vex: to irritate, annoy; confuse, puzzle

Viable: workable, able to succeed or grow

Viaduct: series of elevated arches used to cross a valley

Vicarious: substitute, surrogate; enjoyed through imagined participation in another's
experience

Vicissitude: change or variation; ups and downs

Vie: to compete, contend

Vigilant: attentive, watchful

Vignette: decorative design; short literary composition

Vilify: to slander, defame

Vim: energy, enthusiasm

Vindicate: to clear of blame; support a claim

Vindication: clearance from blame or suspicion

Vindictive: spiteful, vengeful, unforgiving

Virile: manly, having qualities of an adult male

Virtuoso: someone with masterly skill; expert musician

Virulent: extremely poisonous; malignant; hateful

Viscous: thick, syrupy and sticky

Vitiate: reduce in value or effectiveness

Vitriolic: burning, caustic; sharp, bitter

Vituperate: to abuse verbally

Vociferous: loud, vocal and noisy

Void (*adj*): not legally enforceable; empty

Void (*n*): emptiness, vacuum

Void (*v*): to cancel, invalidate

Volition: free choice, free will; act of choosing

Volley (*n*): flight of missiles, round of gunshots

Voluble: speaking much and easily, talkative; glib

Voluminous: large; of great quantity; writing or speaking at great length

Voracious: having a great appetite

Vortex: swirling, resembling a whirlpool

W

Waive: to refrain from enforcing a rule; to give up a legal right

Wallow: to indulge oneself excessively, luxuriate

Wan: sickly pale

Wane: to dwindle, to decrease

Wanton: undisciplined, unrestrained, reckless

Waspish: rude, behaving badly

Wax: to increase

Weather (*v*): to endure, undergo

Welter (*n*): a confused mass; a jumble

Whet: to sharpen, stimulate

Whimsy: playful or fanciful idea

Wily: clever, deceptive

Windfall: sudden, unexpected good fortune

Winsome: charming, happily engaging

Withdrawn: unsociable, aloof; shy, timid

Wizened: withered, shriveled, wrinkled

Wraith: a ghost

Wrangle: loud quarrel

Writ: written document, usually in law

X

Xenophobia: fear or hatred of foreigners or strangers

Y

Yoke (*v*): to join together

Z

Zealot: someone passionately devoted to a cause

Zenith: highest point, summit

Zephyr: gentle breeze

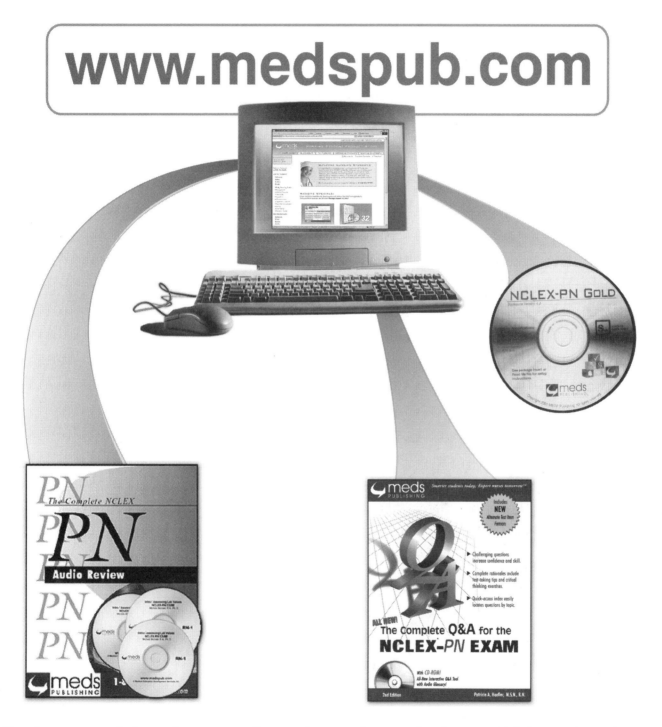